TRÈS RICHES HEURES

TRÈS RICHES HEURES

Lydia Chamberlin

1992

Published by Madison Books
4720 Boston Way
Lanham, Maryland 20706

The paper used in this publication meets the minimum
requirements of American National Standard for
Information Sciences—Permanence of Paper for
Printed Library Materials, ANSI Z39.48–1984. ∞™
Manufactured in the United States of America.

Library of Congress Cataloging-in-Publication Data

Chamberlin, Lydia.
Très riches heures / Lydia Chamberlin.
p.   cm.
1. Chamberlin, Lydia, 1923.   2. United
States—Biography.   I. Title.
CT275.C4548A3   1993
973.9'092—dc20   93–23030 CIP
[B]

ISBN 0–8191–9239–2 (paper : alk. paper)

The trick in life is not to avoid
error at all costs, but to give
triumph a chance.

— Huew Weldon
former head of the B.B.C.

Contents

Dedicated to
Lyn and Margot

Foreword

My story, *Très Riches Heures* is a far cry from the horror of today's headlines, and indeed from the increasing dangers that now threaten everyday life. Yesterday's newspaper headlines featured the conflagration in Waco, Texas, and the immolation of its Davidians, the capture of the crazy Washington man who randomly shot eleven people point blank from his car window, and the continuing mass atrocities of ethnic cleansing in Bosnia.

In recent months violence has hit even closer to home. When our oldest daughter Lyn was caught in the midst of the crossfire during the demise of Monitor Television at the Christian Science Church, as a professional lay person and not a member of the "Mother" Church, she received ugly threats, had obscene notes pinned to her windshield, and had her tires slashed. Not funny! Not Christian!

Eric MacLeish, our youngest daughter Margot's husband, who has successfully prosecuted some bad apples who molested children, received alarming death threats that necessitated hiring a personal bodyguard. That was last year. Not funny! And just this March he received at home a very terrifying call saying: "I threatened you before. Now I am going for your wife and children." They have hired a bodyguard round-the-clock to protect themselves. This guard, (who crayons with Alexandra, aged four, at the kitchen table when all is quiet) formerly was a body-guard for Henry Kissinger.

When Ward and I cruised through the Suez Canal to Malaysia last fall we stopped at Aden in Yemen and saw hundreds of impoverished people, many of whom were emaciated refugees from Somalia. Later when our boat pulled into harbor at Safaga, Egypt our tourist party had to be escorted by an armed guard on the way to Luxor and the Valley of Kings. On the way back to the ship, the bus passed a crossroad where the very next day Muslim Fundamentalists shot at nine German tourists. When we left Colombo, Sri Lanka, also the very next day a local army chief of operations was murdered on the porch of the hotel where we had previously stood waiting for a taxi. The world indeed is full of terror.

I have written my *Très Riches Heures* hoping that happiness has not gone out of style, and that like the eye of the storm my story might have a calming effect no matter how temporary. I have written this without notes of any kind. Only what I remembered. Although there is no sex or violence herein, and although I am not a person of "special eminence" or fame, my "normal" life has been blessed by very rich hours.

If I do say so myself, I am gifted beyond measure in the unfailing ability to spot good human beings, and the sensitivity to metabolize beautiful things. I hope you can recognize these lighting up the pages.

L. G. C.
April 1993

I

Très Riches Heures

I start writing this journal at sea on the Atlantic, about 30 miles off the east coast of South America, having left Rio de Janeiro two days ago, and approaching Salvador, Bahia, Brazil. We have traveled nearly 2,000 miles already from Buenos Aires and are between worlds. This is a golden opportunity to write, and something I have wanted to do for a long time. We are in a state of suspended animation on this floating pleasure palace, The *Royal Viking Star*. As Ward is a lecturer and part of the ship's "enhancement" program, we get the whole package free. Three weeks of sun, gourmet food, entertainment, without any money passing hands, except for buying Bingo cards, the coiffurist, the slot machines, and what we spend when we go ashore. The skies are blue, the seas are perfect. "This is my *Apologia Pro Vita Mea.*" Apologia does not mean "Apology." It is a description of life, and thus a life-scape. I undertake this in hopes that it will be an illuminated manuscript for Lyn and Margot, casting light on Ward's and my wonderful life together, and providing some insights as to how I got to be so lucky. I always wanted my Mother to write her memoirs. She had such a marvelous slant on events and people who were part of her fabric. She could walk to the mailbox and make a fascinating event out of it. *She* was, however, a true writer. This also might be entitled *"Who Do I Think I Am, Anyway?"* Perhaps in the course of this, I will find out. Today is Christmas, December 1990. We miss awfully not being with Lyn and Margot and their children. But we have hung up their stockings for nearly thirty-five years, and hopefully our absence, this once, won't be too deeply felt.

My self-portrait is really a reflection of how I believe other people see me. I have always been tall; I never was a little girl. Old Mrs. Randall, whom I feared greatly and who lived next door just up the hill from our yard in Duxbury would come into our house and remark in astonishment at how big I was for my age. I learned to hide when I saw her coming. She had a piercing stare, and though she was probably sixty, I thought her skinny frame very old and wrinkled, and not at all enhanced by rings on her fingers which slipped around as she gestured. But she did allow us to coast our sleds down her front lawn which sloped to Cedar Street. I learned later that she had a flaming correspondence for many years with e.e. cummings. He sent her roses weekly, but they never met as she wouldn't allow him to come see her, ever. The house she lived in, belonging to the Ames family, was a house in which my great grandfather played cards with Daniel Webster. It had been owned by Stephen Nye Gifford and his wife Ada (Winsor). His first wife, our great grandmother was her sister, Florence (Winsor).

I remember two photographs of me at this early stage. One nice one when I was around four with Steve in his little knitted short suit, I in a smocked Liberty dress, which I can remember to this day. It had peaches and pears, and turquoise smocking; my party shoes were turquoise with silk fringed pompons. I remember being desolate when these shoes no longer fit no matter how hard we forced my feet into them like Cinderella's bad sisters. In the other photo, I was standing in a red and white broad striped bathing suit that sagged almost to my knees, in one of those awful khaki-colored life jackets that weighed about ten pounds when wet, with a bathing cap with a large rubber flower attached to it. I must have been six years old because my front teeth were missing, which I tried to cover up with my upper lip. A puddle had collected beneath my long, spindly legs.

I was a day camper at Camp Chappa Challa. I liked this camp, but was in awe of fat Miss Davis who was mean to a little boy who cried all time and wet his bed nightly in his bungalow. His mother finally took him home, thank goodness. Blond Miss Carlton was nicer, pretty I thought, who allowed me to ride the bigger horses to which only the older girls were assigned. At the end of the summer prizes were given out for various accomplishments. I got the prize for the most beautiful nose in camp. I guess my long straight nose that went up into my forehead without pause was unusual. There were some people who called me horseface later, but I took that as a compliment.

I looked like a tomboy. I was taller than all the boys my age, and generally scorned them. But a young blond boy Matthew from Philadelphia, came to visit his aunt nearby. He was my brother Steve's age, two years older than me, but he didn't have warts on his thumb or hairy knees, like Longy who lived with us, or freckly like Prudie, Peter or Harris who were in Steve's ratty pack. In his aunt's kitchen, right in front of the huge black cook, who must be related to Aunt Jemima, Matthew gave me a big kiss. It was surprisingly enjoyable and the black lady shook with laughter and a sly pleasure I didn't understand. "Now, don't that beat all," she said covering her face with her apron. Grownups are funny. The same tittering and side comments occurred when my best friend Warren in the 1st grade at Buckingham School came down with chicken pox and I contracted the same dread disease after I had kissed Warren while waiting on the fence for the school bus.

Hair was important even at an early age. When I first went to Derby Academy at about 9 years of age all the older girls had short hair. Franny, my idol, had a beautiful shingle up the back that then burst out into wavy chestnut curls. I had long straight hair of no special style or character, with a part in the middle, fastened with two bows on bobby pins. My Mother reluctantly agreed to take me to the beauty parlor to get it cut à la Franny. The lady cutter didn't understand what I wanted. In one motion she sheared my tresses from ear to ear. Both ear lobes could be seen hanging down on either side of the wedge of hair. When I went to school the next day, my appearance was so shockingly different the teacher made the whole class applaud to make me feel better, which it didn't. A short time later to improve the situation I took matters into my own hands and cut bangs. The frightened hair immediately stood straight up and never came down onto my forehead for months.

In Duxbury, even though the Depression was on, we had one, sometimes two, Portuguese maids. One of them, Agnes, was fascinating to Steve and me. We used to watch her taking a sponge bath. Her skin was blond in some places, like it had been bleached, but dark in others like a mulatto. She had the flattest feet, like two beaver tails. Her hair didn't seem like it was made of single strands, it was homogenized into a rounded mat, and quite greasy. We also watched as she took bugs out of her hair and flushed them down the toilet. My hair had now grown out enough to put curl papers on, which we did on occasion. But when my picture was to be taken in my great grandmother's wedding dress, my Mother blew me to a real beauty parlor and shampoo and curl. The lady who started to do me suddenly disappeared, bringing back the entire staff to examine my hair and scalp. My head was loaded with bugs. It took several nights at home picking these creatures out of my hair and dropping them into a jar of kerosene. My brother Steve told everybody. It took me many months to get over my embarrassment.

3

My Uncle Robert came from time to time to visit us. He was a portrait painter. I shuddered when he came down the driveway as he always wanted to do my portrait. This meant sitting for him in the enclosed porch of our house on the Point in Duxbury. I longed to be out playing touch football with the other kids. I suspected I was chosen because I was a free subject but Steve said Uncle Robert told Mother I had an unusually beautiful face, which was news to me.

The only thought I ever gave to clothing at this time was to not be different from everyone else. This meant blue jeans, sneakers or loafers. And sweaters. I've always loved sweaters, especially the ones Mum knit for me. When we were in Europe for a year when I was eight we bought beautiful Fair Isle sweaters which I remember to this day; the soft yoke patterns on the lovely grey-brown body; the little buttons on the collar. But all through Derby Academy and Winsor I horded sweaters. At Winsor School, we all used to get our sweaters and matching skirts at the Vermont Industry store in Cambridge. This uniform with the pearls was evident throughout in our yearbook. I still had the longish brown hair parted in the middle with bows at my temples. Very symmetrical. Very boring. My face never achieved any special character until later in New York when I had an automobile accident and went through the windshield. The resulting curved scar on my forehead was quite exciting. I am pleased even now when people notice it and ask about it, although few do.

Since I've "grown-up" and settled in to the face and figure that my genes destined, certain people have said that I reminded them of somebody. These have variously been: Virginia Woolf, Julia Child, William F. Buckley, Lady Asquith's granddaughter and Ava Gardner. Good Lord! This list has amused me because none of them were what I was trying to achieve.

I was born in Cambridge, Massachusetts, December 5, 1923. We lived my first six years on Hilliard Street, just off Brattle Street, in a house whose small front porch was held up by rounded pillars. The long French windows with folding double shutters let a lovely light into the living room. I remember the staircase going up to the second floor on which, on separate occasions, Steve and I sat having a contest to see who could get a lamb chop bone the cleanest, and also on which I sat trying to smoke a cigarette that Steve dared me to smoke at 5 o'clock in the morning. There is a picture of me with Mother pushing me in my carriage with little Steve holding on, and some forgettable Scotty dog in tow. Steve looked adorable as usual, like a little British lad. Mother doted on him, and I guess on me too. Generally however, our Swedish nurse, Ingrie, took us to Longfellow Park, that little jewel of a park on Brattle Street, where she chatted with the other nannies in her guttural English. She had terrible teeth and would never allow us any sweets. One night I hid some chewing gum in my mouth when I went to bed. The next morning it was discovered in a tangled mess behind my ear. After Ingrie, we got nice Nelly who was quite old, and then Gertrude from Newfoundland who was young and spirited and whom we adored. Steve and I hid raw yellow chicken legs in her bed in the attic. Mother spanked Steve with her hairbrush.

I have loved male companionship from early on. There were three men on whom I doted when I was six. One was Mr. Carr the postman who gave me a white candy mint out of his sack of mail. I used to sit on the porch steps and wait for him and we discussed affairs of the world. Sometimes I would wait for him hanging upside down like a bat on a branch of the maple tree that grew to the left of the path.

Then there was my friend the policeman who directed traffic from his high box at the cross road of Brattle Street and the road to the Buckingham School. I was allowed to walk to school, as he was there to shepherd me. He would stop the traffic in all directions like in *Make Way for the Duck-lings* and little Lydia would march confidently across.

But my best friend of all was Professor George Lyman Kittredge, the revered famous Shakespeare scholar and author, who lived just across the street from our house. Many an afternoon I would trot over to his house to pay him a visit. As he worked at his big cluttered desk, I would play on the floor with the cigar boxes he gave me, putting my crayons, autumn leaves, marbles in them and making colorful paper dolls for him, which he seemed to like. When Mother took Steve and me to Europe, our first stay was in London. The name of the small hotel we stayed in was Garland's. One afternoon we headed off to play in Regents Park. As we walked down the narrow hall of the hotel, we passed by a room in which a meeting was being held. The door was open as distinguished men were taking their places at a long table. There at the head of the table I spotted my dear friend Professor Kitteridge with his long white whiskers and sparkling eyes. I ran into the room, rushed up to him and climbed into his lap. He then said to the assembled group, "Gentlemen, please permit me to introduce you to my good friend Lydia." It is no wonder that Shakespeare has been an integral part of my life.

By 1930, we had to move all year round to Duxbury, having to sell our Cambridge house on Hilliard Street. My grandparents on Mum's side,

Grandma and Grandpa Young, had died, and the Depression was in full swing.

We had two houses in Duxbury, one on Powder Point, where later Ward and I were married, a beautiful house. Grandpa Young had willed this to Mother. And there was Pup's house, a vintage Cape Cod, in which we were to live those lean years. Pup's wool business was almost non-existent, and we had to conserve our resources in every way. In the summer, we rented out the Point house. Steve and I went to the Duxbury High School in the winter. Grandma Gifford lived with us occasionally, which was good as she read aloud to me and Steve every night before bed. We sprawled out on her big mahogany bed as she read the Bobbsey Twins, all the Augusta Hewell Seaman mysteries, *Treasure Island* and *Kidnapped*. We never wanted her to stop.

Grandma had a friend who went to Atlantic City every year and always sent her back a box of mint candy which looked like a huge bloc of styrofoam. She would break off bits for us. We sneaked bigger bits when she was out in the garden. Also salt-water taffy. Grandma was very beautiful and always smelled deliciously of lavender. Her head, however, shook constantly from side to side. There is a name for this palsy, but we all took it as a matter of course. After supper, we listened to radio, relishing *Myrt and Marge*, *Jack Armstrong*, *Buck Rogers*, *Bobby Benson*, *Little Orphan Annie* (with our Ovaltine "shake up mugs"), *John's Other Wife*, *Amos and Andy* and *Major Bowes*. Sundays the grownups listened to opera which I found awful.

Mother claims that when Lindberg flew across the Atlantic, a dense fog enveloped him over the coastline of Massachusetts. She said she heard the sound of his motors over Duxbury Beach and Gurnet Light. This was somewhat confirmed by radio reports. That was 1927.

Mother was very upset when her parents' huge house in Ashmont had to be sold. She never went back to see it. I remember being there when we went for Sunday lunch, driving from Cambridge. There was a huge parlor, reception room, smaller sitting rooms, and a music room with a large grand piano, and a victrola with that Philco dog cocking his ear. There was a flower room, in which all the flowers from the large garden were arranged for bouquets daily. There were several maids in the kitchens. One maid in the pantry regularly prepared butter pats, rolling them out between two grooved paddles. There was Warren, the chauffeur, who lovingly took care of all the means of locomotion, including horses, but most especially Pa's shiny black open touring car—a Pierce Arrow which Steve called *Mr. Red Wheels*—with horns he allowed us to toot, and lap rugs and running boards. Grandpa Young's car was a large buick Sedan. Grandma Young's presence was awesome. When I remember her I was about four years old, and she was always in bed, but she looked far from sick. She could have led a battalion, which is about the way she ruled the roost. She had thick, thick, auburn hair wound in a braid, making her head quite massive. On the bedside table next to her huge canopied bed, where she was propped up by pillows, there was a glass jar with huge yellow chewy gum drops in it. These she offered us when we came in to pay court. My mother never mentioned her much, except to say she was wonderfully civic minded, and led many organizations. I don't think they were close at all, especially since Mum was so totally devoted to Grandpa Young upon whom she doted.

Grandpa though gentle, was a smart business man who was a part owner of the *Charles W. Morgan* now at Mystic Seaport. He made a fortune in oil, not oil-oil, but whale oil, and other oils like linseed, doing much business in Fall River and New Bedford. He was away a good deal and wrote touching letters to Mother, his favorite. He counted on Mum to run the household, and she had to take care of young Rosamond and younger Teddy, chauffeuring them to music lessons, dancing lessons, and the dentist. Rosamond, who had a budding career as an opera singer, and showed much promise in recitals and concerts,went to Europe to study. Grandma Young didn't care at all for the bohemian life she was leading, and her involvement with a German concert-meister, and ordered her to come home. How rotten! When Grandpa died, they placed him in a small dark room. Steve and I were ushered in to see him. He looked so still and peaceful, his skin, smooth and white as fine porcelain. He is the only dead person I have ever seen.

It was discovered that in their wills, Grandpa and Grandma had left $2,000 to "little Stephen, and the Gifford girl-child" (that is me because in the period they were making out the wills for a year I didn't have a name). I was called merely Baby Sister. This money, a lot in those days, was to be used to take us abroad for a year, which was a blessing in that it relieved my father from having to provide for us during this dark financially depressed year. Mother and Steve and I headed for Europe on The S.S. Baltic. There is a photograph of us standing on deck which was printed in the Boston Transcript newspaper. We were dressed warmly in kneesocks, berets and heavy jackets. Mum looked stylish enough in a tweed suit, sensible shoes and one of those felt cloche hats pulled down over her forehead. Off we sailed while others stayed home with the paint peeling off their shutters. Poor Pa. He and Grandma kept each other company. It must have been so hard for him that year. But Mother wrote him every week, wonderful long, descriptive, loving letters which I still have. She and he called each other "Boots" (he called her *Boots-hot toots*) and signed them 1.4.3. (Minot's Light off Cohasset flashed 1.4.3, which everyone believed said *I love you.*) This same code was also printed inside Mum's wedding ring.) This European year warrants my attention here as it was one of the most formative years of my life. I have been to France and England many times since, but this trip, when I became eight years old, triggered attitudes and memories that have been abiding. "As the twig is bent, so doth the tree grow."

II

Europe, 1930

We sailed on The H.M.S. *Baltic* (Cunard/White Star Line) from Boston. I loved being on shipboard. In the dining room our steward created all kinds of figures for us folding our table napkins. Walking out on deck, I relished the smell of the sea, and that unmistakable aroma of wet ropes and tar, mingled with fumes from the kitchens baking cakes and preparing fried foods for our meals. I made friends with several stewards who would give me money to bet on the horse races that were held every afternoon in the lounge. The crew was not allowed to bet. I always won, and came back with my pockets bulging with winnings which I parceled out to delighted recipients. They called me *Lucky*. We arrived at our first port of call at Queenstown, Ireland at midnight. Mother woke us up to watch the docking activities, and people boarding ship. It was all very dramatic as the *Baltic* pulled alongside the dock, raining and foggy, with a big sea swell. As the gangplank was lowered, and passengers started to board, a group of people in a party mode came dockside to see one of their lady friends off. She looked funny to me. Mother said it was because she was drunk. Then suddenly as she was waving goodbye she fell into the water. Quick as a wink, sailors jumped in after her, and buoyed her up until the net was lowered, and she was brought up on deck like a large flounder. Although I was fascinated by the drama, this episode was all very alarming to a seven year old and I couldn't get it out of my mind for a long time. We docked in Liverpool, and then boarded a train for London. Our hotel, which was a family type hotel, was at the end of a narrow courtyard. The big square taxi, that I could stand up in, pulled up to the front door and we were warmly greeted by the first Britisher I had ever met, speaking in their beautiful native tongue. From that moment on I was an Anglophile.

Mother's great friends, Ed and Anne Kelly, were in London at this time staying at Claridge's. One very pea-soup foggy night when Mother was preparing to go out to the theater with the Kellys, Steve had a fit of homesickness, and cried and cried, not wanting her to leave. He would not be consoled. I couldn't see what all the fuss was about, for the porters and maids had cookies, and stories, and pampered us like Dicken's Oliver. Later we were taken to a theater where a costumed operetta was playing. We joined the Kellys and sat up in a small gold box overhanging the stage, and I was enchanted by the sounds and costumes. My first theater was mesmerizing. My love of make-believe had its beginning here. Steve and I played in all the parks, we climbed on huge cannons, and fed the ducks and swans in Green Park. We watched excitedly when the King's Mounted Guards came clinking and clattering in bright formation down Rotten Row. We tried to make the guards at Buckingham Palace smile. We doted on the Sunday British funny papers, and poured over all the cartoons lying on our stomachs in the sunny upstairs hall of our hotel. I fell down the stairs trying to do some acrobatic feat of foolishness, and cut my knee on the banister. Much solicitation by all. We even saw Princess Elizabeth with Princess Margaret being wheeled in a large pram by an imposing British nanny, whose veils streamed out behind her in the wind, like the pictures in Bemelmans.

We went on a train overnight to Scotland. I remember trying to sleep in our compartment on the seat with Steve, covered with coats. Mother was opposite. On the backs of the seats where one's head would rest were large crocheted doilies with the letters L.M.S., for *London, Midlands and Scotland*. We determined they had been fashioned especially for us: *Lydia, Marjorie and Steve*. I don't remember much about Scotland, but I remember feeling so sorry for beautiful Mary Queen of Scots being imprisoned at Fotheringay by Queen Elizabeth, being so cold and damp. I cried thinking about the little terrier dog concealed under Mary's skirts on her beheading day. When later we went to the Tower of London and climbed up a narrow circular staircase to the dark room where the little princes were murdered, I felt a strong horror of the absolute tyranny of monarchs. Even the Crown Jewels on dazzling display in another part of the Tower couldn't deflect my thoughts of that awful injustice.

Crossing the English Channel to France from Dover by boat train had its fascination as many of the passengers got seasick from the turbulent waters. All Paris seemed like a huge amusement park to Steve and me. There was *Luna Park* itself, with its many rides and attractions, and Mum was generous doling out francs for our amusements. But what I liked best about this wonderful city were the Luxembourg Gardens right out of Seurat's *La Grande Jette* with the shaded walks, the pebbled paths, the colorful flower borders. There was a pond where Steve sailed his toy boat, pushing it off into the wind with a stick and running to the other side to catch it as it glided in. But above all, I remember the carrousels gaily blaring music and beckoning to us in the gardens; brightly colored horses bobbing up and down with the country organ music emitting from each one. We loved riding on a particular one of these. We received a little stick from the proprietor as we mounted our steed and endeavored to "spear" the ring suspended at just the right arm's length away every time we went around. When one got the ring successfully one would receive the prize of large square chocolate covered caramel. I was frightfully good at spearing the ring, and won over and over again. Finally the proprietor told Mother I couldn't ride anymore as he was running out of caramels.

Our pension was off the Boulevard Raspail on the Left Bank, not far from the cimetières de Montparnasse. We ate in pension style in the dining room with the other guests. Mother ordered milk for us continually to keep our health up, although the French waiters scorned this beverage. Once when I was opening a container of milk it squirted like a geyser all over the Belgian gentleman next to us which endeared us to no one. There was a young count, or a duc, or a prince or some other type noble, about 13 years old who was there with his utterly gorgeous male tutor, who was very stuck on himself. Mother constantly challenged the tutor to games of ping-pong and always beat him very soundly, much to his consternation. He kept demanding a rematch but he never once could win.

Steve announced one morning that he should be allowed, like the young count, to see Paris by himself. Mother agreed, surprisingly I thought. She gave him some money, adjusted his cap and watched her 10 year old boy go out through the revolving door. We rushed back to our room and out on the tiny balcony and watched as Steve disappeared down the street and out of sight. Mother put her arm around me, and gave a big sigh. It seemed like ages that we waited in our room for his return. Mother knitting a bright red sweater. In about two hours he came back. He looked very tired. When he took his hat off his hair was parted in the middle and plastered down like patent leather. He also smelled of cheap perfume. His first stop had been at a barbershop, he got a haircut, which he could afford, but when the barber applied "lotion", that cost extra, which he hadn't counted on. The poor boy lost most of his money down a grate. He only had a little left with which, praise be, he bought a ticket on the underground metro, sitting in the subway car going all around Paris below ground, arriving back where he started. Pretty good for a little kid! He never asked to go alone again, however. Steve's memory of this is that he negotiated the Paris subway system alone in order to follow Mother to the atelier of her Russian dress-maker on the opposite side of Paris.

We had access to an ice skating rink nearby. I adored it, and we skated as Mother sat in the little cafe in the sun, knitting and watching us. I made good friends with a small Chinese gentleman who was just my size, and we went round and round together holding hands which we crossed in front of us. I totally missed the trip to Versailles because I preferred to skate with my Chinese friend. I feel somewhat guilty to this day.

Mother had arranged for us to go to French schools in Tours and Grenoble. We were to stay several months in these wonderful French cities. After Paris, we went by train to the heart of the Loire country to Tours. The Pension Brunswick on the Boulevard Beranger was a family type pension. Students and professors and various foreigners all ate in the same dining room, sharing the good hearty plain food. The atmosphere was very lively and non-touristy. The only other Americans were the Develins from Texas whose daughter, Chicky, became my pal, and Mrs. Nance and her son, Stanley, who was older than Steve. We kids played endlessly together in the large back garden where swallows flew in and out of an old barn. I had my eighth birthday party in the smaller dining room. Mother talked the cook into letting her make macaroni and cheese for me, which was my favorite dish on earth. The French cooks and maids were fascinated by Mother who decorated the table with marshmallows in each of which she placed a tiny candle, and under which she inserted a French franc for every child. Mother made many friends of all nationalities and spoke French more and more as she went along. She had a Russian lady who was a dressmaker make her some gorgeous clothes, very inexpensive. There was a black woolen cape with a gray satin lining, and a smashing black evening dress very low cut in front, with red and pink and mauve embroidery on the puffed black sleeves, very continental and chic. On Christmas Eve, we went to the huge ancient cathedral for the midnight service. I was so taken with the altar boys in their long white satin robes marching slowly down the aisle to the High altar, and lighting all the candles with long tapers. It was snowing hard when we came out of the church. Christmas Day was snowy too. Mum gave me a little sewing machine that really stitched. We bought a lovely engraving of the head of an English setter dog to take home to Pup. Steve missed him awfully. Pup had the picture in his bedroom for years.

As I remember it Steve took drawing lessons from an old man and brought back charcoal drawings of bowls and birds and flowers. Very good I thought. I went to a little école for girls, right down the boulevard from our pension. I wore the usual black smock, buttoned in the back, a dark grey skirt and knee socks. I took my slate with me. At the end of each week, we all got a little certificate for our report card, looking very official indeed with a red sealing wax stamp on it. I did very well, in all subjects, but I can't understand why as there must have been a big language barrier. Mother had to give the report card back at the beginning of each week so as to be reused. After awhile Mother sent me to have an in-depth course at "conversation" with a French family. I remember this earnest, unsmiling family all gathered around a round table firing questions and suggestions, with pas un mot d'anglais which none of them knew.

Steve and I loved the chocolate covered French caramels which we bought whenever possible at the local patisserie just off the boulevard. Every day as spring came and the weather was more favorable Boulevard Beranger became a bustling market with farmers and merchants setting up their wares on the broad central strip of the promenade. Once Steve made friends with an old donkey that was harnessed to a cart of cabbages and potatoes, and fed him one of those large caramels. You have never seen such a sight as the donkey's jaws opened and shut with stringy blobs of candy sticking to his enormous yellow teeth and getting tangled in his bit. We laughed and laughed. I suppose it was mean but the old animal relished every bit.

Mother took us to all the grands chateaux of the Loire—Amboise, Blois, Chambord, Azay-Le-Rideau, Chinon, Chenonceau. We got to feel we had been born as French royal children, and projected ourselves into the past with utter unselfconsciousness. We darted through mazes, gardens, dropped stones in moats, peered through slits in towers, gave orders like French generals for drawbridges to be opened and closed. I began to know Jeanne d'Arc, and nowhere more vividly than at Chinon. After all she was only a few years older than I, and I was big for my age. Jeanne d'Arc was my idol, and I used to practice on bended knee in my tights, with sword at rest by my side demanding the King help me raise an army to fight the English.

We went to a movie in Tours which still chills me to remember. It was called *"The Yellow Canary Murder Case."* In the movie, every time something awful and dire was to happen a black cat appeared silently and would sit strategically on a window sill, or staircase, or balcony with menacing eerie music as accompaniment. I was simply petrified never having experienced fear before, and could not sleep in my little room alone at the pension for many nights.

After Tours we moved to the mountain city of Grenoble. This pension, Belles Alpes, was situated above the city in the village of La Tranche. It was also a family establishment. There was a long driveway going up to it lined with those linden trees like gnarled fists. At the street end of the driveway there was a large water trough filled with icy cold water from the mountains where horses and donkeys stopped to drink. On warm days the sun melted the snow and ice and small torrents would rush down into the culverts on either side of the driveway. I remember seeing four Friars walking to town from their monastery on the mountains. They wore dark brown habits, like bathrobes, I thought, tonsured heads, feet clad only in open sandals. Through the snow and slush their toes looked pink and pained.

I remember young French boys filling their bicycle baskets with unwrapped long golden loaves of French bread they had bought a little way down the street at the boulangerie. Mother had come to this university city for the perfect French that was to be had at the University and enrolled in an advanced class to which she went regularly. Little Steve went to a Lycée in Grenoble. The two of them boarded a lumbering green bus at the end of the allée that took them down the steep village street to a trolley which then took them into the bustling city. I on the other hand could walk to school just beyond the nearby stores behind a forbidding iron gate, clutching my slate and feeling miserable. I walked slowly past all the delicious shops, with the aroma of fresh bread, chocolate, sausage and wines filling the cold March air. The school was all dark, with a cement courtyard, run by a very terrible lady who couldn't understand me at all. I was supposed to be in the third class, but because of my nationality and the language barrier, I was placed in the first grade among what I considered to be babies. I was as conspicuous with my height as a giraffe, and was made to sit in the front row. When I couldn't do the required penmanship exercise that awful teacher would hit my hand with a ruler, very hard. The reason I was not good at forming the required letters was that I was left-handed. I wasn't allowed to write with my left hand. When it came time for recess the children all went out to the dark dank play yard to play red light, or something corresponding to it. I remember the first game when I was "it." I counted my numbers slowly, and when I looked around, everyone had vanished. It was like a Fellini movie. Every day when I came back to the pension, I threw myself down on Mother's big oak bed and cried and cried, so much so that she eventually removed me from the school. But not until she had given my teacher a large piece of her outraged mind.

14

Steve's schooling was disappointing, although he wasn't persecuted. The plan that he would go to school among all French children did not come about, for there were no French boys in his class which consisted instead of Orientals, enrolled at the University and the Lycée to learn the French language. We both left these schools and Mother hired a young male student, Jean-Claude, as a tutor for us both. I can remember sitting in the glass pavilion attached to the back of the pension sipping chocolate and declining the verb être, and fumbling over the "subjonctif." But some afternoons, there was a "thé dansant", and a little orchestra would spirit-edly play familiar danses and marches. I sat entranced as couples gyrated and swooped vigorously over the dance floor. I especially loved the polka. Jean-Claude endeavored to teach me the waltz and the polka, and although he was no expert, it instilled in me the love of dancing which I have kept all my life.

I also became crazy about this young Frenchman. But I think he was more fond of Mother. I would watch them in the pavilion at tea time talking animatedly in French, with beaucoup de gestures, and laughing conspira-torially as grownups are apt to do.

The lovely French Alps loomed up behind the pension, and we would take glorious walks into the foothills, up a steep road, where on the sunny side the spring snow was beginning to melt. Tiny flowers like edelweiss, anemones, primroses and mosses bloomed in the small crevices and cracks of the high retaining walls on the mountain side of the road. Lizards bright-ly colored and iridescent sunned themselves on little ledges, still sleepy from their winter's rest. One early morning we boarded a bus and went up into the Alps to a ski village. The bus was filled with students headed for a day of skiing. The sun was bright, and the huge pines and firs that lined the route were loaded with newly fallen snow. We carried with us the picnic the pension had prepared. It was invariably the same, and invariably good, a lovely loaf of crusty bread, several slabs of cheese, some cold meat, small apples that weren't photogenic but juicy and delicious and some bars of chocolate. Mother ensconced herself on the outdoor terrace of an inn at the foot of the mountain, and sat in the sun whilst keeping an eye on Steve and me. She had rented a small toboggan for us, and we laboriously dragged it up quite a ways to where we could get a good ride down. The snow was packed by the skiers as this was the bottom of the ski run. Mother recount-ed later our descent which was hair-raising. She was alarmed when she caught sight of our sled gathering speed as we hurtled out of control straight down. Skiers screeched to a halt, and watched as we crashed into a snow bank that lined the parking lot. We thought it a triumph. But Mother had to pacify the discombobulated skiers who complained vigorously. That night we went back on the same bus tired and happy. The students sang songs as we rode through the dark. And I fell asleep in one boy's lap.

As spring bloomed fully, the meadows appeared increasingly verdant as the snow cover receded up the mountain. French housewives replaced their multitude of pots of geraniums out on front stoops. We now packed up and headed by bus for the Riviera. The Kelleys had rented a villa in the hills above Fréjus. We were to stay nearby in St. Raphael in a little hotel au bord de la mer. The route we took from Grenoble was the route through the Alps that Napoleon took, scenic but tortuous and winding, and there were icy conditions in the elbow of curves and dark valley. Steve and I monopolized the broad back seat of the bus, peering out the rear window at the retreating scenery. Our attention was riveted on a young man on a motorcycle. He had goggles and a muffler scarf trailing behind. He stopped when we stopped, and kept close to us all the way to the Mediterranean. Steve and I noticed him in the lobby of our hotel. It developed that he was following Mother. We thought that romantic. Mother denied it hotly. But we never saw the young swain again.

The beach at St. Raphael was wonderful and we played in the sun and sand for hours under the watchful eye of a "mamselle" who sat in the shade of a palm tree. I don't know what it was that Steve and I did that was so bad, but a situation developed. We were too much for the management. Mother had a heated talk with the propriétaire insisting that we were not "enfants terribles." She got so mad that in high dudgeon, she announced we were leaving and going to the *Grand Hotel*, which we could not afford. This establishment was very large, but it being not yet "le saison" was not very full. In the large dining room, there were more waiters than diners. In the silence broken only by the sound of dishes and glassware clinking, Steve and I could not suppress our giggles, and had to be sent away from the table by Mum several times. We were fascinated to silence, however, by an elderly gentleman who had ordered screens placed around him to keep off the draft. The waiters hovered around him responding to his every whim, of which he had many. But what most particularly fascinated us was a huge parrot that sat on a roost in this little enclosure, receiving choice tidbits. The two of them clucked at each other like the most amicable married couple. The Grand Hotel was grist for Steve's and my adventurous spirits. We roamed all through the vast service rooms, laundries and corridors.

Our most dramatic exploit, however, ended badly for me. Our rooms were on the top floor. All floors were joined by a circular staircase. When we leaned out over the brass stair rail we could see way down the spiral to where the concierge stood at a desk to conduct all the hotel business. He had a large guest ledger open in front of him. Steve bet me that I couldn't spit and hit this target. Well I did. Bulls eye. Everyone was furious. I've never seen Mother so mad. When asked to explain who had done it, Steve said I had. I was marched by the ear to the hotel manager to apologize, which I could hardly do out of fear and trembling. To this day, I think it was as much Steve's crime as mine, but he got off unscathed. Drat!

Not only was it Mardi Gras time, but the Grand Prix bicycle marathon was careening through every village and hamlet and came along the Boulevard des Anglais in Nice. The promenades were dazzling with brilliant flags and ornaments. As the parade got in full swing the streets were thronged with gaiety, the climax of which was the Mardi Gras parade. Mother got us very good seats in a grandstand lining the route, and we donned masks such as fencers wear to protect us from the shovels-full of confetti and flowers that were pelted at us from those on the floats. One afternoon when Mother was involved in a bridge game with new friends at the hotel, Steve and I went down to the boardwalk and sat on a curb stone to watch the touring bicyclists streaming through town exhausted and sweaty, bent parallel to the ground over their handlebars. When there was a slight break in the flow we dashed across the street hand in hand, and went into an inviting little tea shop which had outside cafe tables where one could sit in the sun and watch the parade. When the waitress came to take our order Steve very enterprisingly ordered "un pot du thé avec deux tasses." We only had enough money for one, which we had counted out carefully beforehand.

This sojourn in the South of France formed an impression on me which has been indelible. All the Matisse-like scapes of flags, the deep blue Mediterranean becoming turquoise as it approached the shore, the bleached curve of the beach disappearing towards Spain, the white stucco architecture, pink tiled roofs, bougainvillaea tumbling from balconies, soft mimosa everywhere, the cafe tables with red and white table cloths studding the boulevards like jewels, the gorgeous clear, clear sunlight that made one forget that leggings, scarves and mittens ever existed. But I loved best the umbrella pines that enveloped the villas perched on the hillsides above Cannes. I had always loved the New England pines, vertical and stoic. But these pines were like graceful parasols, not quite blocking out the light which was softly protective. The Kelleys' villa was set not only among lovely trees, but being near Grasse, was amid vast fields of flowers, which basked in the warm benign light. The aroma of freesias, hyacinths and narcissus was so delicious. But best of all was the scent of acres of lavender buzzing with bees. And also thyme which was bursting in poofs among the terraced loveliness.

We were asked by the Kelleys to a luncheon party on the terrace of their villa at which were assembled all kinds of glamorous grownups. The Kelleys' daughter Jane had arrived from the States. She was the most beautiful individual I'd ever seen. and she soon became surrounded by adoring men. She was dressed in a cool lime linen dress with a white collar. She was like Grace Kelly, with pale blond hair drawn back in soft knot, a downy peach complexion, and the softest speaking voice you ever heard. I marvelled at her conversation, which was never over-animated, but which riveted her admirers as she looked at each one with steady blue eyes. I later often practiced in front of a mirror; my hair drawn back with an elastic: "Oh, isn't that fascinating," "How could anybody be so amusing," "Tell me that again, I want to remember every word." But I was never to be such a "femme fatale." To this day, however, if one mentions "mimosa," "lavender," "umbrella pines" or "villa" I become an entranced eight year old again basking in the dazzling environment of the Riviera which has drawn so many adorers from the time of the ancient Romans and before. I have been many times to France since, but no French impression has been so abidingly vivid as on this visit.

III

The Thirties

The thirties were my school years. The year abroad had discombobulated all continuity, for I had missed normal grades and teaching methods, and when I came home no one knew where to put me nor at what level. They wanted to put me back into the lower school with "infants." I was mature socially and tall physically, and threw such a fit that my mother became alarmed. I would have none of it, and with Mother's full support was enrolled in the third grade, with the older kids at the High School, thereby skipping second grade altogether; also skipping a certain level of arithmetic, geography and spelling. These gaps I bluffed my way past all through school, never knowing what a fraction was, or the source of the Nile, or the whereabouts of the Himalayas. But I did know how to speak French; I intuitively understood the persuasive magic of a peasant girl from Orleans. I had intimate kinship with Mary Queen of Scots, having inherited her height, her love of golf and her fatal fascination with romance.

In this third grade, I saw some of the same tyranny of a teacher that had been inflicted on me in Grenoble. A young Portuguese, Domenic Fernandez (who later ran the multi-million dollar Fernandez Super Markets in Plymouth County) was humiliatingly placed in the front row of our grade. He was fourteen years old, and very big amongst the little kids. He was so dumb scholastically that for years he didn't get advanced to the next grade. He was also bad, and little wonder that he kept running away, not showing up at school. The teacher hit his knuckles hard with a ruler also, but he didn't wince. I made friends with him, and many years later I bumped into him in his huge store. He remembered me.

Eddie Frasier and George Davis were Steve's best friends in his fourth grade class, just ahead of me. Eddie's father ran the golf shop at the Duxbury Club. George's father was the chief lighthouse keeper at Gurnet Light. George's sister Olive was my friend, and I was asked on occasion to visit out at the Gurnet. It was a great adventure. We would be taken by the Davises in their truck with its huge balloon tires across Powder Point bridge and then through the dunes to High Pines and from there to a sandy road that bumped its way to the foot of the lighthouse. Once we were picked up by a coast guard van, and because the tide was way out we could speed along the hard smooth sand for several miles until we had to cut back up to the rocky promontory on which the lighthouse was built. The beach at Duxbury is a magnificent white sandy marvel with the energetic Atlantic Ocean on one side, and the more serene Duxbury Bay on the other side. It is about nine miles long from the bridge, but about fourteen from the Marshfield end at the left. The Davis family all lived in the lighthouse which had roomy living quarters. It was a spooky and awesome experience to go to bed in the little room under the lighthouse structure, where all night long every two minutes the whole room would light up as the powerful beacon circled overhead for ships at sea. On foggy nights with the foghorn blowing incessantly I could hardly sleep for the drama of it all. One night when Olive's Mother made her sleep in another room on account of her bad cold, I was left alone. I was feeling a little lonely in this situation, with the foghorn's basso profundo blaring, and the constant light change, when into my room came George and climbed in bed with me. I was really so pleased to see him and we sat up in bed side by side chatting like magpies, and trading stories. But our innocent nocturnal rendez-vous came to an end when the search light lit up a dark massive figure standing in the doorway. It was Mrs. Davis shocked at the two of us in bed. She registered strong disapproval which we didn't understand. It was quite exciting. The next day George and I walked way out on a long sand spit at low tide just off Saquish Beach. We wrote our initials in the sand and watched as the incoming tide washed them away. We walked back hand in hand, feeling a marvelous bond.

Duxbury in the winter was totally different from Duxbury in the summer when all the summer people came from Boston. Then the wicker furniture was placed again on the porches, the floats were reattached to the long piers jutting out into the Blue Fish River and along Standish Shore. The post office was crowded as was Sweetser's Store, and all the boat yards were busy with yachtsmen sanding and scraping and preparing their boats for launching. I simply adored the summers there, especially later as a teenager revelling in the picnics on the beach, singing around fires, dashing in our cars to the Plymouth movies, attending the yacht club dances, turning on our victrolas to our endless records of Glen Miller, Artie Shaw, Benny Goodman, Larry Clinton, Harry James, etc. We danced all the time. Our group sang harmony throughout the summer, with nary a thought or worry in our heads. That is, till the war came.

But before that in the early thirties, when we were living in Duxbury we were "townies" all year. I experienced another Duxbury which I loved, when my friends were Peggy Nathan whose father ran the fancy grocery store and Jean Horsefal whose father was head groom at a small riding stable. Peggy had two horses herself, and she and I would ride all over the back sandy roads, cutting up hidden paths back of the railroad tracks, barreling down Mayflower Street and relishing the cold winter air and the soft feel of the horses' thick winter coats. The cranberry bogs were flooded after harvest, and these made wonderful skating ponds, safe, not deep, and frozen before any other body of water. In early April, Pup used to take us to pick mayflowers back of the town dump and the cemetery. He knew where the biggest and most fragrant clumps occurred underneath the oak trees, and like truffles, lay quietly hidden beneath a light cover of oak leaves. There was one cold January when Arctic air moved in and totally froze the bay. Steve and Pa and I walked almost to Clarks Island on the frozen salt surface. Pup used to get some of the scallop fishermen to take him out to Clark's Island where the only "pink turnips" were to be found. And once I went with him to collect these sensationally sweet wonderful root vegetables which only existed in this particular soil, and like Videllia onions could not be duplicated in another environment. On Saturday afternoons we often went to Plymouth to the movies. One unforgettable afternoon Mother took us to see *Naughty Marietta* with Nelson Eddy and Jeanette MacDonald, and it happened. I fell deeply in love with Nelson Eddy. It wasn't at all fun, but it was unmistakable. I couldn't eat or sleep for days from thinking about him, and "tramp, tramp, tramp along the byways" coursed through my brain. I was totally bouleverseed by *"Ah Sweet Mystery of Life, At Last I've Found You."* Of course it wasn't Jeanette walking down the long staircase as she is reunited in bliss with her lover, but me. My emotions came as quite a shock to me, and being so unrequited, were awfully frustrating. Mother noticed, besides my not taking nourishment, that I roamed around the house humming to myself, and not speaking to anyone when spoken to. But soon my affections were turned in another direction. The Duxbury High School for their senior class play put on *Peg 'O My Heart* and the lead was played by dark haired, handsome Gilbert Redmond. The title tune then replaced *"Ah, Sweet Mystery"* and I was well into my fickle nature, now adoring from afar a real life idol, Gilbert. Probably his first and last appearance on the musical stage.

Steve's and my educational life took a turn for the better when we were accepted at Derby Academy in Hingham on scholarship. This involved going 40 miles from Duxbury each day to Hingham by train, which we soon did as a matter of course, picking up other children at stations along the way headed also for Derby. A very nice gentleman got on at Seaview, a few stops beyond Duxbury, who was going into Boston for business. I always saved a seat for him and for some reason he liked to sit with me. We talked like mad until I got off at Hingham, waving goodbye from the platform. I think he must have liked children, and didn't have any. He had kind of a sad, gentle face, and I tried to cheer him up. I think I did.

There was a girl, Ann Converse, who made the trip to school on the train with us. She was a year younger than I but very crafty. Once we set up a lemonade stand on a card table in front of our house. Mother provided all the fixings plus delicious homemade brownies. We were perfectly situated to lure the evening businessmen returning from Boston who drove past our house. Mother gave us some nickels and dimes to make change. We did a fairly brisk business, and when it came time to close up shop, Ann ate the remaining brownies, washed down with lemonade, divided the money including the change in half and went home. That was a slick business manoeuvre.

Mother used to have to drive to Hingham to get us every Wednesday afternoon which was a half day at Derby. Ann and I and Steve went back with her to Duxbury. Ann's Mother never made the trip, why I don't know. One day Mum couldn't come for some very good reason, and we all had to wait a couple of hours and take the evening train. As we boarded the train, Ann mumbled something awful about my Mother under her breath. I don't remember exactly what, but it so enraged me that I wanted to kill her. Strong emotion! I waited for whatever action I was going to take! We got almost to Marshfield, and the train car we were in had emptied out. As the conductor finished turning the seats around the other way for the next day's trip and went to the next, I headed to where Ann was sitting. She saw me coming and dodged my first attempt at killing her. We jumped over seats, leaping and crashing, me yelling "you take that back what you said about my Mom." Just as we were pulling into Duxbury, I caught her trying to get out the door. I let my fist fly at her face, and gave her a marvelous bloody nose. It fills me with utter satisfaction when I think of it now. I'm glad I didn't kill her. I have never hit anyone before or since.

Kids will be kids. But there was a pack of us at Derby that did some really bad stuff. We stole candy. The opportunity arose every afternoon after school when we walked down Burditt Avenue, to the railroad station. We had over an hour to wait for our train, and we spent much of that time at Dykeman's Drug Store just on the other side of the track. If we had money we bought root beer, or ice cream, or a frappe. If we didn't we wandered through the store and "unseen" lifted chewing gum , Mr. Goodbars, Charleston Chews, Necco Wafers, etc. We got really good at it, we thought, judging by the pile of stuff we all pooled together on the train. But I can see the headmaster's face now. Mr. Cherry looked like Abraham Lincoln, only sinister. He called us all in and announced that he couldn't run a ship if there were those who were rowing the wrong way. Nothing more happened than admonishment, not banishment. I can see the Dykeman's Bros. faces to this day, and Mrs. Dykeman watching us all the time, and then calling school. I never again ever stole anything, not even hardly a bar of soap from a hotel, although occasionally a hand towel.

Before the Hingham "heists", my little friend Joffy Maxwell and I found a small coin collection in Mother's living room closet in Duxbury. We took out several coins and marched up the hill past the Blue Fish River bridge to Peterson's drug store. Mr. and Mrs. Peterson were both mean and stingy as could be. For instance if you bought an ice cream cone, they would scrape off all the extra ice cream on the side of the cone. If you bought a little pleated cup of peanuts that sat on the counter in a huge glass jar they would shake off any peanuts that rose above the rim of the cup. This day Joffy and I presented the coins in payment for our cones. Mrs. Peterson called to her husband and they examined the coins silently. Nothing was said, but they did give us a "free" cup of peanuts. We thought this a triumph. The Petersons probably retired to Florida on our coins. I don't think Mum ever connected us with the lost coins. We didn't realize what a dishonest thing we had done. I felt the real criminals were the Petersons.

Another aspect of our "bad" youth was to torment other kids younger than ourselves. I had been teased unmercifully by the older Lawsons' girls who lived on the hill on the way to the post office. When I arrived to play everybody hid and never appeared at all, forcing me to walk home, miserable, not understanding. The Lawsons had a lot of children. Mrs. Lawson was a painter and painted in a barn down the slope from their garden. The atmosphere of the studio was quiet, and I was reverential as I passed it, going down to the marshes with Joanny, my friend. Often Joanny had to sit for her Mother, and I would wait patiently for her on the ramp going into the barn. Her grandfather was Frank Benson, the famous American painter of beautiful family portraits and landscapes. I didn't realize this till later when I became involved myself with art when we were at Mother's house on Powder Point when it wasn't rented. Another Joan and I, who lived directly behind us, found a wonderful culprit in Midge whom we discovered would do anything we asked her to do. There was a marvelous evergreen tree next to Joan's house with huge cascading lower branches which touched the ground, forming a splendid dark vault inside which we used as our club house. We told Midge she could join our club if she would let us tie her to the trunk inside like an African slave. If she cried out the natives would surely come and kill her. Poor Midge with her arms in ropes around the tree stayed there silently for a long time. It was very satisfying.

Our house on Cedar Street which we lived in most of the time, had a studio over the ell back of the kitchen. This contained all of Uncle Robert's paintings and the paraphernalia that Mum allowed him to store there. It being locked always, I had to find a way to get in, which I did by going through the garage and out to the back where a window in the studio could be pried open. I spent many hours pouring over his early art school drawings, his later nude still-lifes, his water colors of nymphs and satyrs, and some lovely paintings of Duxbury. The paints, somewhat dried, smelled of linseed oil, some palettes still contained hardened puddles of beautifully mixed colors. Most of the brushes were sable and soft in a variety of shapes. I liked best the one shaped like a fan. But this dusty studio, full of cobwebs and easels and art, was as magic to me as the Forsaken Garden. It was clearly why I became a painter, not because of any great talent I had, but for the yearning to be associated with what I considered to be beauty. Also there was mystery and romance and I'm afraid tragedy in Uncle Robert's life, which lacked complete fulfillment as an artist and as a human being. I felt very sorry for him and he became something of a hero for me. He was my Father's youngest brother and when it became evident that Robert wanted to pursue an artistic career, all the Giffords, including my Father, loudly voiced their objections. Why couldn't he be like other boys and play football. What a sissy. Poor Robert. But he did make a career out of painting despite the family disapproval. He mostly did portraits, some of which were charming, especially of children. He created quite an enviable life style where he would travel to Virginia and get commissions to paint all the members of one family, joining the household for weeks on end, relishing the soft southern hospitality. When he finished one family, he would move down the James River to another plantation and sock in for another stint. He was a very handsome man and must have been welcomed by his hostess as a desirable extra. There was a rumor that he was living with a Russian countess in New York but that was never proven. As I grew older I lost track of Uncle Robert until I eventually moved to New York myself to live, but more of that in another section.

At the end of the thirties some recovery had taken place economically. Pup's wool business was never stable, but it did have some ups. Steve was enrolled at Milton Academy, and I was at the Winsor School in Boston. This entailed moving out of Duxbury for the school months and renting in Milton. We rented four different houses these four years, Blue Hill Road, Canton Avenue, Randolph Avenue and Brookside Road. These were our teen years. Our living room was always full of Milton boys, sprawled all over the sofas, Steve's cronies, particularly the boarders who practically lived at our house craving home-cooked meals. I never paid much attention to any of them. Crocker and Pud, and Howie and all seemed just part of the family and not at all candidates for a beau. I was picked up by a chauffeur every morning who worked for the Mathers, and he drove Phyllis Mather and me to Boston to Winsor, appearing in the afternoon punctually to take us home. And one year it was Dorky Hovey's chauffeur who did the transportation. Mrs. Hovey thought I would be a good influence on the younger Dorkey who was a bit vague and willful. She was over six feet tall.

I loved the Winsor School. My four years there were very contented ones full of friends and friendships which have abided for fifty years. As of this writing, I am preparing for our 50th reunion in May. All of us old girls are so enjoying the preparations for it. I am impressed with the lasting qualities of straight-arrow niceness, good judgment, decent values and humor that my best friends have maintained over time. None of us has set the world on fire, but we have lived caring about others, and from time to time have put back in the earth what we took out.

I chose to go to Winsor rather than Milton because it had a swimming pool, which I thought a good enough reason. Also Mother wanted to keep Steve and me apart in our schooling which was probably wise. The school was very civilized and I loved all the maids in their black uniforms and white caps and aprons, especially Jenny who stood by the front door like a concierge. I was not a great student by any means, but I managed to metabolize some of the fine teaching that was based on a revolutionary concept of Mary Packard Winsor, the founder. It was that all subjects should be taught on a pyramid of time, and all were interrelated. French history should be allied with French art, Latin should be intertwined with Roman civilization and math, and the pyramid was constructed on layered foundations. Nothing was isolated. When Ward and I chose the Thomas School in Connecticut for Lyn and Margot, the same principles were applied. Miss Thomas and Miss Winsor had been best of friends and engineered their curriculums with an identical concept.

At one point in my senior year when my marks were not quite up to

academic snuff the teachers felt I couldn't afford all the extras I was involved in such as glee club, drama club, all sports—hockey, swimming,
tennis and basketball. I didn't mind curtailing some of these, but I cared
awfully about playing the part of Sir Robert de Baudricourt in Shaw's *St.
Joan*. Although I had prepped myself all my life for St. Joan, I was no
competition for the beautiful Lanny who was a real actress and even had
that Galahad type hairdo that you see in all the paintings of Joan, especially the ones done by N.C. Wyeth. But the teachers relented and I played Sir
Robert with such gusto that my "throne' toppled into the wings with me
in it when my scene commenced. "No eggs, no eggs, thousand thunders
man, what do you mean no eggs," I bellowed at poor Pouligny. Then came
the crash. It made quite a stir in the audience, but evoked much laughter
backstage among my fellow actors.

Winsor had a student government which was built on the principle of
a city. There were a student mayor, chief-justice, traffic department, health
department, and other city government officials. As a younger student, one
was always in awe of the elected officials, and especially when arrested by
a senior policeman for running in the hall, or not keeping to the right of
the big black dot at the curve of the hall leading to the library. I am still
amazed at the Pavlov response that a clock reading 11:07 a.m. evokes in
me—salivation and total loss of concentration on whatever prior matter
was at hand. That was the magic time for recess, and everyone piled up to
the dining room for orange juice and the most delicious oatmeal cookies
as large as saucers. The food at school was frightfully good, served by tidy
uniformed waitresses. Friday noon we relished succulent spaghetti and meat
sauce, with gooey fudge squares for dessert.

My friends at Winsor have been abiding. Although I haven't seen very
much of Jib and Buddie and Margie since I moved away from Boston, I
have kept up the friendships in one way or other. Anne Williams (Willy)
was my closest friend and she and I eventually went to Europe together for
a year. When we were at school she lived in Chestnut Hill and I often
visited her there, spending the night after dances, going to skating parties
at the Country Club, and always being enchanted with the lifestyle of her
household. Her father was Ben Ames Williams the writer, a massive man,
rather awesome, who had been reared in Tennessee as a young boy. I remember Willy saying his family all slept together in one bed in a cabin
when he was a youngster. Now that he was a well-known author of such
books as *Leave Her to Heaven* and *House Divided, Comes Spring*, and
many more, the family was very comfortably situated in Brookline. Willy's
Mother, Aunt Floss, was such a contrast to Uncle Ben. She was very petite

with black curly hair and pink cheeks. She had been brought up in China, with missionary parents, I think, and had an oriental exquisiteness about her. Then there was wonderful Kaye, the tiny general factotum who had been nurse to Willy when she was a baby, and been with the family ever since keeping everybody and everything in perfect order. She even ironed our underwear. She drew baths for us with bath salts, pressed our dresses for parties, and although there was a cook, Kaye made specialties like toll house cookies, fresh bread, and always kept the cookie jar full. She made a simply splendid green salad which was like nothing I had ever experienced. The big wooden salad bowl was rubbed with garlic which I had never tasted before, and to which I am addicted to this day. The salad dressing was merely lemon and olive oil.

I loved being at the Williamses for meals. Especially if Willy's brothers, Bud and Chuck, were at home from Dartmouth. I was crazy about Bud which all started on a sleigh ride around Chestnut Hill one snowy winter evening. I thought that he paid a bit of attention to me, especially later when he danced with me as we all gathered in the living room for hot chocolate where we rolled back the rug to dance. The song we danced to was "In the Still of the Night." I used to "gaze out my window" with thoughts of Bud. But I didn't stand a chance. He was courting Jamie Marshall whom he eventually married.

The conversation at the Williams dinner table both in Chestnut Hill and also at Searsmont was fascinating to me, although I couldn't contribute to it. Uncle Ben talked so knowingly about current events and world affairs with the assembled company. My family didn't discuss politics or any controversial subjects at our dinner table. My father and mother blamed so much of their reversal of fortune on Franklin Delano Roosevelt that we couldn't bring his name up without them getting angry and upset. Democrats were ethnically different from us Republicans. When we were at Searsmont all kinds of literary people came for dinner. I remember one large lobster feast was held at a long table set up in the barn. Kenneth Roberts was there and he and Uncle Ben, who were good friends, carried the conversation to what I thought were dazzling heights, erudite and witty.

I remember the utter joy of visiting them in Searsmont, Maine, at Hardscrabble Farm. The peace on earth of lying for hours in a blueberry field, just reading, with Willy. The fun of piling into the car with Bud and Chuck heading for the swimming hole in the woods which had a waterfall. We stood on a ledge under the fall, soaped our hair with Ivory soap and dove through the falls far down into the deep black water below, the bubbles cascading up behind us. Then the hot afternoons when we helped with the haying up at Mr. Mariner's farm on the ridge above Hardscrabble. I was introduced to obstacle croquet which was set up all around the property. Not a normal lay-out, but like a miniature golf course with many obstacles to overcome. The games all hotly contested lasted a couple of days, often being called on account of dark, and resumed immediately after breakfast. There were several smashing penalty shots one could execute. One was to send the opponent's ball up the ramp and through the barn where it dropped off into a field. Another was through the garden gate and into the road where the ball could enter a culvert and practically go to the next village. Aunt Floss's beautiful garden with its hollyhocks, roses and delphiniums was out of bounds totally. One had to be super careful and deft not to get in it, as the penalties were extreme.

Hardscrabble had no plumbing for bathrooms. One went out into the ell behind the kitchen to a very civilized privy. I thought this was great. Sears Roebuck and Montgomery Ward catalogues were there for good reading. When we were at Hardscrabble in winter it was mighty cold on one's bottom to sit for any length of time, so one didn't read much then. Kaye would heat up flat irons, wrap them in flannel and put them in each bed for needed warmth. The windows were open at night and I remember snow had come in on the foot of my bed one morning.

As I was leaving to catch the train at Rockland, and Chuck was driving me, I passed through the dining room to collect my bags which I had put by the door. Uncle Ben was eating his breakfast of cereal, blueberries and heavy cream. I said "Do I have everything, Uncle Ben?" He said "You *do* have everything". I think it was meant as a compliment. One summer afternoon Uncle Ben and Willy and I carried a blue canoe over the back-fields and down a mossy bank to a small river. We paddled down stream past dense woods, winding along farmland listening to Uncle Ben's tales of this territory, of which he knew every inch. I felt I had gone back in time as he told of the Indians who lived there and recounted wonderful adventures of the sturdy souls who braved the wilds to make settlements. When we came to an old mill, we portaged the canoe around the stone fixtures and resumed our course.

Uncle Ben worked every morning from 5:30 for three hours in a small study he had built in the loft of the barn. A wooden staircase went up to it. It had that wonderful smell of new pine boards, mixed with old barn smells. He had a secretary in Chestnut Hill whose name was Miss Plunkett, but I don't think she came with him to Maine.

IV

Bryn Mawr, 1941–45

The last summer I visited at Hardscrabble, my brother Steve sent me a telegram saying I had gotten into Bryn Mawr. This astonished everybody, including me. But I was very happy as I was anxious to get away from the Boston environs. Most of my class at Winsor went to Smith or Vassar, only one other than me going to Bryn Mawr.

Although I felt quite sad leaving Mum and Pup who put me on the train for Philadelphia at Back Bay Station in Boston, I was excited and never once felt scared or homesick. This was the autumn of '41. I came home for my 18th birthday on December 5th of that year, and after a lovely weekend in Boston, Steve drove me in his car to the South Station to return to college. The music on his car radio was interrupted as we approached the large railroad terminal. *"The Japanese have bombed Pearl Harbor."*

My college days were bracketed by the war. The peace was signed four years later at the time of my graduation. All of our male friends and relatives and some females were in uniform. The ROTC at Harvard was loaded with Steve's friends who subsequently scattered to all parts of Europe after training and Steve went to Fort Benning and later to France and Germany. Dick Winslow went to Fort Dix and then France I think. My greatest beau Bill Floyd joined the ski troops' 10th Mountain Division and went to train in Colorado, and later was among the first groups to land in Italy at Anzio. Many guys joined the Navy and went to even remoter spots on battleships and carriers etc. like Guadalcanal, the Phillipines and Corregidor.

When the mail came in to Rhoads Hall at Bryn Mawr all the girls clustered around to get their beloved letters from APO locations, from far flung corners of the world.

I threw myself into all activities at Bryn Mawr. I joined all the teams, tennis, hockey, swimming and basketball, and eventually became captain of most of them. But field hockey was the pre-eminent sport in Philadelphia, as it was at Bryn Mawr, held in about the same esteem as soccer in Italy. There were many rival clubs. Our coach, Miss Grant, was English and she vigorously carried on that tradition of field hockey started in England. I made the varsity my freshman year which was unusual. There was a newspaper picture of me shooting a goal past the famous all-Philadelphia goalie M. Elliott at one of the games. My father was so proud and carried the picture around in his wallet. It became pretty tattered as he showed it so often to his cronies. I wasn't the greatest athlete, but I was tall and energetic and could pull my weight on the teams. Mother was very proud of the fact that I, too, was awarded the yellow flannel Bryn Mawr blazer when I was a senior for athletic achievement. She had gotten one 25 years earlier. I promptly lost mine when I took it to a tennis match, and left it behind when we got on the bus. Chris Waples was the star athlete at college, I think on the all-American or all Philadelphia hockey team later. She was a senior when I was a mere freshman, and I looked up to her with great adoration. She wore her yellow blazer constantly, and looked mighty swell in it. I never dreamed I would be good enough to get one. They didn't give them out every year, by any means. Chris befriended me which made me proud.

I had gotten into Bryn Mawr on the strength of my two college exams, one English, and the other Scholastic aptitude. At Winsor I was part of what they called the New Plan which allowed you not to be tested for Science and Math, etc. This was a blessing, as I scored very high in English and Scholastic aptitude, but would have failed if tested in those other departments. I only had one high point in my scholastic achievement at Bryn Mawr and that came my first year. I won the freshman English prize for my paper on Virginia Woolf, and beat out all the real brains from Shipley and Brearley and Westover. Actually, I shared the prize with Jane Hoopes who was a genius and who wrote a scientific treatise on some physics experiment. She was so intellectual that her marks were off the charts. I suspect she eventually got a Nobel prize for science or worked at Los Alamos on the Manhattan project. But the curve of my scholastic graph never maintained this altitude. I won't say it was all down hill, but my academic career was checkered to say the least.

I really worked hard to keep up, and the volume of work was extensive. I went home for vacation once on the train with the complete works of Shakespeare under my arm. We were assigned by Dr. Sprague to read *all* the plays for his course. This I thought ridiculous, but had not yet rebelled against the system. I was struggling away in the stacks night and day, writing papers and slavishly trying to memorize my class notes. My study habits were not good. I could not skip and get the gist of things when I was reading, I had to read every word. When in class, I would furiously take down every word the professor uttered. This meant I did little thinking of my own. I was too inhibited and insecure for that. I would love to go back to college and attend classes now without taking one note. I could then see what stuck and what didn't. I feel I have tremendous understanding, but no memory. Perhaps there is much I learned at Bryn Mawr that I metabolized deeply that only later came to the fore in my being. I have always felt that education should not be vocational. Its purpose is to make known the unknown along the paths of life one chooses, to illuminate the mind with the light of good judgment, to make order out of the chaos of infinity, and to bless the mind's eye with a capacity for sensing beauty in the world. And furthermore for those few lucky souls who are creative, education should be the catalyst for converting that inner sense of beauty into a re-creation of it, which is art.

I rebelled against the intellectual approach to learning whose main goal was the amassing of knowledge in the attic of the mind. How much tin was imported from Bolivia, not important. The gross national product of Uganda, not important. What was Tchaikovsky's state of mind when he wrote his Fifth Symphony? Was Van Gogh crazy? What were the dates of the Boer War? Examinations, it seemed to me, dealt with externals. And how much one knew never correlated with what one felt and understood.

Furthermore, at the time I was at college the war was ever present. For those of us left at home when all the horrible news of D-Day, the invasion of Normandy, the ghastly treatment of Jews in concentration camps, seemed to minimize the importance of Descartes, Spinoza, Shakespeare's sonnets, and Schopenhauer. Besides I disagreed with much of the philosophy I was learning. Descartes said, "I think therefore I am." I believed, "I feel therefore I am."

Halfway through my sophomore year I wanted to leave college. My poor family was so distressed, Mother especially hoped I would follow in her illustrious footsteps. When I arrived home on Beacon Hill with my friend Sue Coleman after a short ski vacation and announced my decision to leave Bryn Mawr, my father said, "A Gifford doesn't quit." So I didn't. Mother always thought that something very traumatic must have happened to me to come to such a conclusion. Her college experience was nothing but happiness. I plowed through to the end and got my diploma without any distinction. I was proud, however, that I made it.

Two traumas did occur that weren't world-shaking in magnitude, but did contribute to my malaise and unhappiness. Mother called me on the phone one morning. I took the call in the public phone booth off the smoking room at Rhoads Hall. The 10th Mountain Division had invaded Southern Italy and was bombed by the Germans. My great friend Bill Floyd was killed. He and I had a falling out just before he went overseas, nothing too serious, but I always felt we would be together again after the war, and amends would be made. But now there was no chance, and my lovely boyfriend of four years would never return.

Then there was the situation of several girls in my dorm being caught drinking on campus down in the meadow below Rhoads Hall. The situation was serious as the Student Government was going to kick them out. I was a sophomore, but I knew many of the self-government officers with whom I was on good terms from athletics and the choir, etc. I took it upon myself to attend the crucial self-government meeting where the girls' fates were to be decided. I made an impassioned plea for their defense, and asked for leniency in that it was a first offense, and they were of such good character, that the college would be strengthened more by pardoning them than ex-pelling them. They were campused for a time, but that was a minor punishment. Word got out, however, that I had gone to the meeting and squealed on them. I was injured by this enormously, and never could bring myself to stand up in my own defense. Just last year, 1990, the girl that perpetrated this injustice on me, Adelaide Burnett from Louisville died. She surely went to her grave with the thought way back in her mind that I had squealed. I wish I could have set the story right after punching her in the nose.

There were many wonderful things, however, at Bryn Mawr. One was President Katherine McBride. This tall, gentle, compassionate lady became President after Miss Park during my sophomore year. I was waiting on table at the Deanery when Miss McBride was given her first welcome by the faculty and trustees. She handled herself with great dignity among the old guard which was trying to size her up. Mrs. Chadwick Collins, an arrogant self-centered old lady, who was head of development and public relations, I think, fired all kinds of questions at the new president, endeavoring to secure her own territorial power. Miss McBride took no offense, and deftly kept Mrs Chadwick Collins at bay. I was appalled at the rudeness. As all were leaving the table after coffee, I got a big wink from Miss McBride. She must have known I was on her side.

When I was contemplating leaving college, I got a note in my mail box from Miss McBride inviting me to lunch with her at the Deanery. I was quite surprised when I found myself sitting at the small table across from the president. I couldn't figure out why she asked me, but the conversation was easy and I found her fun to be with. She shared little human things with me such as how she coped with new people who sometimes seemed hostile, or how distressed she was that she could never keep her desk in the President's Office from being a perfect mess. When we got to dessert she alluded to my discontent and seemed so knowing and understanding. I feebly tried to explain my malaise. She listened attentively, and then said to me, "Lydia, if my big oaks fall, whatever shall I do?" From then on I was determined to stay and graduate. What a wonderful difference one person can make in your life by just believing in you. Miss McBride had polio, or something that gave her a slight limp. But she charged all over campus, and walked to and from her house in the dell nearby. Sue Coleman and I often went to tea with her. She liked us and we were among her first students when she came to college. She had the most beautiful face which lit up when she was speaking at assemblies and functions. Not a traditional beauty, but with a glow and inner conviction.

In my senior year, our May Day festivities with May Poles and Morris dancing, etc. was completely rained out so we had to move everything into Goodhart Hall. I assumed the role of May Pole because I was so tall. I stood on a high stool and the May Pole dancers did their thing, enveloping me finally in a messy web of yellow white streamers. Miss McBride sitting on the platform got the biggest kick out of my improvisations, and referred to it with a chuckle often, later.

Bryn Mawr was not big in the creative arts. There was little offered in painting, or theater or dancing. Any theater activities seemed to have occurred in the past, where Cornelia Otis Skinner and the Skinner Theatrical clan had starred and been prominent in productions. That was in Mother's era. Also one of Mother's great friends was Theresa Helburn, who later started the Theater Guild and was its head for many illustrious years. But in my day the arts were only *appreciated* with courses in music appreciation and art appreciation, which I took and loved. But my greatest pleasure came from joining The Choir and Choral Society. We sang in chapel every Sunday, we went to other colleges with our troop, we sang all over campus at Christmas and Easter, and when two or more of us got together we would burst into song and harmonize at the drop of a hat. I remember once after a concert at Princeton, the choir got on the train at Princeton Junction and completely took over the car we were in. We sang our whole repertoire all the way to Philadelphia, and were applauded by the passengers and train conductors as we got off at 30th Street Station. We really were hot stuff, or so we thought.

Just before Christmas vacation, the chorus serenaded the neighbors and all the faculty members who lived on faculty row. We started outdoors and more often than not were asked indoors for hot drinks, cakes and cookies, and sat on the floor around the fires that burned brightly in our honor. We knew carols in all languages, Portuguese, Latin, German, Welsh, and French, and of course the harmony was delicious. I loved hearing the sopranos do the descants to Adèste Fidelis, and Minuit Chrêtien. Also from my four year experience with the chorus I learned much about the language of the Bible and the Liturgies of music. Everything I know about the New and Old Testaments I can hum along with some chorale or oratorio. Agnus Dei, Kieri Elisons, Stabat Mater, "Lift Thine Eyes, oh Lift Thine Eyes, to the Mountain", "And All the Flesh is as the Grass", etc. There was a strong bond among members of the choir, and I will never forget how wonderful it was to "make a joyful noise" together.

At the end of my freshman year, I went to the Harvard Summer School to take French and German so as to be prepared for the dreaded required language orals early and so that they wouldn't interfere with my regular academic schedule, which was heavy enough as it was. You could take the orals any time during your four years, but some otherwise brainy seniors left their exams to the very last and were in danger of not graduating.

I had a splendid time living in Cambridge in a little house off Brattle Street with Sylvia Winslow and my cousin Barbie Coffin. I joined the Harvard Glee Club and The Radcliff Choral Society. Under the superb leadership of J. Wallace Woodworth, we rehearsed diligently the gorgeous Brahms Requiem, presenting it at Boston Symphony Hall with Serge Koussevitzki directing. Imagine! We later performed it outdoors in the Hatch Shell on the Esplanade. I was part of the alto section, and as such we were placed very near the tympani and kettle drums which throbbed with ominous regularity in the doleful sad sections. One's heartbeat kept pace with the dire beat. I was so moved that I burst into tears as the words drummed into my heart: "And all the flesh is as the grass, and all the grass withereth," etc. But in the triumphal section when the spirit overcomes all the preceding misery, and the chorus shouts "Death, death, oh where is thy sting?" a most extraordinary acoustical miracle happened. The lawns in front of the esplanade shell were jammed with people. Every inch was taken with blankets, folding chairs, picnic baskets and bodies. The backdrop of the audience were the buildings of Charlesgate East which faced the river. (I knew them intimately as our family dentist, Dr. Wesson, had his office in the first section of buildings.) It was a marvelous, windless, hot evening. You could hear every word, every note of the beautiful Brahms masterpiece. When we got to the "Death" part, we shot the first "death" out over the heads of the audience where it confronted the buildings in the background and bounced back "Death" again. We shot it back. The same suspended animation. Then a third time. When this reverberation returned to us, we countered with a triumphant, "Where is thy sting", and we could hear it fill the lawn and like a disembodied spirit, fly over the shell to the Charles River and into the cosmos. I will never forget that moment.

That summer was wonderful. I enjoyed taking my classes at Harvard in the Yard and in the huge Memorial Hall. That fall I passed my orals on the first try.

Bryn Mawr had some pretty colorful people, not all of them the bespectacled grinds one imagines. One memorable character was Claudie Cléjas, a glamorous French gal. She was noticed by the faculty as well as the student body for her chic and French sexiness. When she walked into the library you knew she was coming because of the heady exotic perfume that wafted in her wake. At Christmas vacation, she went to Sun Valley to ski. At the end of the holiday, she sent a telegram to Dean Nepper saying: "Doctor advises me to stay one more week." Dean Nepper shot back a telegram, "Dean Nepper advises you to come back immediately." Half the college went to the Bryn Mawr station on the Paoli Local to see if Claudie would conform. With much luggage and two pairs of skis preceding her, Claudie descended from the train. The assembled crowd burst into applause.

Some noteworthy faculty members, some only on a sabbatical, were William H. Auden, ascetic, pale, and kinetic who invited his friend Stephen Spender for a visit. Then there was tiny Edith Finch whom I had for a while in freshman English, who looked like a fragile finch-like bird and who later married Bertrand Russell, of all unlikely combinations. Then there was the bachelor Arthur Colby Sprague the Shakespearean Professor and scholar who seemed older than God to us in his class, but who ended up marrying Posy Kent from Boston who was in our class. Then there was Dr. Herben, the Chaucer professor, who rode from London to Canterbury on a horse. He was clad in full armor with lance and all to see how it felt. He was a big man, and I didn't know armor came in such large sizes. Helen Taft Manning was acting dean for a while. Very imposing and frightening, more like a marine captain, big, with fuzz all over her face. We freshmen were lined up on the stairs outside her office waiting for an interview. Scribbie (Nancy Scribner from Winetka) was next to me and she complained that her father was here for a visit and knew Mrs. Manning long ago, and wanted to see her. In he bounded past all the waiting girls and much to Scribbies embarrassment burst in to the Dean's office. As the door was closing we could hear the shouts "Scribner!" . . . then "Pootsie!" and an ensuing embrace.

Nantucket, September 30. Tomorrow night we fly to Paris for our 40th wedding anniversary, to spend almost two weeks, first in Paris for three nights, then touring Brittany and Burgundy. We will fly from here to Boston, then New York, and have lunch with Mary Ahern before taking off from JFK at 7 p.m.)

I am continuing my Journal in this new book, for I feared the other book might get lost and I would hate to lose it, as I have not yet had a chance to get it duplicated. As I remember it, I had not yet finished with my Bryn Mawr years.

I had a student ticket to the Academy of Music in Philly every other Monday night to hear Eugene Ormandy and the Philadelphia Orchestra. Sue Coleman and I went together. We rode in on the Paoli Local to the 30th Street Station, and walked to the concert hall. We sat in the front row right by the orchestra pit, which involved much craning of the neck upwards to see the performers on stage. But we doted on Ormandy with his gorgeous romantic style, who played to our mood perfectly. Tchaikovsky, Brahms, Rachmaninoff and Chopin under his loving baton were memorable. On occasion the soloists from the front of the stage looked right down at us, and I had the distinct impression that the dashing young first cellist knew I was there. He was so handsome, and as passionate as a Chopin or Liszt with his smooth black hair, deep eyes and fair skin. Our eyes met often, and I felt sometimes he was playing for me. But that certainly must have been my imagination. Sue said she hadn't noticed.

I was made Secretary General of The Model League of the United Nations which convened at Bryn Mawr my Junior year. This was a huge and fascinating undertaking. Various colleges from all over America each represented one of the United Nations. I was the U Thant of the League. I went to New York to get indoctrinated in procedures, working closely with Edgar Fisher, a lovely man and head of the Model League of Nations. The organizing work was time-consuming and it was difficult to get all the bodies and groups coordinated on campus. It took a good deal of my time which could have been spent on my studies.

I think I was class president all four years. My Father and Mother were very proud of this, but I began to like it less and less. Being everything to all people, keeping control of others and courting popularity, I began to feel was superficial. I was good at running class meetings, and had a knack at bringing the best out in others who were shy and lacked the confidence of some of the more obvious leaders from Brearley, or Westover, or Fox-croft. When after gradation I was elected permanent class President, it occurred to me that I really didn't want it. I wanted to get on with my own life, unstructured, not beholden, no carry-overs. So I resigned. My family did not understand.

Ward is such a super graduate of Princeton, active in all Princeton activities. He was made a trustee for three years, is a prime mover in the Washington Princeton Club, and does his university great credit with love and devotion. I, on the other hand, found no great continuity with Bryn Mawr, nor did I look for it. My best friends dispersed to other parts of the world, and I found I had much closer ties to my school than my college. Also I moved to New York and immersed myself in that huge and exciting city, never looking back on Philadelphia and the war years.

V

New York, 1945–49

As I contemplated living in New York, I was really very naive, but confident as I anticipated all the wonderful opportunities that this great city could provide. I left Bryn Mawr in June 1945 immediately after graduation having called Mum and Pa in Boston to say I would be home in a very few days after I had found a job. Not a doubt in my mind that I would get one, and soon. After all I was a Bryn Mawr graduate and an English major! My good friend Pat Castles Acheson had very kindly offered her duplex apartment on East 79th Street for me to stay in while I job hunted. She gave me a key and told me that the Irish maid Lena would be there, who was told I was coming. I arrived late one evening and let myself in with my key.

I was awakened the next morning by a vacuum cleaner being pushed around my room noisily, and there was a jolly lady.

"Aw," she said, "sure and I've waken ye." (Her Irish accent was thick.) Then she said, "And what might ye be doin' in New Yaawk?" I told her I was looking for a job. "And what might ye want to be doing?" I hadn't ever been asked that question, nor given it too much comprehensive thought.

Quickly I said, "I want to be a writer."

"Awk," she said, "that's very interesting. . . . This very afternoon I'm working for a very nice man who is in the 'pooblishing business.' I could put in a good word for ye."

"What does he publish, Lena?" She thought a moment.

"He wurrks for the New Yaawker Times."

"Lena, there's no such publication as that. You mean the *New Yorker*?"

"No, that's not it."

"You mean *The New York Times*?"

"No, that's not it."

"You mean *Time Magazine*?"

"Yes, now that's the one."

"What's his name?"

"O, C, H, S, Ochs" A very luffely gentleman. I'll tell him you are going to call. His number is CI 6-5000. And just tell him that Lena sent you!"

The first day I made a couple of unsuccessful phone calls trying to get my job bearings, and later in the afternoon called *Time Magazine*. I was getting nowhere with the call, and finally in desperation said, "Uh . . . er . . . but Lena sent me."

The secretary burst out laughing and said, "Yes, I know." She set up an interview, bless her heart, for ten days later, but things worked out so that I didn't have to cash in on it.

The next day I began in earnest to job hunt. The only parameter in my mind was to do any job that was non-academic, and non-intellectually oriented. It occurred to me that the opposite of intellectual was "entertainment," and whatever that might mean I would pursue it. I got on the Fifth Avenue bus and headed down toward St. Patrick's Cathedral. Not knowing much about New York City I did know that Rockefeller Center was nearby, and so also the Radio City Music Hall. I walked down 49th Street, to the Rockefeller skating rink, and on this beautiful sunny day watched the skaters. How miraculous to be skating in June. The wind was blowing the huge colorful flags behind the rink, and the sound of their flapping was loud and energetic. Right behind was the 30 Rockefeller Plaza building stretching up impressively to the sky. I walked through one of the revolving doors into the large lobby where a huge directory listing all the hundreds of offices and businesses located here bouleversed me with choices. It started with a listing in the upper left-hand corner of the American Broadcasting Company, and ran the alphabetical gamut down to Zabriski Aircraft in the lower right corner. Whew! The range was too great, and I felt in need of a cup of coffee which I saw I could get in the coffee shop just at the right of the lobby. I sat at the counter and asked a nice looking lady if she would pass me the sugar.

As she did, she said, "What are you doing in New York?" I must have looked like I didn't belong. I told her I was looking for a job. "What kind of a job?" Again I had to gather my wits.

Having only the recollection of American Broadcasting, or Zabriski Aircraft from the directory outside, I eliminated Zabriski as out of the question, and responded, "American Broadcasting Company. I would very much like to work at ABC."

She smiled, and while she was paying her check she gave me her business card. "Come and see me after you've finished your coffee." I looked at the card which said, "Ruth Tours, Director of Personnel at the American Broadcasting Company!" I had a job half an hour later. I telephoned my parents that night to tell them the news,and they seemed quite surprised. I couldn't understand why.

This job at ABC started simply, low down in the Script Routing Department where I proof-read scripts for typos, etc., *This is Yr. FBI*, *Gangbusters*, *Walter Winchell* and many more. Gradually I moved up to the *Continuity Acceptance* Department where we processed scripts, directing them to the right studios and into the hands of the actors and directors. I loved being in the center of things. This was mostly radio, but television was just emerging. I remember seeing my first television set on display in a RCA window on 48th Street. What a miracle. And ultimately I got to know Robert Saudek who was head of the Public Affairs Department as I did some writing for the *Closed Circuit*, the inter-office organ. I did features like reviewing Fulton Oursler's *The Greatest Story Ever Told*, and I even did a Profile on the big managers Robert Kintner, Edward Noble and Justin Dart. Saudek's assistant was Mary Ahern.

After she had read one of my stories, she called me into her office. She said, "Lydia, you interest me very much. Tell me about yourself." It was the beginning of my friendship with this wonderful human being. She was my maid of honor at our wedding, and to this day is the best friend I have on earth. And Robert Saudek also is one of my oldest and most abiding friends. And all this came about due to a cup of coffee in a coffee shop.

I loved New York, and have so many memories of my four years in that exciting city. I lived with Holly on East 72nd Street, in a stylish and civilized apartment. I had met Holly through a friend at ABC. She was unlike anyone I had met to date. Her parents provided the apartment, but wanted her to have a roommate of stable disposition and normal wholesomeness. They didn't feel comfortable with her lifestyle which involved theatrical and operatic types about whom she was very secretive. I don't know why Holly put up with me invading her privacy, but she did, and we became good friends. But she made sure that I understood the ground-rules. She said that whenever we spoke about her gentlemen friends when we were on a bus or at a party, we would have our own language . . . aliases. For instance Henri would be Flower Pot, Michel the Flag, and Bax the Ice Bucket. Furthermore I was to be absolutely sure when I answered the telephone that I knew which gentleman it was, and didn't get them confused. I did once, saying confidently, "Good evening Michel," and it was Henri. In the course of time I met these gentlemen and they were dazzling to a young, rural, Bostonian girl. Once when Mother was visiting, she had just applied fingernail polish when the doorbell rang. In came Henri in full dress French naval regalia with gold, etc. He kissed my Mother's hand ceremoniously and there under his chin were the pink Revlon traces of the undried lacquer.

One afternoon I came home from ABC around four o'clock—I worked the 7:30-3:30 shift. As I let myself in with my key, I noticed a man's scarf and umbrella on the hall table. As I walked into the living room which, facing south was full of afternoon sun, a tall figure stood up from his seat in the big wing chair. I couldn't see his face at first because the bright sun behind him silhouetted his outline. With an unforgettable sonorous deep, mellifluous tone he said, "Good afternoon, my name is Ezio." It was Ezio Pinza. I became very useful to this romantic affair as a go-between. Being on the premises of the studios which NBC and ABC shared at Rockefeller Center, I could pass notes to the principals. One morning Holly entrusted me with a note to deliver secretly to Pinza. I went up the back stairwell to the third floor where the NBC studios were, carrying a script to make me look part of things, and sat in the wings just off stage while Pinza rehearsed for *The Bell Telephone Hour*. He spotted me as he went off stage, and I hastily handed him the note. Another time I was already in the elevator when it stopped at a floor and Pinza got in with a group of four or five others, including his wife Elizabeth. When he spotted me a look of apprehension came across his face which said, "Don't dare acknowledge me," which of course I didn't. But as he turned to face the front of the elevator, he put his hand out behind him, and I took the note from his palm.

All this was very heady stuff. Holly was not a traditional beauty, but she had an ethereal magnetism, I guess you might call it sex-appeal, but not of the ordinary pin-up variety. She looked almost pre-Raphaelite, with fair skin, fair hair and huge green eyes. When all the girls I knew studiously sat in the sun to get their thighs tan, Holly would studiously avoid the sun, wearing large hats, and gauzy veiling. She most often wore black, even in summer. Her closets were lined with cedar, and there were fragrant sachets in every drawer. She always wore beautiful underwear in case, as she said, she might be carried off to a hospital. Holly and I called each other Roma. It was a sad day for me when Wolff moved in. Holly had decided to quit playing the field and settle down. Her love affairs were always stormy and ended unhappily. The last one was Bax, a doctor, who unfortunately took a shine to me. But Wolff adored her and knocked himself out to carry out her every whim. He irritated me with his unctuousness, and I soon realized they would be married, and I would be out of an apartment. I have lost track of Holly and have tried several times to locate her. I think she moved to Rome.

Mary Ahern had now become a close and dear friend. As she was soon to be out of a place to live, we decided to live together. After a lengthy search for an apartment with one near disaster as we were about to sign a lease on a totally dismal flat on Lexington Avenue, I was lucky enough to see a moving van on West 11th Street loading up as some people were moving out of a basement apartment. I dashed up the steps to find the landlady, Mrs. Paganelli, a cautious but friendly Italian lady, who agreed to let us move in. There was a little triangular garden out back, and the small living and sleeping area was fun and a bit bohemian we thought. The kitchen was also triangular which made for a rather awkward cooking dynamic, but we loved it, and after I moved out, Mary lived there for several years. Greenwich Village was lively and the small restaurants fun and very accessible.

Robert Saudek called me into his office one day and said that there was an opening at Steuben Glass for an assistant to the special librarian in the design department, would I be interested. I jumped at the opportunity, not knowing what it entailed, being intrigued by this finest of glass companies, and a chance to be involved in design research for glass, whatever that meant. Before my interview with Mary Fisher the librarian, I boned up all night on the Dewey Decimal System. I loved the whole atmosphere, the quality of Steuben, its people and its product. When Mary left I became head of the library and the design research department. This entailed working closely with the designers both for Steuben design, and Corning design, the art glass, as well as the commercial glass such as Pyrex baby bottles, Corning Ware and pie plates. Both sets of designers worked in a large room on wonderful blond drawing tables, in modern bright surroundings, and made use of my library with its colorful Eames chairs and glass partitions. I scanned daily all the art magazines and glass trade publications, forwarding them to the designers when I found something of interest. I also had on my shelves a Neri 17th century leather bound book *The Art of Glass* which was a treasure collected by Arthur Houghton, president of Steuben. I had other rare books under lock and key. Outsiders wanting to use my library for research work were often seated at the tables.

The designers were very varied in personality. There was the immensely shy but gifted George Thompson who designed the famed "Merry-Go-Round-Bowl" which was presented to Queen Elizabeth on her coronation, but also the sublimely beautiful "Gazelle Bowl" whose superbly engraved gazelles coursed gracefully around its circumference. There was Lee Goldman who was hugely fat and always produced glass designs which were elongated and thin. Then also there were Jean and Don, and Jack and Lloyd. Jack Ward was head of the design department and although he lived mostly in Corning, New York, there were many evenings he stayed in the city, and on numerous occasions he gathered the designers together and headed down to my place at 38 West 11th Street. We had such companionable and jolly times sitting out in the garden laughing and talking. One night all of us headed to Astis Restaurant where all the waiters are frustrated opera singers and sing constantly while supper is served. The climax of their offerings was the Anvil Chorus where the cash register played a big role with the drawer banging in and out and bells ringing and glasses being struck sonorously. Jack Ward asked one young waitress to sing "Summer Time," which she did. It was lovely and her voice perfect. Our camaraderie was great, and we almost created a little salon.

I will never forget a party during one of the first days I was at Steuben on Fifth Avenue. It was a fancy party given to introduce some new glass designs. There were some very spiffy people there, naturally all drinking from crystal goblets. All very snazzy New York types, and there were photographers snapping pictures everywhere. The curtains in the showroom window which fronted on Fifth Avenue were closed. Then to everyone's surprise Arthur Houghton, Jack Gates and Sidney Waugh, impeccably dressed in black tie, climbed into the show case, seated themselves in cross-legged positions and assumed the monkey roles of speak-no-evil, see-no-evil, and hear-no-evil, and ordered the curtains to be opened. The passers-by were stunned to see this unusual display.

I loved the exquisiteness of Steuben glass. I admired the design concept which capitalized on the clearest "metal" ever devised by scientists, and was of the same quality and batch as the Palomar telescope. No color was ever allowed to interfere with its clarity, and as a matter of great pride the crystal was designed with thick form which revelled in the lack of striations, bubbles or other imperfections. When I went to Corning to the Corning Glass Factory and watched the hand blown glass made, I was stunned with the craft and the artistry of this most ancient of art forms. The fiery furnaces were like the jaws of hell. A "shop" consisted of servitors, gatherers, and the ultimate gaffers, all performing with precision and the choreographed mastery of the moment. The molten red hot glass goes from stage to stage at the precise instant of its optimum development, being finally blown by the gaffer into a rounded glass, twirling all the time so it doesn't fall on the floor in a liquid heap, or harden before the desired shape has been achieved. It is truly a miracle!

The glassblowers are Czechoslovakian and they take enormous pride in their work. All hand blown glass is intrinsically round—square shapes are done in molds, which is manipulative. Waterford crystal is cut glass, cut originally in order to eliminate the faults in the metal—the cloudiness is camouflaged by the prismatic reflections of the square cut facets. But Steuben is smooth and thick. I thrilled when I watched as the delicate copperwheel engravings were added to the glass later. One slip of the wheel and the glass could shatter. One thinks because Steuben is so heavy that it is strong and sturdy. It is not. It is very fragile and can break easily.

My days at Steuben came to an end, however, as I was fired. To this day I don't really understand why, but they said for "insubordination." I had been independent when working with some people who came to my library to do research from the extensive material I had. One man relied on my help for a project he was doing, and I did not clear his material with Jack Gates or Jack Ward. It never occurred to me to do so. But the man was an important man, whom I've now forgotten, whom management thought valuable to some on-going project that I was unaware of. But that did not explain my dismissal totally. I suspected that my research library was going to move to Corning along with most of the designers. Even that notion did not quell the unhappiness I felt, or the unfairness, particularly in that Jack Ward, my friend, turned against me. I was pretty miserable.

At the end of my tenure at Steuben I was involved in an automobile accident. Four of us had been together at LaRues for an evening of dancing, etc. Afterwards, my friend Bob Longstreth had driven alone back to his apartment uptown as Jack and Pat were headed down to the village and could drop me off at 11th Street. As we were heading south on Park Avenue, a car jumped an intersection and rammed hard into us. We all hurtled forward, my head went through the windshield, Jack broke his nose, and Pat hurt her leg, which we later discovered was broken. The ambulance arrived and carried us off to Belleview Hospital, I suggesting I didn't need an ambulance, not realizing that my forehead was badly cut and bleeding profusely. As I lay waiting in the emergency room in a little cubicle with screens, and I shut my eyes for a few moments, I soon sensed that someone was standing by my bedside. I couldn't believe it. There was a Catholic priest praying for me like mad with his bible open, and his eyes focused heavenward. I didn't know what last rites were, but if he was doing them he'd better stop immediately. Whereupon I told him to get out—vamoose! Poor guy. I felt like Bette Davis. But if I was in danger (I wasn't), I would like someone around I knew. I had the nurse call Bax, at 3 o'clock in the morning, who was a doctor sometimes connected with Belleview. When I went finally into the operating room I had lost much blood, the surgeons dressed in green had to start sewing me up before the anaesthetic took effect. They said I had been brave. Bax did arrive and later told me he was responsible for saving my eyebrow, for if they had shaved it off it would never have grown back again.

I was put on the women's ward, which was pretty grim. All shapes, nationalities and sizes. I had several friends (other than Bax) who were doctors at Belleview. One of them was Chuck Webster who I had gone out with several times. He looked very impressive and handsome as he went up to the battle-ax nurse who was in charge of the ward. She manned her post at the entrance like a Marine sergeant. Chuck came up to her with a long stretcher on wheels. He said he was "instructed" to get "Gifford." Nurse allowed him in reluctantly. As he came to my bedside he whispered, "Look really sick as we go by Matron, we're going to a party." It was New Year's Eve, 1948, and we went down a couple of floors to a room where a party of doctors, a couple of whom I knew, were eating and drinking merrily in a very festive mood. Pat Jarman was there with her leg in a cast.

The upshot of all this was that the course of my life was to change forever. Indirectly, my automobile accident was responsible for my meeting Ward. Directly it was responsible for my having some money for the first time in my life, as my Father saw to it that I was properly compensated by the insurance company. The timing was perfect as far as Steuben was concerned, for I could practically say, "Don't bother to fire me, I quit, and what is more, I'm off to Europe." Which I did.

I wanted Ann Williams (Willy) to go with me. I wrote her in Boston at Houghton Mifflin where she worked. I told her my plan and that I wanted to go in October. "Can't possibly go in October," she wrote back. "Worst time for publishing." I sent her a telegram: "Have 2 reservations on the

Liberte sailing Boston Oct. 6th—must come." I got a telegram back: "Ok—coming," and off we went for almost a year.

But before I stop telling about New York, a few more observations about my life there. In the four years I worked in New York, there was never a dearth of companionship, male and female. I had enough beaus to take me places I wanted to go. But I had no great romance. I really would have liked one, but no single one person added up to the total human being I desired. I told my brother Steve one time when he asked, rather nosily, I thought, how my love-life was, "One loves me cuz I'm funny, another loves me because I'm intelligent, and the third loves me because I'm artistic."

One of my most cherished memories of New York was going up to the Lewisohn Stadium to hear a summer concert. On the most beautiful warm night, with stars out and no wind, I went with Bleeker to hear Arthur Rubenstein playing "Rachmaninoff's Second Piano Concerto." There sitting in the wooden seats, gazing up at Rubenstein, I thought I had died and gone to heaven. Even the airplanes flying in and out of LaGuardia overhead couldn't break the magic spell. I felt totally in step with the brave piano marching triumphantly against all odds, its voice being heard above the determined orchestra, and found myself in tears as wave on wave of the main theme finally crashes into shore, lyric, exquisite and triumphant. To this day I think it is the most beautiful piece of music ever written.

Another special musical treat was to hear the Trapp Family Choir singing at Town Hall at their first-ever concert just after they had escaped from Austria to this country. I went with Rod MacLeish who also was working at ABC, and as we sat there listening to this remarkable family dressed in their colorful native lederhosen, dirndl skirts, bodices and ribbons, little did I realize how Rod's and my lives were later to be intertwined. But more about that in a later chapter. Countess Maria von Trapp was impressive and beautiful and after one glorious full family number sung in German, she comes to the center of the stage, and in her rich Austrian accent said, "Und now vee vill hear from leetle Hanzie." And the smallest of the Trapps broke from the family which was lined up according to height, and with the greatest dignity, played a little piece on his recorder, the sweetest sound you ever heard, his white-blond head gleaming under the stagelights, his little knees pink above the grey tasseled stockings.

One of my great friends during college and the post-war years in New York was Al Perrine. I had first met him in Duxbury when Mother had

47

organized an officers' USO at the YWCA where Navy and Army officers stationed in Boston could have a bit of local fun, being far away from home with no social life. About 20 Navy ensigns and lieutenants came to Duxbury for an outing. We girls knocked ourselves out to be charming and friendly, which wasn't hard as the men were very attractive and we were hard up for males, as all our boyfriends were off in the war.

I immediately took to Al who was from East Elmhurst, Queens. He was not at all a Boston type which was a relief. His wonderful personality was enhanced by his New York Bronx accent, and perfectly delicious sense of humor. The many laughs we had together, and his wry manner made for great companionship, and although no ultimate romance was in the cards, we dated and danced for years. He took me to a Navy Ball one time at the Roosevelt Hotel in New York, attended by many of his New York cronies, and several ship-mates. He introduced me to a couple of girls who were friends of his sister.

In the ladies room where we were powdering our noses, one of the girls said to me, "You better watch out or you'll break his heart, you're not his type." I knew just what she meant, and it didn't make me feel good. Little did she know how un-upper crust I really was.

"Prune," as I called him, wrote to me faithfully all during the war from the Solomon Islands and elsewhere—wherever his LCI ship took him in the Pacific. These letters were welcome when they came into the little concierge at Rhoads Hall and the warden read out the mail call. My friend Bill had by then died, and letters for me were now few and far between.

One afternoon in New York when Prune was on leave, we were walking to Central Park on a wet sloshy day, and he had me in stitches imitating the little children in the custody of their nannies, returning from coasting, their cheeks bright red, and their noses dripping like mad. It was the way he brought his tongue up to his upper lip and snuffed in deeply to catch the flow from his nose and then flipped his forearm up to finish the job that struck me as so funny. Prune was wonderful at imitating people. He loved my Mother a lot, and she him, but I winced always when he referred to her as "Mother." He was a wonderful dancer. I am glad he is married and has two grown boys. For years he would call me from wherever he was on my birthday.

VI

Europe, 1945–50

As plans for my trip to Europe were being formulated, I met Jim at a party. He worked at Pan American, and we became instant friends. As our friendship quickly developed, he impulsively decided that he wanted to meet us in Europe during his winter vacation. But most important, Willy and I could take his Hillman-Minx with us, thereby relieving him of caring for a car in New York. It was a bonanza for us, this nifty little dark green convertible, and we put many miles on it before we were through.

It was very exciting as we boarded the "Liberte" in New York that October morning. Nat Marston from Boston was also sailing, and she and Willy and I were in a state of glorious anticipation of our great adventure. Mum and Pa had come to see us off. As the deep foghorns blew deafeningly, the gangplank started to lift, streamers billowing in the wind, Nat and Willy disappeared to another deck, and I stood at a railing alone looking down at the multitude of people assembled to see the passengers off. I spotted my Mother and Father way below and moved over to where I was directly above them and waved furiously, which they saw. For some inexplicable reason I reached into my pocket and found a nickel. I threw it down at them, and lo-and-behold, Pa caught it! Unbelievable but true. He carried that nickel with him for the rest of his life, placing it carefully on his dresser each night when he got ready for bed along with his gold watch and his gold pocket knife.

There were a lot of young people on shipboard and we had a blast.

There were three of us in a tiny stateroom, but it was okay, as there was much to do elsewhere. I don't remember too many specifics, but the night before we landed there was a huge party that lasted till 3 in the morning, and by the departure time in the wee early hours of morning we had no sleep. We watched the cargo being unloaded at Plymouth where we landed, and there was our little Hillman Minx in its canvas cradle swaying in the breeze as it was deposited safely on the dock.

Nat left for London by the boat train, Willy and I climbed into our Hillman piled high with luggage and skis. No sooner had we pulled away from the dock in our somewhat dazed state, we realized we should be driving on the left-hand side of the road. Our first uncontrollable laughter occurred when we came to a traffic circle and were forced by the laws of eminent domain to go around clockwise rather than our accustomed opposite. The signs were blurred by our tears of laughter, and we decided immediately to pull into the large forbidding Plymouth Hotel that loomed up to our left to catch our bearings over a cup of much needed coffee. The concierge was very formal, not at all convinced we were respectable. When we asked if we could use the bathroom there was a large whispered consultation, and we were ushered into an elevator where we were whisked to the fifth floor and led into a room which they unlocked with a key. In it was *only* a bathtub. We were in the *bath* room. Again our laughter was uncontrollable, and our sobs were only to be presently equalled by our visit to the large dining room for coffee. There were several sedate English couples having breakfast in total silence, all of whom kept eyeing us. Even the sugar lump made a loud noise when dropped into our coffee. Well, that did it, and for a third time in less than an hour we laughed until we were nearly sick. We disgraced ourselves our first moments in England.

I will not recount a step-by-step of our trip, but our hearts were young and gay, and we had nearly a year of European roaming. From England to Scotland to Belgium to Paris to Austria, to the South of France, to Rome, to Ravello and finally back to England. It was some experience, but I will only hit the high spots. The English countryside, London, Cornwall, Bath, the Cotswolds, all were beguiling, and we moved as our fancy dictated, stayed where an inn beckoned, ogled at castles, the Tower of London, Buckingham Palace, Salisbury Cathedral, Lake Windemere, martinis in the bar of the Connaught Hotel, and points north to Scotland. Before we left London to go north, we rather reluctantly obeyed both our mothers by paying a courtesy visit to the English Speaking Union to which they belonged. There we were overwhelmed by the courtesy of Miss Briscoe who on discovering we were headed to Scotland asked if we would like to stay with families on our visit. She produced four names and addresses in various Scottish locations and told us that these would be confirmed by letter at our Hotel Roxburghe in Edinburgh. Sure enough. One from a Lord and Lady in Roxburghe, where we later went on a partridge shoot, and one from a splendid lived-in castle near Glamis where we watched from our window and saw a full dress hunt assembling in the courtyard below. "The sounds of the horns brought us from our bed," the pink coats and the baying beagles. Another family in Ayrshire, Robert Burns country, where the manor house in which we stayed was adjacent to the Burns property.

But best of all was our visit to the Highlands to Rosshire northwest of Inverness to the home of Sir Michael and Lady Peto. As we approached their town Dundonell by Garve, we came from a coastal road that had gone through tiny fishing villages. Our eyes were already dazzled by the lovely lochs with their reflections of ruined castles and the rugged, purple mountains covered with heather. The most beautiful loch of all was Loch Linhe. As our little car turned inland again, we went up hill and down dale, and beyond each turn in the road was another more gorgeous vista. We passed two lady walkers striding along with vigor, dressed in vintage tweeds and tartan scarves looking for all the world like Peggy Ashcroft and Margaret Rutherford. They planted their feet and walking sticks down with much determination and relish. The fog soon enveloped them from our rear view mirror. We found Dundonnel House across a little bridge over a burn after waiting for some unconcerned cows to make way for us. We were greeted by Lady Peto who was charming, and Sir Michael and their daughter Serena later joined us as tea was being set up before a roaring fire. It was instant passion for both Willy and me—and our friendship with the Petos lasted many years and through many letters and Christmas cards. We had never seen such an idyllic lifestyle. Sir Michael was laird of a vast area, and he described how to his house every year at Christmas time all the population of Crofters would file in to pay their tithes, as had been the custom for centuries. He would greet each one separately behind his large oak desk, ask them their troubles, and give them a wee dram of whisky. Everything was created on the property. Lambs gave wool which Serena dyed and carded and spun, she made butter from the heavy cream, all vegetables were grown and harvested, and trout and salmon gathered from the many fishing streams. One day we walked way up into the mountains and saw with Serena and her three black Labs as guides, stags and several eagles soaring from on high into the valleys looking for rabbits. And of course there were pheasant, grouse and partridge practically outside the back door.

As we sat at tea in front of the roaring fire that first afternoon, the drizzle had turned to snow. There was a knock at the door and in came the two ladies we had passed many miles back on the road. They promptly sat down to join us at tea. The next day another visitor arrived, Sir John somebody, the head of the Royal Academy in Edinburgh, who had come to paint Serena's portrait. As he sat down he looked pale and in need of a brandy which he got. Although he looked like George Bernard Shaw, he was not a hardy type, having come from the Lowlands in the south. He announced that this place surely was remote. I'll bet he made fast work of the portrait of lovely Serena. Willy and I were nothing but exhilarated by this magic place which Sir John thought was the end of the earth.

We later crossed the channel from Dover to Ostend and into Belgium and Holland. In Holland we visited friends of Willy's parents, the Polis, who lived in Maastricht, very near the German border. We played bridge in French as it was our only common language. At night I thought of the Nazis who had swarmed over the land, and dreamed about Ann Frank. After all, the war had taken place only five years before, and its aftermath was still vibrating. We loved Bruges in Belgium with its enchanting old medieval buildings and the swans swimming in the tiny canals. The Memling Museum was memorable, and we were shown around by the nuns in their seagull hats in the convent where the museum was located. The Memling paintings were marvelous and transcendently calm.

And on to Paris. It was getting to be late November or early December. We stayed with Jean Paul Carlhian's parents on the Quai D'Orsay in one of the most sumptuous houses imaginable. Monsieur et Madame were wonderful to us and gave us lodgings for three weeks, imagine. Josef the butler in his red and black striped vest brought us breakfast every morning in bed, and often we ate lunch with the Carlhians in their beautiful dining room, which had Fragonards, scenic wallpaper, and objets d'art of museum quality. The rotunda entrance hall had a black and white marble floor modelled after the tombeau de Napolean, around its walls and up the marble staircase were the finest Japanese woodcuts, the actor series of Sharaku and many Hiroshiges. In Madame's boudoir was a large priceless set of Utamaro's ladies. All these were the genesis of my great love for these Japanese treasures called Ukiyoe. Monsieur Carlhian was the head of a renowned decorating firm on the Place Vendome. We met Jean Paul's sister Brigitte who could be the heroine in a Flaubert novel. A heartbreaker she, as we could see from Alan Jacobs, an architect who was hopelessly in love with her. Jean Paul made my brother Steve take her to the Harvard-Yale game on short notice. Steve was at first furious, but later was boulevèrsed by this femme fatale who lost her shoe in the snow outside the Harvard stadium, and Steve had to carry her the rest of the way through drifts to the AD Club after the game.

It was getting to be the Christmas season and we were planning our ski trip to Austria. We were also expecting the arrival of Jim who was to join us skiing. On a snowy night in Paris I headed off at one o'clock in the morning for Orly Airport to meet his plane. I got royally lost and did not know how I made it in the driving snow. His plane was late, but at about four a.m. it landed and I rushed through the barricades to meet him, much to the consternation of the security guards. He presented me with a large orchid, which looked very pretty with snow on it. We drove back to the Hotel des Ministères, back of the Invalides where I had gotten him a cheap reservation. It was too late for me to go back to the Carlihains, and although I knew Willy would be worried, I had no alternative but to spend the night with Jim. Both of us were too exhausted to be romantic. It soon turned out that Jim had quit his job at Pan Am. He was not on vacation to make this trip, which I heartily disapproved of, and so this was the beginning of the end of our relationship, which disintegrated by slow degrees.

One degree was activated by my meeting Harriet, an old friend of Jim's, a real live-wire, fascinatingly energetic, who happened to be in Paris. The afternoon before we left for Kitzbuhl by train, I met Harriet at the Lotti Bar off the Place Vendome for a drink. She was called "Choo." There, over more than one martini, she cautioned me about Jim, nothing too awful, but that he was below standard. I was torn because I was beholden to him for the Kneese which had now become indispensable to us. I never saw Choo again, but she was quite wonderful enough to make me lose track of time, and nearly miss the train that Willy and Jim were already on. As it was just starting to pull out of the Gard du Nord, I was running along the platform with my skis. Jim was leaning out the door and pulled me on board in the nick of time. He was not at all pleased, and was alarmed that I had been with Choo. We were in a crowded compartment with a family of Russians and several others of undetermined origin who spoke no English. When we got to the border they all looked apprehensive. On we went through the mountains and the night was spent mostly on the floor huddled in our coats.

We arrived in Kitzbuhl the late afternoon before Christmas eve. We had no reservations and the hotels were jammed full for the holidays. Jim tramped up and down looking for lodgings and finally found rooms for us with Herr Uberall, the shumacher meister, who lived just below the old stone bridge near the old gate that led into the main square. Herr Uberall made ski-boots and also was a ski instructor. His little house was charming and we had the top floor with two bedrooms and a lovely sunny other room that had a beautiful blue and white tiled stove or "furnace" which warmed us deliciously and on whose raised hearth we dried our ski boots at the end of the day. Our breakfast of fruit, croissant and hot chocolate was served to us by Frau Uberall who smiled a lot and had no English. Often when we were skiing and Herr Uberall would spot us from afar, or on another trail, he would call loudly "Huwee, Yup-yup-yup" and we knew who it was. We often later used it to signal each other.

On Christmas Eve we walked to the ancient 11th century church with the onion shaped tower on it. The snow was very deep and the church yard was mounded high with drifts. It was very clear and as we looked to the surrounding mountains we could see the parishioners skiing down to the church for the Christmas Eve services. They carried flares and torches, and lit up the mountainside. They deposited their skis in the drifts and went into the church. We stood outside not feeling it was our place to go among the crowded congregation and take up family space. The last person to enter the church just as the services were beginning was an old, old lady in black silk who barrelled down the path on her skis at top speed, came to a screeching halt, her silk ribboned headdress streaming in the wind. She took her skis off, went to the half-hidden tombstone nearest the entrance, and genuflected in front of it. She planted her flare firmly in front of the stone, and marched smartly into the church. The mountain became quiet in the moonlight as we joined in singing "Stille Nacht, Heilige Nacht" which resounded from inside the church, the old bell tolling serenely.

Christmas morning we woke to find the little Uberall children, Fritz and Friedl, dropping incense over our threshold from a decorative little bowl, as good luck, and Frau brought us cakes. Later in the morning we walked through the snow to the railroad station to meet Jim's friend, Tom, who had come to join us for the holidays. But before we got halfway down the road we spotted a horse and open sleigh merrily jingling its bells coming fast toward us, and there in the vehicle, sitting under a fur lap rug, with a black persian lamb hat on like a Russian noble, was Tom, grinning like mad. Tom was a Tolstoi or a Noel Coward type, more parlor-oriented than outdoors, very rich, and very good company, though a bit stingy as some rich folk are. But he was a welcome addition to our trio. Extremely intelligent and well-read, he and Willy got on fine.

We had met a young Austrian, Fritz Gitzel, in the Sport-Alm where he worked selling ski equipment. He took a liking to us, especially to Willy. He was a marvelous skier, being a ski-instructor as well. One Saturday on his day off he took us way up into the mountain where we hadn't yet dared to venture, and, instructing us to follow closely, skied ahead of us. We went down behind him through large snow fields, across little bridges, through farmyards and even a little village where the ducks scattered as we passed. We skied way beyond our ability and were exhilarated by the adventure. When our descent ended we were two villages beyond Kitzbuhl and picked up a tiny train chugging through the valley to get home again. Fritz asked us all for supper one night at his chalet which was on the outskirts of town, and which he had built himself, all blond wood and smelling of pine. We had much sausage and sauerkraut and bread and glüwien. His wife was charming in her dirndl. A very loving and generous evening which we cherished. We did not give a thought to the fact that Fritz had been conscripted in the war by the Nazis into the crack Panzer Mountain Division, as many Austrians were.

We had decided to also ski in the Arlberg at Lech. The day we left Kitzbuhl it was snowing heavily. We were very sad to leave the Uberalls who assembled to see us off. Frau Uberall was crying as she said, "Auf, wiedersehn, liebchens," and hugged us as we got into the taxi. We hadn't realized how much she cared, as there had been little verbal communication. The children also were sad to see us go, and Herr Uberall looked away quickly as he shut our taxi door, wiping his eyes with his sleeve. The snow storm that was developing was a big one. By the time the train pulled into Langen, the cars in the station parking lot were buried, and the passengers who were to have gone up the road, through the pass and over the other side of the mountain, decided not to and stayed in the station hotel instead. But a young Austrian boy came up to us in an old beat-up station wagon that had seen many trips overland. He said he could make it over the pass into Zurs and Lech easily. We got in and started off. The visibility was zero as the snow was coming down so heavily. Before we had gotten very far we came to where eight or so cars were collected, each one helping the front car that was mired in the deep snow drifts. We also helped dig. The progress was very slow. As we got up higher on the winding road that clung to the side of the mountain, every now and then we would hear a terrible roar overhead, and then a crash from far down at our right as a "lavina," an avalanche, thundered into the deep chasm way below. When we got to the Arlberg tunnel we had to dig out the cars that got stuck as they emerged from the other end. We just made it past the tiny town of Steuben, whose lights were barely visible, and it was tough going from there another mile to the top. As luck would have it, there was a snow plow that was working valiantly and we followed it into Zurs where even it got stuck. We were lucky beyond belief to have made it that far and blessed the little inn that took us in. The next morning we followed the plow down into Lech. We were the last car in or out of this area for two weeks. We learned that Steuben had been swept away completely an hour after we had passed.

We stayed at the Gastoff Schneider. There was no electricity, no ski tows worked, and Britishers who were on a travel allowance (rationing) and had come to the end of their resources, did odd jobs to pay for their over-extended room and board. One of these looked for all the world like Anthony Eden, as he waited on table at our dining room. The village was beautiful at night with nothing but candles illuminating the scene. The old church tower with its onion dome looked like a delicious dessert topped with a huge serving of "schlag" (cream). It was a memorable time to be there, and no one will forget it. The camaraderie was wonderful, and although eventually the tows and lifts got running, the road was altogether impassable, blocked by huge fallen trees and powerlines snapped by the weight of the snow. When we finally did make it out, we were piled into a vehicle which was a half-track that could move like a caterpillar up banks and around trees. But a man had to sit on the front fender and kick the front wheel into position as it balked from time to time.

Jim's and my relationship was getting strained. The lack of respect that I felt was confirmed in little ways, for instance, he had run out of money and Willy and I had to help out as best we could. He eventually got a bit more sent to him in Paris, but for the time being he was broke. The three of us hired a ski instructor one Saturday morning to take us high up into the mountains as Fritz had done. This Austrian was very un-charming and scornful. At the end of the ski session we came to a place where the only way down was along a steep shoot that looked like a ski-jump,two tracks ending in a small landing area. No chance to turn or escape. The instructor did look a little apprehensive, but he wanted to get to the bottom quickly by noon for his Saturday afternoon off. He said, "Now do just as I do." And he sped sharply down the shoot, making a tidy christie at the end before the steep drop behind. I was petrified and knew I would have to go immediately or not at all. I went charging down with an untidy christie at the end just in the nick of time. Then good old Willy, who didn't ski then quite as well as I, had even more courage to do the same, and safely. We looked back up the hill to where Jim was. He was taking his skis off and walking down.

After leaving Lech on the perilous journey, which was nevertheless terribly exciting, we left the mountains and headed back to Paris. Brigitte Carlhian was throwing a large party in her own honor to which the three of us were invited. A very elaborate affair, it had many smart and aristocratic guests, none of whom we knew or dared speak to. Jim was in a foul mood, petulant and gloomy, as he was heading back to New York in a few days. He was also very upset at the deterioration of our relationship. During the party he asked me to go out into the large hallway to discuss our future. The spiral staircase going down had an ornate wrought iron and gold railing, and in the course of the argument that ensued, I became terrified that he wanted to push me over it. It was threatening but not actual. Only, I suppose, designed to scare me. It did. I ran back into the party and up to our room where I hid in the secret room behind our room and Monsieur Carlhian's study. I sobbed for quite awhile.

It was in this room that Nanny Conway the nurse had hidden the Carlhian boys during the Nazi occupation of Paris when soldiers came to the house searching for Frenchmen. Nanny was a remarkable English lady who somehow got passports forged for the three boys. She got them listed as girls—Marie Josef, Marie Jean Paul, and Marie Michel—dressed them in girls' clothes she made out of the dining room curtains, and whisked them off to the south of France.

The day before Jim left, we went up the Eiffel Tower to have lunch. While viewing gorgeous Paris from the top, I again felt that Jim wanted to push me over. In fact my back was pressed against the railing as his anger emerged again. I tried to keep this from Willy, but I think she sensed it anyway.

She and I proceeded to go south to Grenoble in the Kneese (guilt, guilt) to ski at l'Alpe d'Huez, high up in the French Alps. The road up to the station to ski was hairpin curves all the way, and the old bus driven by a French maniac sapped our courage at every turn. But once there it was glorious. Our little inn was one of several above the town perched on the side of the mountain. It was fun and we soon made friends with two young guys who worked as waiters and bartenders, Ian an Englishman from Chichester, and Lucien a Frenchman from Bordeaux. We skied with them when they had time off. Ian made a pie bed on me, and once brought me a boiled egg for my breakfast that had no egg inside. I later visited him in Chicester and went sailing with him in the beautiful harbor. Often after skiing we sat at the little bar before supper. One evening an old drunk stumbled in and sat at the bar precariously on a stool right next to mine. He didn't make a nuisance of himself, he just smiled. His cheeks were bright red and his eyes watery. I smiled back at him. A couple of days later he made his way to the bar again. I asked Lucien if he was okay or to be avoided. Lucien replied, "il n'est pas mechant." I subsequently learned that this wreck of a man was once a famous architect who had built grand houses for wealthy people all around the world. He picked l'Alpe d'Huez to build a fine hotel up the mountain for his new wife and himself to run. But in the process of building, his beloved wife died and he never completed the project whose ruined foundations could still be seen above in the snow. He also never built anything else and lost his mind, wandering around from inn to inn getting handouts and subsisting on town welfare. They called him Totosche. When our skiing was over in l'Alpe d'Huez, Willy and I boarded the bus in the town square to go back to Grenoble. The window beside my seat had become steamed up, and as I wiped it with my scarf, I could see a figure standing down below looking up at me. It was Totosche. As the bus started its engine he waved and shouted to me, "Au revoir ma grande Bretagne!" I vowed I would sometime have a French poodle and call him Totosche—which I did, living in London after I married Ward.

And on now to the south of France and thence into Italy. We did all the famous chateaux, loved the Loire, and when we hit the Riviera we went to Hyères hoping to visit the lovely Iles de Hyères. But when we arrived at our little hotel au bord de la mer such a rain storm was in progress that the streets became flooded and we were marooned in the hotel for three days. I remember seeing fields of artichokes totally submerged in water with only the tips of the plants showing. My Father had said in a letter when Mum told him when we were marooned in snowy Austria, "If only the girls would get out of danger and go south." Here we were again at the mercy of the elements. After the "inondation" the sun came out and we were off again, this time to sunny Italy.

I realize as I am writing that my most abiding memories are of special people who made an imprint on me, and who have shaped my life. The places I have seen, however, have made a strong impression on me, and although in this journal I am not dwelling on Arles, Avignon, Nimes, Juan Les Pins, the Matisse Chapel in Vence, the gorgeous vistas of the French and Italian countryside, the Colosseum in Rome, the Medici Chapel in Florence, the Ponte Vecchio and the Uffizi, all these are indelibly in my memory. It was Wordsworth who said, "I am become a part of all that I have met." I have revisited many of the lovely places since, but one's first impression is often the most nourishing. I believe I became a painter because of the need to put back in the world some of the beauty I had taken out.

It was April as we crossed the border into Italy, and one of those springs to die over. Wildflowers everywhere and geraniums tumbling from windowboxes or lined up on stone steps. Florence was dazzling in the sunshine and we marvelled at the rich treasures we saw. The Duomo, the bronze Baptistry doors, the Piazza del Signore, the Michelangelos, Santa Maria del Croce's beautiful cloister, and the Bernozzo Gozzoli's journey of the Magi. But I lost my heart totally to the exquisite Byzantine Church of San Mineato al Monte across the Arno on its proud mount. This experience was enhanced by meeting the Francises from Cleveland on the broad steps leading up to the church. They adored the place and had been there many times. He was an art history professor and a director of the Cleveland Museum. They shared their love and insights into this church with us. I had never been exposed to anything Byzantine before and was stunned at the intricate inlaid designs of the marble and tile interior, all so beautifully conceived and abstracted. It was dazzling. This was not "plain geometry."

On the way south we stopped at an American cemetery where I was looking for Bill's division that had been so decimated during the war. The graves, however, were unmarked, and although I had assumed he was buried there, I couldn't get it confirmed. The countryside had burst into full-blown spring and the silent white graves contrasted with the exuberant beauty of the surrounding olive groves and vineyards whose vines were bursting with green energy, and fruit trees in full pink bloom parading up the steep banks. It was a gorgeous final resting place for those poor dead boys, and very moving.

I cannot do justice here to Rome, for that city above all others needs time to visit, and time to write about. Furthermore my classical knowledge is limited to school Latin, scant familiarity with the Roman civilization and some meager knowledge of Aristotle and Plato. I have always been turned off by Plato who is so logical, so abstract, and so stuck on himself and his coterie. I felt more at ease with the crazy Romantics, and the classical turn of mind seemed to me unreal. But that didn't keep me from being awed at the Colosseum, stunned by the Vatican and dizzied in the Catacombs. The Italians do everything in jumbo size. At best they are monumental and heroic as the Michelangelo paintings in the Sistine Chapel. But they can miss terribly, as for instance, the huge monument to Victor Emmanuel at one of the piazzas. Willy and I stayed in a smashing villa at the head of the Spanish stairs belonging to some countess who occasionally took in guests. There was a sensational roof garden on the top of this charming building where we could look out over all of Rome and count the seven hills.

After we left Rome we hastened to the Italian Riviera. In Ravello, above the Amalfi Drive, we discovered we were in the most beautiful spot on earth. At the top of a frighteningly steep and deeply curved road was this tiny town clinging to the side of the mountains. There amid the lemon and orange groves and the terraced vineyards was the unforgettable Hotel Palumbo, and we swooned over the vista from our balconied room down over the Salerno Gulf with its sapphire blue sea. The terraces were festooned with huge pots of flowering plants, and roses climbed profusely over entrances and arbors. At dusk as we sat on the terrace after dinner we could see the fishing boats returning to port, and the lights of Positano coming on to create a beautiful silvery crescent which followed the shoreline of the gulf.

The first night in the dining room we noticed with relish a marvelous couple sitting at a small table by the windows. I had never seen two people so engrossed in each other's company, chatting animatedly, and obviously very much in love. They spoke to us after dinner on the lower terrace where we had coffee. We became great friends and found them fascinating. It was Lily and Antony Hornby, and they had come here on an anniversary, as they had each year for four years. They were English, or at least Antony was. Lily was Czechoslovakian, I think, or maybe Romanian, and had been a ballet dancer. Before the war she had traveled with a corps de ballet all over Europe, dancing before royalty and the elite. She was dancing in Monte Carlo when she was spotted by Lord Beaverbrook, who had quite an eye for the ladies. He subsequently gave her his card and said, "If you ever come to England I insist you look me up." When the Germans invaded Czechoslovakia she escaped to England ahead of great trouble. When she got to London she had no money, no belongings, and remembered Lord Beaverbrook.She found herself calling him from the Charing Cross Station with much trepidation. He told her to come immediately. She was his mistress for several years. She was fascinating looking with hair parted in the middle and drawn back in a ballet dancer's familiar coiffure. Her accent was delicious and I was glued to every word as she recounted the story of her amours and intrigues when she took me to the Ivy Restaurant in London later. The waiters at this celebrated restaurant treated her as if she were a countess and showed us to her special table in the corner.

During that lovely first evening at the Palumbo, she told us that she and Antony had fallen madly in love while she was still with Lord Beaverbrook. She said Lord B. had other women, but none that he counted on more for advice than her, and indeed had made several crucial decisions of national consequence due to her suggestions. I guess I believed it. As we were sitting there in Ravello she said how Antony embodied all the wonderful qualities of Great Britain at its best, and indeed he did: handsome, brilliant, compassionate and amusing. She turned to him and said,

"Darling, please turn around so that Lydia can see the back of your head." He did obediently. "There, what did I tell you, does not that strong shape suggest Britain? I shall get him sculpted when we get back to London."

Pasqual Vuilluimier ran the Hotel Palumbo, and he was quite a charmer with all his guests, especially the ladies. After dinner the next night he took me down into the rose garden and cut a huge bunch of roses for me which I took back to our room, it continuing to waft its fragrance for all the days we were there. Lılı said that he had amorous intentions toward me, but I wasn't interested beyond being flattered. All the children in town looked just like Vuilluimier.

Around the Gulf toward the south, about an hour away, we journeyed to Paestum with its ruined Greek temples. I almost became converted to classic form when I caught sight of the Temple of Diana sitting serenely on its plain, looking out over the sea. It was simple and lovely, and the doves that wheeled in and out amongst its graceful columns enhanced this sunlit scene. I got an impression from this one example of what great beauty was inherent in classical Greek form. I dare say that it prompted as wonderful a response in me as the Parthenon would on first viewing. And without all the crowds and the hype.

Sharing the crest of this hillside, this idyllic spot, was the Villa Cimbrone, an extraordinary elaborate Italianate villa. With its many statues, terraced walks, ornate gardens, and marvelous promenade overlooking the sea, it inspired all who visited it, including Wagner who was said to have composed *Parsifal* here while in residence. So also came Greta Garbo. It was so encompassing that it looked out on the neighboring hilltops, including the one on which Gore Vidal chose to build his own home.

Willy and I took long walks up into the mountains. One day we passed a procession all costumed in festive native garb celebrating some holy day. They were coming to the little 12th century church in the town square.

We hated to leave Ravello. We headed along the perilous but gorgeous Amalfi Drive taking our lives in our hands, and often there were only millimeters between us and sure death as the wild Italians screeched around corners, and buses passed us on blind turns honking loudly. The sea was far below, beneath steep precipices. We went from Sorrento by ferry to Capri. All the Italians were seasick, but no one else, on the comparatively smooth hour's boat ride. Capri was better than even a picture postcard, more lovely than we hoped, although touristy. We went by a small boat into the Blue Grotto, shimmering in the light reflected from the calm seas. We went up the steep path to Axel Munthe's wonderful house in Ana Capri.

As we left Italy, our eyes and senses had been given a real treat, and the beauty we saw would provide a lovely standard and parameter by which to measure subsequent delights. France had been in my life as a little girl. But now I could add Italy to my recollections, evoking it in my mind with the greatest relish.

It was early May. We stopped in Nice to pick up any mail that might have collected for us at the American Express office. I went in to get the mail while Willy waited outside on the Boulevard d'Anglais in the car.

There were quite a few letters including a telegram which said, "Arriving May 15. London. Meet me. Love Mother."

I said, "My God, its my Mother."

Willy said, "No goddam it, it's my Mother," which was confirmed by the fact that it was addressed to Ann Williams. This was not what we had in mind. We had not contemplated going back to England so early.

By the time we had rushed back to Paris, Willy had decided to go and meet her Mother while I would stay in Paris a while longer to look for a job. This would allow me to prolong this wonderful experience. I had almost run out of money and had to wire Pa for just a bit more. After Willy had gone to London, I did look for a job at the Paris Herald Tribune, and the American Embassy, but there wasn't enough promise of one to delay my inevitable departure. Besides I was quite lonely in Paris the few days I was there by myself. So I decided to go to London and meet Willy and Aunt Floss, her Mother, and we toured for several days in the south of England. We took a picnic in Cornwall high up in a field full of daisies and wild flowers overlooking the coast. Aunt Floss delighted me as she always had, although Willy was a bit miffed with her for coming. I remember this feminine, pretty, tidy lady taking her shoes off, putting daisies in her hair, and with a chiffon scarf trailing from her upstretched arms, ran through the field pretending to be one of the Three Graces. I thought it wonderfully funny and liberated of her. Willy was not as amused.

As I was leaving the Hotel de France et Choiseul to go to London, I received a long fat letter from Pat Jarman in New York announcing she was getting married in June and would I be a bridesmaid. (This is the last thing I wanted to do.) She had my dress already ordered at Rosette Pennington (Ugh, and cantaloupe-colored). There would be twelve ushers and three bridesmaids (good ratio, I thought).

And then she added in a P.S. at the end that a wonderful guy from Washington was coming to the wedding whose name is Ward Chamberlin. (That does it. Goddamit! Why won't everybody allow a single girl to stay single. They always have to sew you up with some "wonderful guy." All I want to do is to go back to New York, make enough money to come right back to Paris, buy a really French poodle and live happily ever after, and *Single*.)

We sailed on the United States line, we in tourist and Aunt Floss in first class. She asked us up to all the swell parties, and we had quite a ball, for there was again a fairly good group of young people. I made friends with a young man called Bill something who was training to be an undertaker. The night before we landed, we were all terribly merry at a first class gala, and Bill and I under the influence almost became entwined for a night. It was fortunate, however, that we went to our separate berths in time because Mary Ahern nearly talked her way onto the pilot's boat which came to meet us in the harbor, and it would not have done to have me absent and unaccounted for. Mother and Pup did come to meet me, and looked a bit disapproving as I had a clinch and embrace with Bill at the foot of the gangplank, never to become an undertaker's wife.

VII

Ward and Me

Pat Jarman's wedding reception was at the Cosmos Club with all the trimmings. The twelve ushers were nice, and the orchestra good. The cantaloupe bridesmaids' dresses with pastel colored bouquets were hideous. But as our receiving line was winding down and the last aunts and uncles came through, I was looking forward to the dancing. The last person to come through the line before we broke up, rather disheveled, as he had missed his earlier train, was Ward Chamberlin.

I made a mental note that he was not too bad-looking, and dashed off to the dance floor with the others. A bit later Ward came and cut in on me. I was not displeased. And after a brief time moving to the strains of the society orchestra, and some inconsequential chatter, the most extraordinary thing happened. I knew I was going to marry him. This was not a sensation of blood rushing to the head, knees crumbling, sudden chemical changes of love at first sight, but just an honest-to-goodness unavoidable fact. I had not been looking. I had not contemplated this happening, but there it was. I found myself later asking him to join the wedding party for dinner in the Village at Enrico and Paglieri's which he did. It was a bit fresh of me, but Pat didn't mind. She even beamed. Ward and I sat next to each other at the end of the long table, and held hands under the red and white checked table cloth.

After dinner Ward and I escaped and went dancing at LaRues, and my own suspicions were confirmed. He was the one for me. It took him a couple of weeks longer. He wrote me a letter stating that he felt we could successfully put our lives together. Not the most romantic proposal, but good enough for me. We were married four months later.

And what a wedding. I've never been to a better one. We both enjoyed ourselves hugely. It was like a provincial village wedding. Everybody participated, and much great generosity bestowed on us. Power Point, where my parents' house was in Duxbury, opened its houses up for ushers and guests, luncheons and dinners thrown for us, and local ladies prepared the best food imaginable, simple but delicious. The bridal dinner was donated by friends at the Winsor House, and the many toasts and skits were outstanding and original.

I had brought Aleese, my black cleaning lady from New York who I loved, to Duxbury for the event. She had purchased a bright pink satin uniform with starched cap, apron and collar, and was dynamite. Little Mrs. Gibson, our cook, looked quite startled behind her thick glasses when Aleese got dressed for the reception. The next day after the wedding, good old Mom, even though she was dog-tired, took Aleese on a sightseeing trip. When Aleese caught sight of the tall Myles Standish Monument silhouetted against the sky, Myles Standish standing on top, she said to Mom in her southern accent, "Who's dat standing up there, it must be General Lee."

The wedding was spirited and ebullient throughout. A glowery, damp day threatened the garden ceremony, but I insisted on having it outdoors, and we lucked it out between showers. A huge flock of geese flew over honking like mad as we took our vows. I had gotten a tiny portable pump organ which we placed in the entryway, and Cousin Addie, aged 84, whom I had asked to play the wedding march, came up to practice every day for a week. She over-practiced and I was soon sick to death of the melody. By the time all the guests had assembled around the little pool, and Dr. Vivien Pomeroy, our wonderful Unitarian minister from Milton, had taken his place under the rose arbor, Cousin Addie took up her position at the tiny organ. I came down the stairs and joined Pup who was waiting for me in the living room and off we started to the first strains of the Wedding March. But as we passed Cousin Addie, the music seemed to stop, and although she was playing the organ keys vigorously, with her head uplifted in ecstasy, she was forgetting to pump with her feet.

"Pump, Cousin Addie, pump," I whispered as we passed her, and the music resumed.

My bridesmaids were Mary Ahern, Willy Williams and Sue Coleman. They were smashing. Ward had as best man Billy Sloane, his brother-in-law, who exercised his duties admirably, romancing all the old aunts and the single ladies, and gave marvelous toasts at the opportune moments. Ward's ushers were his dearest friends Sam Bell, Newt Schenck, Alex Stumpf, and Bill Farelly. The names Schenck, Stumpf and Farelly sounded like a Mafia law firm and were a bit much for the Boston brahmins, but they were sensational. When it came time to throw my bouquet, Ward and I stood on the little porch above the garden. All the single ladies were lined up below and as I tossed the bouquet at Willy, out of nowhere came Auntie Mamie, aged 84, and grabbed it. In doing so she got knocked down and was lying there amongst the rhododendron bushes, her little black red-cross shoes sticking up in the air. Sam Bell, who was a doctor, rushed up to assist her, found her glasses nearby, and she stood up triumphantly with nary a scratch.

As I was in my room getting dressed to go away, I heard peals of laughter coming out of the room where the guys had assembled to dress and toast Ward. After a very sentimental and loving toast given by Pup to Ward, there wasn't a dry eye.

But quick as a wink Alex Stumpf who has a hare-lip jumped to his feet and said about Ward, "Mitha Giffud, he ain't much, but heth the bethte we gut!" Alex has to be one of the most comical of human beings, and has always been so. Newt Schenck had come to the wedding by train from New York. He was to take a taxi from Kingston, which was near Duxbury. Newt got off the train at Kingston all right, but it was Kingston, Rhode Island, and he was astonished when he asked the cab driver how much it would cost to go to Duxbury, and the driver responded $65. Newt realizing his error got the next train to Kingston, Massachusetts, after a couple of hours delay.

It was pouring torrentially as we left the wedding on our honeymoon in the Chamberlin's little black Desoto. We headed for our wedding night to the Ritz Carleton in Boston. Amid all the luxury of this gorgeous hotel we felt marvelous and festive and got all the room service we could.

About 2:30 in the morning our phone rang and it was Steve who was still partying with the wedding party. He said, "Oh, hi! How's everything going?" I could have killed him.

We headed to Manchester, Vermont, with a stop-over at Aunt Rosamond's Inn in New Boston, Massachusetts. She gave us the whole inn, which was empty, as she and Uncle Russell were staying in an adjacent cottage. Her instructions to us were that there were no guests expected that night, and if anyone arrived not to let them in. No sooner had we settled down for the night in the largest suite than there was a loud insistent knocking at the front door. It was still pouring rain, and Ward took pity on whomever it was and dashed downstairs clad only in my trousseau satin negligee. A bearded man dripping wet said he had a reservation, he must stay over-night. Behind him stood a peroxide blond, looking like a wet white poodle. Ward found himself showing them rooms he had no idea about, searching for one with a huge double bed.

When Ward told Rosamond the next morning she had a fit. "He's a first-class sponger, never pays his bill!"

After our honeymoon we drove to Washington, our car loaded with wedding presents and trousseaux. Ward had found a small apartment on Que Street in a brick apartment house in Georgetown. We were on the ground floor which was good, and I immediately painted it cocoa-brown. Ward was working for the Economic Cooperation Administration, and lo-and-behold, after we had been in residence only a few weeks, we were offered a position in Paris with the ECA. I chuckled when I thought that the only thing I wanted six months earlier was to go back to Paris, single, and get a job. Now I was going double and tickled to death.

We had no money. And in order to get overseas with any pocket money at all, we had to sell some of our wedding presents. What we didn't sell we packed and gave to a friend to store who had a large barn in Virginia. We did not need eight dozen crystal goblets or ten hand-painted trays, etc. Unfortunately, the packers packed my list of presents and this went to Virginia without my realizing it. I had written about one-third of my thank-you notes and the rest of the people never heard from me because the barn in which our presents were stored burned to the ground and along with it my list of who gave me what.

I'm always ashamed to go to Boston even to this day to meet some family and friends for I can just imagine what they are still thinking: "Isn't Lydia terrible, how awful not to thank me for my wedding present to her!"

We were so happy taking off for our new life in France. We left Washington by plane, and stopped in Boston before going across the ocean. It was late at night in Boston and there assembled at the airport to say goodbye were Mum and Pup, Tinny my cousin, and Barbara, Uncle Chandler and Aunt Maizie, and, believe it or not, old Auntie Mamie. What good sports! I was very touched. I can see them now all waving as we pulled down the runway.

In Paris we settled into the Hotel du Quai Voltaire on the Left Bank near the Pont Royale. Sitting in bed having croissants and coffee in the morning I looked out at the Louvre, saw barges moving slowly down the Seine, and could see Ward walking over the Pont Royale headed to work at the ECA offices in the Hotel Wagram on the rue de Rivoli. One Saturday, as he had to work, I suggested we take a picnic in the Tuilleries; we would meet under the statue of Eros. I had such fun shopping for the bread and fruit and cheese and salami. I wanted to add hard-boiled eggs and asked the concierge if the kitchen might boil me up a couple. There was no restaurant, only breakfast served. The cook and the chambermaid and Madame et Monsieur were only too happy to join in providing my eggs, and with great ceremony added them carefully to my picnic basket. They were very excited at the prospect of a picnic.

"And where is Madame going for the picnic?" (thinking perhaps Fontainbleau or Chantilly or Honfleur) (all in French)

When I answered, "Aux Tuilleries," they nearly died with laughter.

We relished Paris, its everything—its museums, its restaurants—and loved discovering little bistros and cafes. One of our favorites was "Eddie's" on a little street back of the Place Vendome, to which Willy and I had gone many times before. We made friends with Eddy and his wife, and Eddy took us back into his tiny kitchen one time, when I asked, to show me how he made his superb veau au champignons à la creme. Once when Ward and I had gone out to Marly to play golf and were standing in a large busy square waiting for a bus, as another bus was pulling out, I noticed a man waving at us like mad from a window. It was Eddy.

Each day I would venture forth from our hotel looking for an apartment to live in. It wasn't easy as we didn't have much money to spend and apartments were hard to come by. Furthermore it was difficult to plow through the French real estate sections of the newspaper. But I finally found a real studio with a sleeping balcony above the main room. It overlooked the cemetiere de Montparnasse. It suited me to a tee, and Ward liked it also.

But a few days before we signed the lease, Ward came back from work in a high state of excitement. "Guess what! We are moving to London!"

I was not pleased. How can I become fluent in French, be a French cook, and a French Impressionist in London? Drat! But the dye was cast. Ward also was excited because he had met a lady at a party who offered us her flat in London. Her name was Maryse McLaren, and she was the daughter of General Freyburg. And we were to move in June into a flat without ever seeing it.

Earlier when we first were in Paris, Ward had to go to Vienna on business. I figured out that I could go to ski in Austria in St. Anton while he continued on by train, did his work in Vienna and then joined me on the way back. The only way this would be possible would be if I could exchange his first class ticket for two second class tickets. The French officials at the Compagnie Generale de Chemin de Fer, or whatever it was called, looked dumbfounded when I tried to negotiate the deal. But I finally succeeded after two days and many hours of bickering. Or is it dickering? As the train chugged through the Alps the snow was deep, and I was enormously pleased to be returning to the Arlberg again. To this day I regret not seeing Vienna, but the mountains called. I got off the train at St. Anton in the middle of the night, dressed in my ski clothes, and Ward in his business suit waved at me as the train huffed and puffed off into the darkness. I walked carrying my skis to the Schwarzer Adler Hotel. The next morning I skied alone, but after lunch as I was preparing to go up the mountain again, a lady asked me if I would like to go with her. She was quite intimidating with a snappy expensive ski outfit, jet black hair, and the deepest tan you ever saw. I was worried that she would be too expert for me. When we got off at the top of the cable she took forever to fix her skis and bindings. I skied a little way down and stood waiting for her in the sun. But she never appeared. I finally gave up and skied half-way down. I looked all around for her and I saw a figure way over at the right of the snow bowl moving very slowly, hardly going down hill at all for the angle chosen. It was my friend.

And as she passed me in a full snowplow she shouted, "I'm not very speedy, but I'm steady as a rock."

Ward did join me later in the week. I was careful of where I took him to ski. Though he wasn't terribly experienced, he was too game for his own safety. The second outing we approached a rather steep trail which joined a gentler terrain. I went down ahead, cautioning him to take it easy as it was icy. I looked back for an instant to see how he was doing, and caught my ski in a rut, and took a big spill. He came after me just fine, but I thought I had broken my ankle. It was me that ended up in the medical dispensary. Though painful, it wasn't broken, but I hobbled around for days, even back in Paris.

We packed up and left Paris for London. I was sad. We had been given

70

keys to 19 The Boltons, London SW I and arrived there in South Kensington. It was a very fashionable area, a small oval park with the old church, St. Mary's The Boltons, perched in its middle, and large houses, some converted to flats as ours was, stationed all around the perimeter. Douglas Fairbanks lived three doors down. The second evening we were there, a splendid entourage pulled up in front of the Fairbanks' house, and out of a long sleek black limousine emerged the Queen who was coming for dinner.

Almost as soon as we arrived and were taking our luggage in, Ward began exploring the premises and much to his delight found our neighbors had a grass tennis court! He peered over the stone wall and further discovered there were very good players playing doubles, the men in long white flannels. Before you knew it, Ward had made his presence known and the Couplands asked him over. Within twenty minutes, while I was unpacking inside, he rushed in demanding his tennis clothes. Ian Coupland had asked him to play. We became very good friends, and Ward was a great addition to their tennis, which he doted on. It was July, and a lovely one. I was pregnant.

We had the two bottom floors of this grand house. There were two other families in converted apartments on the upper floors, including Andrew and Isabel Crichton who lived on the top floor. Our living room, dining room, with a kitchen overlooking the garden, were converted from the once ballroom. The three bedrooms were downstairs including ours which had French doors going out into the garden. Our garden was beautiful and the exact same size as the adjacent grass tennis court. We had been told by Maryse McLaren that a gardener came every week and that we must keep him. Soon Dutton showed up on his bicycle.

He said to me, "Does Madame like Dye-les?"

"Oh yes, very much," I said, not knowing what he was talking about. The next time he came he had the rack on the back of his bicycle filled with plants. They were Dahlias. He had lifted them from the Kensington Gardens where he worked other days.

Shopping was great fun along the Fulham Road, and the Old Brompton Road, but time-consuming as one had to go to the Fishmonger, the Green Grocer, the Meat Monger, the Bread Monger, etc. Very different from en Amerique. Only one unpleasant occasion when I took Ward's shoes to be re-soled at the Cobbler, and after showing the cobbler the shoes I asked him sweetly if he could give them a nice proper shine when he was finished. He practically threw them in my face. "Shine them yourself Madame, I'm not your servant." I was stunned.

We became very good friends with Marie-Ange and Bill Underwood who was also working with Ward at what was now called DMPA, the Defense Materials Procurement Agency, formerly ECA. Bill and Marie Ange had a smashing little flat in Mount Street. It was on the top floor that you got to by a little glass and iron elevator. Bill looked like Charles Laughton, but was wonderfully sweet and kind, not like Captain Bligh. He would have been a perennial bachelor had he not met Marie-Ange who was an Egyptian brought up in Paris. She was one-of-a-kind, fascinating, funny, original and totally European in her fine taste and chic sensibilities. She called him "Beel," and "Beel" was devoted to her. She pursued many interests, and often left him for extended trips to Cairo, or petits vacances, which was probably good for the perpetuation of their marriage.

We had our first Christmas in London alone as I remember it because I refused to have Christmas dinner with General Lewis who was Ward's boss and a male chauvinist pig. Also I was encumbered by my burgeoning size, being seven months pregnant. Ward's great friend Newt Schenck had been in Paris with Luke Finlay on an assignment, and he fell madly in love with the daughter Anne Finlay. Newt announced they were coming over to London to stay with us. Newt and Anne became engaged on our front door steps at four in the morning, sealing their troth as the milkman arrived to deliver milk.

I couldn't go to their wedding party in Paris being too great with child. It was then that the Great Fog hit London. One couldn't imagine the impact of this unless one had been there. It was so serious that instant legislation was soon thereafter enacted to ban all peat fires, and other smoky combustible emissions from fireplace chimneys and commercial smokestacks, etc. It was the last Great Fog. For three days the airports were shut, and all traffic in and out of the city had come to a complete halt. The dense pea soup fog trapping gases was yellowish and eerie. Ambulances could not get to hospitals and people with respiratory ailments suffered. When an elderly friend of ours emerged from the Underground to go home to Chelsea she became completely disoriented and stumbled from lamp post to lamp post. The theatres had to be closed down as the audience couldn't see the stage beyond the first row. The silence of the city streets was nerve wracking. In our flat the dishes in the cupboards became sooty, and even the clothes in the bureaus and closets were covered with grime. Ward was supposed to come home on Sunday night, but we realized that that wouldn't happen.

So the Crichtons asked me upstairs for dinner. Just as we were sitting down to a roast lamb, the door bell rang and in came Ward. What a miracle! Just like him to conquer the odds. He got the last airplane out of Paris before it too was shut down as the fog was drifting into France. The passengers commandeered a bus into London from the airport, and it was Ward who directed it on foot, walking along the road with a flashlight behind him to indicate the way to the bus driver. They made it! I was relieved because my baby was due at any moment, and I didn't relish the thought of giving birth at home alone.

Beautiful Carolyn was born on February 6 at the Wellbeck Street Nursing Home. She arrived on my Father's birthday. We chose the nursing home over an impersonal hospital and it was full of personality. I felt like one of the Barretts of Wimpole Street, the street adjacent to Wellbeck Street. I had to bring a whole hamper of baby equipment, nappies, etc. It all looked very unfamiliar at first. Sisters in their nun's habits, with great sea-gull-type starched white hats were in attendance, and they all looked right out of the cast of "Sound of Music." Mr. Jackson (you don't call surgeons Doctors) made a flying trip from a party to deliver my baby. He had on a morning coat and striped pants. He also was the head baby doctor to all the Queen's ladies-in-waiting. But he was nice, although the nun on duty was cross with me for not telling her earlier that my labor pains had started. We were thrilled with our gorgeous, perfectly formed baby. A very imperious older nun came one morning into the room holding a small object in her hands as if it were a dead mouse. "I think this belongs to the American mother," she said scornfully. It was an orange and black booty that had fallen off the baby when she was being brought up the staircase. Mrs. Finlay had knit it in Ward's Princeton colors, and the youngest and nicest nun had put it on Carolyn with a sense of adventure. The first person on the scene was Bill Underwood who ran pell-mell down Wellbeck Street that sloshy morning bearing a huge bunch of tulips. He had been called when they couldn't get hold of Ward. Ward arrived soon thereafter in an excited dither.

Ward and I had earlier decided on hiring a first-class Nanny in that we knew absolutely nothing about babies. So we went to the best agency in town, Miss Austen's, and asked for the best they had. This was a mistake. Miss Holmwood arrived in full Nanny regalia with starched everything, including her personality. She wore nursing emblems on her chest like an admiral, and these were horizontal on her ample bosom. She came to the nursing home as we were leaving with our cherished baby bundle, and whisked the baby right out of my arms, taking complete military charge of affairs. It was a very uncomfortable situation back at the Boltons because Holmwood was used to aristocratic houses with staffs and butlers. Here there was only me, and I knocked myself out to cook well for her, and complete the chores she wouldn't do—like washing the hundreds of linen nappies in the bathtub weekly. We had no washer and dryer, and laundromats were non-existent. The diapers were hanging to dry all over the house, which they never did. February was cold and damp. There was one heater in our bedroom about the size of a large toaster, that was all. Miss Holmwood was, however, very adept at forming the newspapers into hard clumps like bricquets, and they were quite effective lighting the coals in the fireplace. Wood was not available since the war. She was not keen on my nursing Carolyn, and tried every way she could to stop the system and the flow. For her amusement after I had fed her a nice meal, she would sit back and read the racing sheets. She was a big gambler.

One day when Miss Holmwood brought the baby to me to feed I noticed the baby's fingernails were very long. I asked her to cut them, please.

"Oh no, Madame, not today, it's Friday," she announced. "What's the matter with Friday?" I said.

"Bad luck," she retorted firmly.

"You take Carolyn down immediately and cut her nails. I don't care what day it is," I yelled.

Minutes later there came a piercing scream from the baby's room. She had cut the end of the baby's finger. That did it! I put in a call to Ward at his office on Oxford Street. "You must come home immediately and fire this terrible lady." I was too afraid of her to do it myself.

We notified Miss Austen's Agency that we needed another Nanny, this one to be less grand, more down-to-earth and provincial. They said they had just the right type who was immediately available. Miss Whitehead arrived. Oddly enough she had bright white hair. Middle-aged but wiry and strong. She told us she came from southern England where she lived in a van. She was a gypsy! But her nice white uniform and bright pink cheeks made her look wholesome enough. Several days after she had arrived, I heard rather strange noises coming from the baby's room. It was night, and there was a full moon. I went in to find Miss Whitehead standing at the window holding our baby, who was stark naked, up to the moon and chanting some unearthly song. Ward was away in Liverpool until the next day when again I called him at his office and made him come home and fire Miss Whitehead.

We finally got a real jewel in Zia, a lovely young girl who was studying to be a nurse. We all adored each other, and hated to leave her behind, which we did when we returned home just at the time of the Queen's coronation.

During the Nanny episodes we had acquired a beautiful, large standard poodle, apricot colored, and I named him "Totosche." Bunny Coupland and I had persuaded Ian and Ward that we must drive up to Nottingham-shire to a farm that advertised a new litter of poodles. I'll never forget driving back after dark in Ian's small, snappy black Humber Hawk with two squirming adorable creatures in our laps. The Couplands got Peaches, and we Totosche. Peaches was a holy terror, just as mischievous as their young daughter Bambi and the two were very hard to manage. Fortunately ours had a benign and loving un-bumptious personality and we were crazy about him. I felt so proud strolling with Lyn (as we call her) in the gorgeous Cadillac of baby carriages (that Ward had gone to a great deal of trouble to buy) with Totosche on a leash beside us. We really stopped traffic. Besides, Lyn was the most dazzlingly beautiful baby you ever saw.

When our stay in London was almost over we had decided to rent a house in the country for the month of May. Ward came home one Saturday afternoon after playing tennis in St. John's Wood with the news that he had met a lady who offered to rent him her house in Sussex. (What again! Ward is fatally attractive to real-estated ladies!) Ruth Tours had a house which she would rent us for a month. She would move into the village of Pull-borough while we were there, and stay with a friend. The deal was that Ward would drive her car to the station every morning and leave it for her, and it would be waiting at night when he returned from work in London. The house was enchanting, sitting amidst a gaggle of old thatched-roof cottages, with a lovely huge lawn and beautiful garden full of irises, daffodils, roses, tulips, etc. And beyond the garden were the undulating Downs that stretched to, and were sentinels of, the sea. You could even smell the sea when the wind was right, and the cloud shadows that moved over the smooth green downs were beautiful.

When we arrived Ruth was there to show us around. Zia was with us too. The house was very old, and the kitchen had hundreds of gadgets in every drawer that should have been in the Victoria and Albert Museum. Ruth took a large key out of her pocket, and showed Ward where it went in a door half-way up the curved staircase. As she opened it we could see an arsenal of guns and rifles, one of which she took out, and taking Ward to one of the front windows, opened the casement and fired expertly in the direction of the garden. The baby howled and the dog disappeared under a bed.

"There," she said to Ward, "that's what you must do to keep the rabbits out of the garden."

We put the key away and never went near the closet again. Ruth's car was very ancient, and not too loveable. I could see Ward pulling down the lane each morning, coaxing it into action, and I could hear it for several miles coughing and sputtering. Ward said the train trip to London, which took just under an hour, was a swell experience with all the tweedy be-mustached old commuters reading their horticulture journals.

We had several guests. The Underwoods came, and the Crichtons, and the Couplands. There were several good golf courses nearby, one of which we played on a couple of times. But in this lovely part of England was the most charming little village called Thakeham, which was within walking distance from our house. One got to it down a pretty, winding road, over a couple of fields, and there it was nestled in the crease of two hills. An old 11th century church, half-timbered houses with flowers tumbling over walls, and a marvelous old Pub, which was also the post office. We went in one Friday night, and all the natives and locals were there. It was very merry and friendly. We were very happy in this country environment. I will never forget the peacefulness of sitting around the big fireplace in our house, with Lyn having gone to sleep upstairs, Zia doing some needlework, To-tosche stretched out exhausted after running through the fields all day, and Ward reading "The Forsyte Saga" aloud to us. It was bliss.

We were very sorry when the month ended. We were to take "The United States" liner from Southampton, which wasn't very far away. Ward had rented a black limousine to carry all of us and our belongings to the dock. When we drove right alongside the huge ship and prepared to board, a very impressive officer of the ship came to greet us. We were very startled, as he looked like the Captain, with much gold braid and smart blue uniform.

He walked up to Ward and said, "Where is she?"

We didn't know who "she" was—me? Zia? It turned out he was the kennel officer, and had come to get Totosche whom he thought was female. And off he and the dog went to a luxurious kennel on top of the ship. I must say it was the last time Totosche would ever eat dog food, having been fed leftovers from the first class dining room, and forever after preferred steak and roast chicken to Alpo. We all cried when Zia left us. And we waved at her tiny figure below as the ship pulled away from the dock.

VIII

New York, Connecticut, and Our Daughters, 1955–75

These were the growth years, years of stretching and identifying with new and often perplexing forces. McCarthyism, Kent State, Woodstock, Rock Concerts, "Hair," Hippyism, the Kennedy assassination, the Beatles, the emergence of the drug culture, oil crises, Vietnam and all other surrounding changes. But they were years of happiness for Ward and me because of the steady, good growth of Lyn and Margot, and our own relationship.

I doubt if there was any couple in this world that knew less about "birthin' babies," or bringing them up, than Ward and me. But we must have done something right. In their own individualistic way Lyn and Margot are fine human beings, both as beautiful as can be, as well as intelligent and committed. They have really evolved like a Darwin species of their own accord, and I guess if any credit to us is due, it's that we have given them the latitude to be themselves and tried to provide a nourishing environment in which to do so. Ward said one time that the most important quality one could have was good judgment. They have it, and I can think of no better two people to be on a desert island with. When they were grown up and living in the Boston environs, one day they both took me to lunch at the St. Botolph Club.

As I sat there looking at them and hearing their laughs and enjoying their wonderful conversational slants, I said to them, "You know, I would rather be with you two than any other people I can think of."

I got a nice appreciative squeeze from Lyn, and Margot said, "Do you realize Mum, how rare that is?" Well, it's true.

Margot was born in New York City two years after Lyn at the Lennox Hill Hospital and I was overjoyed to have a second daughter. We were living in an apartment on East End Avenue in the Eighties, and we could stroll in the Carl Schurz Park along the East River, Margot in our English pram, Lyn and Totosche bouncing along beside us. Often we would stand near the railing looking out at the busy tugs and wave at them. Sometimes to our delight we would get a loud responding toot. But New York City was not easy to live in with two small children, and we moved out to Connecticut near Ward's Mother and Father. We found a swell little house with a yard in Rowayton, which was an attractive little town on the Rowayton River that came in from Long Island Sound. There were boat yards and fish markets and wonderful views of the river running alongside the stores. The best view of all was from our dentist's office where his chair was aimed for the scene out over the moored boats to the attractive lawns and houses on the other side of the narrow inlet. I later had a studio over the old Fire House which was smashing, and very atmospheric, right on the river.

It was also great to be near to Ward's Mother and Father, who lived at Wilson Point, the next point of land after Rowayton. They had a fantastic, friendly and comfortable house. They doted on us, and provided us with much loving care and generosity. We loved to go there especially for Sunday lunch, often having roast beef and Yorkshire pudding, and invariably finger bowls. Their Scottish cook, Mary McTaggart, was one of the great ladies of this world. She would put oodles of butter on the morning toast because as a little girl in Glasgow she was allowed one small dab in the center of the dry bread. Wilson Point had been practically settled by Ward's Father who discovered it in the twenties. It attracted many like-minded people who enjoyed all its many natural attributes, views of the Sound, a little wonderful beach club where the children spent many happy hours digging in the sand and learning to swim. It sure beat New York, although Ward had to suffer the terrible commute into Manhatten on the New Haven railroad. "Boppie" Chamberlin, as his grandchildren called him, had built the first paddle tennis court in the East, outside of the original one at Fox Meadow in New York. All of us played this super game avidly, and would collect on weekends wrapped up in woolies and mittens waiting our turn to play. Everyone got a chance, and we doted on this marvelous winter activity. We had to shovel the snow off the court on snowy days, but this enhanced the fun. All our best friends were involved, our neighbors the Schwarzenbachs, the Keefes, the Cotters, the Wadlows, the Devens, McDowells, and although the children weren't allowed to play at key times of the weekends when they were little, eventually most of them got to love the game also, and were good additions.

There were good tennis courts down at the beach and periodic family tournaments were arranged. Also much looked forward to were the annual clam bakes. Wilson Point was a private property owners association with its members and management eager to preserve its unique quality. I am ambivalent up to a point about private clubs, but they sure are nice when you are in them. Eventually with the growth of Norwalk and the encroachment of urban sprawl on the Point, there was a guard and guardhouse at the gate, traffic bumps to impede speed on the roads, and police patrolling at intervals. I didn't like it, however, when a black friend of Lyn's bicycled all the way from Bridgeport to Wilson Point (after we had built our house) to see her, and a lady spotted him coming down our road and called the police, saying he had a knife in his backpocket. How rotten of her. It was his comb sticking out.

Our girls both went to the Rowayton School, which handled its elementary grades well, particularly if you got Miss Sherman in the first grade. She looked like Margaret Chase Smith and she had a tolerant, benign quality which the children responded to, and though no pushover, she brought the best out in them. It was quite a switch for Margot to then get Miss Cohen in the second grade who was a real stickler. Neatness and punctuality were high on her list of virtues, neither of which Margot observed as priorities. On Margot's seventh birthday, I had planned a birthday party for her, and the children could walk to our house after school. About ten of Margot's cronies all filed in as expected, but no Margot. We waited and waited. I jumped into the car thinking the worst had happened and dashed to the school. There sitting alone in the classroom was Margot. You've never seen such a thunderous expression, her hands were clenched into round fists, her mouth a determined slit. Miss Cohen had kept her after school because she wouldn't clean out her "cubby." When the teacher walked into the room, I didn't have time to choose my words carefully, but I let her have it, and Margot and I stomped out in high dudgeon. Margot looked up at me with admiration. I in turn admired her determination and steadfastness to principle even in the face of her own birthday party.

Rowayton was a fine place for us to live. Its charm was obvious, enhanced by the colony of artists and writers. The painters, Gabor Peterdi, Jimmy Ernst, Alfred Chadbourne, Paul Nonay all lived in the area, plus Harry Marinsky. When we first moved there from New York, I asked Dr. Trubowitz (Shelley) if there was anybody giving art classes in town. He said that Marinsky was, and if there was room, a summer session was just starting. So I went to Marinsky's studio with some hastily assembled examples of my work. His white stucco house and adjoining modern studio sat behind a high hedge, concealed from street view. It looked more as if it should be on the Italian Riviera, not the folksy village vernacular of Rowayton. There were many flowering shrubs, nude statues and a swimming pool, all very selective. I walked into the courtyard, and there was a man in a long, brown Franciscan robe, sitting on the tile floor peeling a huge pile of oranges. It was Paul, and Paul and Harry were a couple. He pointed to the studio door and said to walk in, class was in progress. I came in on an upper level, the students were down below working at easels.

Harry in a smock, dark-haired with flashing black eyes, looked like a Spanish grandee. "Who the devil are you?" he said. I told him. "Do you know how to paint?"

"A little," I said. "I'm here to learn more."

When I showed him my works he said, "These are awful."

"That's why I'm here," I said, and he smiled and pointed to an empty easel in the front row. The still-life was one of artichokes and dogwood blossoms in an awful white vase. I felt capable of the artichokes, at least, and set to it. A bit later he came up behind me and said, "That must be the worst rendition of artichokes I have yet seen," and he took the charcoal and, like a fencer with a sharp rapier, attacked my paper with brilliance and panache. I recognized immediately that he could teach me, and instead of crying or being insulted, I started again with new vigor.

The class was mostly local ladies, and one man, Dick. Harry twitted Dick at every turn. "You are so up-tight and stingy. Squeeze a lot of paint and apply it with abandon," Harry said, and would ruin Dick's painstakingly tight painting by slathering on more paint. One of the ladies in the class was Otis Griffiths, the wife of Dick Griffiths, the producer of "Damn Yankees," "Pajama Game," etc. They lived on the river just down the road. Harry was at his cruelest to her when he said, "Look here, my dear Otis, you are wasting your time and mine. You better go home and be a housewife." Otis left in tears. By the end of that summer session, there were only three students left: Molly, who was really good; Dick, who hung in there; and me. I really learned a lot and he was one of the best teachers I've ever had.

I didn't admire Harry's painting as much as his sculpture, which was wonderful. Several years later, when he had been asked to show in Palm Beach, he paid me the compliment of asking me to exhibit my paintings in conjunction with his sculptures.

Harry and Paul included us among their carefully selected friends. Fairfield County was not a climate for these two highly creative and original men. One time Ward was standing on the Darien railroad platform waiting for the train amongst a crowd of locals. There was Harry adjusting his trailing silk scarf, and snapping his white kidskin gloves with a flourish. The two of them eventually moved to Italy, to Pietra Santa, near Lucca, where there was an ancient foundry and a congenial artists colony. I have visited them there twice, once with Margot and once with Ward.

My studio over the old Fire House was a joy to me. I gave painting lessons myself to some very devoted ladies who lasted the course for several years—Cacky, Mary, Jean, Yolande, Mrs. Kilbourne, and others. I also took a bunch of children outdoors to paint the attractive local scenes. Some of the kids later went on to major in art at college. I had a feel for teaching. In a class of 15 you should have 15 different paintings. The goal of the teacher is to bring out the individual's image and help him realize this view. The trouble with art schools is that there is a formula, and therefore rights and wrongs. Normally, I don't care for any works of the teacher, and don't want to paint anything like him. Georgia O'Keefe had the same opinion.

I took one of my paintings in to show Chip Chadbourne who had the big studio next to mine which overlooked the river.

When I asked his opinion, which I valued, he was quiet for a long time, and then he said: "Lydia, one of the best compositional devices is the saw."

Chip later gave a series of classes which I took. I loved his wonderful sense of color and his freedom with form. I benefitted from him, too.

We moved to a larger house in Rowayton, and the girls were now to go to the Thomas School, about a half mile away. Our new neighbors were the Roses, Gil and Ann, and four children, which made things sociable for our girls. Gil was a psychiatrist, and when I first met him we were both putting our garbage out our back doors. I was trying to be oh so casual, normal and nonchalant, but missed the top step and the garbage spilled all over me as I cascaded to the bottom.

The Thomas School at Rockledge was in a glorious park surrounded by a wrought-iron fence. It was like an English Manor House, and as such built a special memory for all. There were oak-panelled libraries, huge fireplaces, silvered scenic wallpaper, etc. The first location of the school when started by Miss Thomas, was just underhill overlooking the Norwalk River and Wilson Point. This was atmospheric, suggesting "Wind in the Willows" or a Beatrix Potter locale, and some of the teachers looked like Nurse Jane Fuzzywuzzy. But there was nothing quaint about the teaching which was excellent and carried on the marvelous educational principles of Miss Thomas. I said before that my Winsor School was founded on the same precepts. Miss Winsor and Miss Thomas had been great friends.

Ward became Chairman of the Board of Trustees, a position which was fraught with frustration and anxiety. There were many "chiefs" among the trustees and not many Indians. Also it was a time of enormous educational flux what with student sit-ins, Kent State riots, and you could feel dangerous winds blowing. The old order changeth, and Thomas made a big effort to maintain its established customs, while adapting to the new. From time to time I was hired as a substitute teacher in Art, and in Sports. Thomas girls weren't terribly athletic, but I did the best I could with coaching field hockey and basketball. I dreaded rainy days when we all piled into a bus to go to a gym in Norwalk. The girls were completely unruly and noisy no matter how much I threatened and blew my whistle. And the bus ride was deafening.

Lyn and Margot developed their tremendous love of reading from Mrs. Ide. Everyone should have a Mrs. Ide for a teacher. When Lyn was in her class they put on a play in the small assembly hall, called "Otto and the Silver Hand." Lyn had the lead, and as Otto, had pages and pages of dialogue to learn. She was ten years old then I think. I sat at the performance and marvelled at her, she never missed a word, she moved gracefully around the tiny stage, and generally was convincing in her acting.

After the school had moved up to the big estate, Rock Ledge, there was a whole new lease on life. After Mrs. Opie left as headmistress, several new heads came in who were a source of great disappointment: one was Arthur Harper who ran off with his neighbor's wife; another was Jean Harris, the murderess of the Scarsdale Dr. Tannhower, or whatever his name was. These heads weren't bad while they were at Thomas, and generally provided good leadership. The school did not operate in the summer, and I asked Arthur Harper if he would allow me to run an acting and dance school for young people on the premises. I would bring in directors and teachers and professional actors from "The Long Wharf Theatre" in New Haven, on whose board of directors I sat. It was agreed and my "Theatre Thing" was a great success. Arvin Brown, Michael Youngfellow, Ken Jenkins and others came and participated. Mildred Dunnock and Arthur Kennedy advised, and the young thespians had the time of their lives playing theatre games and learning improvizational acting and dancing. It was quite an operation. I think it got a bit druggy, but not overtly, although I'm sure that Jennifer, one of the students who lived in our house, was a bit suspect. Sally from Philadelphia also lived with us, and our house that summer was very lively.

I will never forget in Gen Casey's dance class, when she gave a recital of her students' own choreographed dances. Lyn's performance was spellbinding. She brought out a tall step-ladder and, dressed in a black leotard and to the music of Mozart (Elvira Madigan), climbed up one side of the ladder, each step delineated, till she got to the top, where she performed an arabesque, and held it breathtakingly long. Then slowly she descended the other side, all choreographed. William Schuman, the composer, met Lyn once at our house, and after talking to her for a while said: "She has star quality." I knew what he meant.

One time when Lyn and I were driving up to Duxbury to visit Mum we were in a new black Rambler which went just like a bird, and as we were barreling along chatting like mad, I was pulled over by a policeman who arrested me for speeding. I think I was going about 74, no big deal. But my license was revoked for a month. I was furious, and wrote a four-page letter to the Commissioner of Motor Vehicles complaining of unjust sentence. I did get a personal letter back from him but it was to no avail, and I found I had to ride my bicycle everywhere. This wasn't too bad, except it was hard to carry groceries, and infuriating when once after I had just had my hair done in the village, it poured rain and drenched my coiffure on the way home. One afternoon I had bicycled home from Thomas where I had waved at our school bus loaded with students coming back from an outing.

At supper that night Lyn and Margot said: "Mom, please don't ride by school on your bicycle, it's too embarrassing."

Another motor vehicle anecdote. Bridget and Bobby Schwarzenbach, who were our next-door neighbors when we built our Deck House on Wilson Point, had a large family, three gorgeous girls, Elizabeth, Sybil, Jessica, and the boys, Chris and Peter. Old Mrs. Schwarzenbach, Bobbie's stately but a bit goofy Mother, lived in a large house above on the hill. She was one of the survivors of the sinking of the Titanic! Being rich and Swiss she wasn't a conformer, and we had to warn the girls to watch out when Mrs. S. came down the road. She didn't obey traffic rules, went through red lights which she considered irritating, and generally drove too fast. When she was about 80 years old, it became time for her to renew her drivers license. Bridget drove her to the Motor Vehicle Bureau in Norwalk. The place was jammed, most of the people looking like migrant workers. In this company Mrs. Schwarzenbach stood out. She was dressed in her Sunday best, hat, gloves, etc. As she was sitting amongst the throng waiting for her test, she talked to Bridget in a very loud voice. Finally it was her turn. After the examiner looked at her written answers to the traffic questions, he said, "Mrs. Schwarzenbach, this is a *multiple choice test*, and you've checked *all* the four choices." She responded that they all sounded like reasonable answers. Then he asked her how many years she had been driving. She turned around and called loudly to Bridget, "Bridget dear, when was it that we got Klaus our chauffeur?" Much laughter by now from all. Then the final straw for the examiner, he took her up to the little booth for the eye examination. As the first card was flashed for her to read, he banged his fist on the table and said, "*Mrs. Schwarzenbach*, would you *kindly* remove the *veil* from your hat!" The room resounded with guffaws. Bridget was covered with embarrassment.

Our neighbors, the Schwarzenbachs, with whom we were very good friends, were like the royal aristocracy of our little enclave. They were marvelous looking, Bobby tall and blond, with the bearing of a Swiss nobleman, Bridget, tall, blond, vivacious and herself related to German nobility. Everybody on the Point knew every movement that the Schwarzenbachs made, because they "Schwarzenbach-watched." The life of this family was glamorous with its rich resources. They flew all over the world, they had a ranch in New Mexico, they skied in Switzerland, they flew their own planes, and were generally of top calibre in all they did. Bobby's Mother had survived the sinking of the Titanic, and was still unsinkable as she lived in her large house just up the hill. The five blond Schwarzenbach children were equally gorgeous, three girls and two boys, one of whom was killed in a car crash on a night that Bobby and Bridget were at our house for dinner. I'll never forget the telephone call Bridget made to us early the next morning with the terrible news.

Bridget looked like a fashion model, and dressed with flair. I honestly never saw her wear the same outfit twice. She managed her five children well, which I admired.

One time when I was having a bad day trying to cope with my two daughters who were being naughty, I said to Bridget, "How do you ever handle your five offspring? I can't control even two!"

Bridget responded, "If we are at the dining room table and the kids act up, I just hit the one nearest to me!" That's perfect justice for you.

When young Peter Schwarzenbach was married, Ward and I went to the wedding, and also to the bridal dinner the night before, which was held at the Wee Barn Club in Darien. It was a very lavish affair, and many relatives had flown in from Europe and California. There was an orchestra which played spiritedly throughout the festivities. Ward and I had driven down from Massachusetts, and I wrote my inevitable song at the last minute in the car as we sped along the Connecticut Turnpike. I hadn't quite finished it when we got to the dinner, but I felt I could manage the few last lines when I got to our table while other family toasts were going on. There were many Swiss aunts and uncles whom we didn't know, most of them quite silent and dour. After one or two preliminary toasts, Ward leaped to his feet and raised his glass to Peter and Priscilla and said, "I'm not going to make a long toast, because the really expressive talent in the family is Lydia, and she has a song." I could have killed him! I was not ready. But I got up and stood by the microphone at the edge of where the orchestra had been playing. The orchestra had left and gone on a break.

There was nothing I could do but commence. The Swiss relatives looked glowering, I thought. Oh well, here goes. And I started my song. It was to the tune, "Something Simple, Like I Love You," a good Sinatra hit. As I got into it I started enjoying myself, I held the microphone like a pro, and focused on individuals in the audience, and swayed rhythmically in time to the music. Without my knowing it the orchestra had reassembled behind me, picked up the song, and came in full force on key. I was simply euphoric. I had never before or since felt such a wonderful "flow" in my public "performances," and I even improvised the last unwritten verse. It was a heady experience. Even the orchestra said they would accompany me any time, any place. I felt for all the world like Bonnie Raitt.

I mentioned the clam bakes at the beach which were held every year. They were always great fun, with a huge bonfire in the sand, authentic cooking in seaweed of lobsters, corn, clams and potatoes, and spirited singing around the fire afterwards. Two of these clam bakes stand out in my mind. One in which the singing quality was markedly improved by the presence of Licia Albinese, Giovanni Martinelli, and Helen Steber. Licia lived with her husband, Joe Gimma just above the beach in one of the houses that looked down on the curve of sand. Martinelli and Steber were visiting. And there in the glow of the fire, the two prima donnas, Helen and Licia, let forth with operatic vigor, each aria competing against the other. The scene was right out of Wagner. It was a quantum leap from our usual motley community sing.

Another clam bake several of us decided to form a small armada and go visit Billy Rose who had just bought "Tavern Island," about a quarter of a mile right off our beach. We thought it would be a neighborly thing to do, and also we were a bit emboldened by liquor. After all we would call on him if he lived on shore. The only difference was he was on an island. We got an outboard and a whaler and set off like Marines for our night landing. The island itself was sensational, lit up like Broadway, with gardens, gazebos, peacocks strutting around, a big pier jutting out to receive us, and a huge low house in the center of a grove of trees. There were about ten of us to start, but some turned back, like Ward who disapproved of this madcap venture. After landing, I got separated from the others who had broken up into groups of two. I found myself crawling up on a high rock from which I could look right down at the house in whose living room a party was already in progress. I was terrified when a huge dog on a chain lunged out at me and growled ferociously. I slipped on the rock and bruised my knee. When I approached the house I looked in the living room window and there were Bridget, Hugh and Peter already with glasses of champagne joining the party and convivial as anything. I went up to the front door and knocked rather timidly. It was opened by a beautiful lady in a light blue turban which totally covered her hair and swathed in a tight matching blue jumpsuit. There were two sleek greyhounds standing picturesquely behind her. She looked me up and down, and then noticed my knee which was bleeding. "You poor dear, come into the kitchen with me and I will fix you up in a jiffy." She sat me on the kitchen table and applied merthiolate and bandaids, very solicitously. It was Joan Crawford. When I joined the others in the living room, our Wilson Point group was easily absorbed among the others, some of whom looked like budding actresses and actors, and there was one "long stemmed American rose," a brunette who didn't say a word, but was very decorative. Billy Rose said we had "made" his birthday party, and he walked down with us to the dock when we left. We sang "Happy Birthday" to him as we pulled away in our boats. Those were our early married years, and we grew up a bit later.

It became evident that it was time to take the girls out of the Thomas School and find a school that was not a girls day school. Lyn and Margot wanted to be where the action was and be a part of the new order that wasn't possible in this protected Thomas environment. We chose to send them to the Barlow School in Amenia, New York, a co-educational progressive boarding school. It was beautifully located in the foothills of the Berkshires, and its many buildings gave the effect of a well-run New England farm. But it was a dramatic switch for all of us, mostly Ward and me.

The free-form environment and the extraordinary mixture of students made for a totally new experience for Lyn and Margot. But it reflected the complexity of the time, and as unstructured as it seemed on the surface, both girls learned some very real values, and above all, how to get along on their own. The headmaster and his wife whom we liked so much, were so totally dismayed by the student culture that was emerging, that they quit. There was a wonderful English teacher, however, Ann Brownell, who better understood the chaotic times and was a bulwark of support to the young students. She gave parameters where they were needed. She was crazy about Lyn and helped her through some difficult times. One of Margot's great chums was Pete Seeger's daughter, and they lived in the same house at the top of the hill which was windswept like on a Bronte moor. You've never seen such chaos and mess as in that dorm, but the girls survived the chaos stronger and wiser in the ways of the world and mastering their own strengths in a way that they never could have in the cocoon of the Thomas School.

Margot, at the beginning, was sometimes sick and had to come home. I would drive up the three hours to get her, and one day as we were coming back home, she was very silent but not very sick. Then she burst into tears saying she felt like such an odd-ball at school. Why, I asked her. She blurted out, "Because everybody at school has divorced parents, and you and Dad are happy and together."

Ward and I often took the girls out for Sunday lunch at a wonderful inn in Amenia, and there we filled them up with a gorgeous meal. At one of these times Margot was contemplating what she could possibly do for her up-coming "Winterim," a period in which the students could go for four weeks off-campus anywhere they wanted to pursue their scholastic interests. Lyn made the brilliant suggestion that Margot go out to join a work-study group in Arizona that the architect Paolo-Saleri had founded. Margot leapt at the idea and soon was on the plane for Arcosanti where Soleri was building his "Arcology," a mystical, imaginative and unrealistic city in the desert. Here she found her goal in life to be an architect. It was a deep and fabulous experience, which she made the most of, living at the primitive site of the construction, learning her fundamentals of architecture, and making a life-long commitment to this profession. She also met David who was a wonderful friend, and a great support for her in this frontier situation in the desert. His steady presence relieved Ward and me of anxiety for our 16-year-old daughter.

Ward was in California one time, and decided to go see Margot at her work. He drove through the mountains to Arizona to Arcosanti and found how to drive up to the site which was near a little town called Cortez Junction.

Actually it was merely a crossroad with a bar and a gas station. Ward walked into the bar and asked the lady if the Soleri building project was nearby. The lady said it was, but hard to get to unless you had a four-wheel drive. But she added, the workcrew always came into the bar after work. Ward asked her if she knew a tall, blond girl named Margot. "Yes," she said, "and if you wait here she will come in soon. She's a great favorite of everyone." Pretty soon the doors swung open, as in a John Wayne movie, and in came the crew—dusty, dirty, hot and thirsty. There was Margot, wonderfully tanned and smudgy with a hard hat on. She was over-joyed to see Dad, although she had no idea he was coming. The experience Margot had was so positive that she returned to Arcosanti during the summer and continued her architectural involvement, as well as being a paid cook for the crew. Although the concept of the "Arcology" was far-out, it was far-in for Margot's development as an architect. Margot has since become an architect, a profession she is gorgeously suited for. Architecture combines two rigorous disciplines, mathematics and art, and Margot is eminently able to coordinate science and artistic creativity into an integral whole. This is a rare quality not given to everyone.

Ward's father, when he learned that we were looking for a house on Wilson Point, generously gave us the property he owned on the waterfront below his house. On this mouth-watering piece of land we built our Deck House. We built a little pier that Ward could keep his sunfish on, and we could swim off it at high tide. Our house was perfect for us, and with five bedrooms and three baths and lots of deck and glass. We had lots of young people in and out, we gave wonderful informal parties, and maintained a very happy atmosphere. The total price of the house was a little over $50,000, imagine. It was a fantastic value, even then.

On the theory that we wanted the girls to feel that home was fun, not always searching for action somewhere else, we built a swimming pool in the curve of the property under the dining room deck. It was a good decision even though we couldn't afford it at the time, because all the kids came over to our house to swim in the pool, which was a great luxury. I could hear "Marco" . . . "Polo" emanating from below as I worked in the kitchen, and the kids cavorting like happy dolphins.

Ward's fiftieth birthday was an outstanding success. I had written the script and planned the event as a "Son Et Lumiere." Ward and all the guests watched from below as the action took place on the main upper deck. I persuaded one of the actors, Terry, from Long Wharf to come and read the script, and he was wonderfully Shakespearean in voice and demeanor. At the beginning our house was totally dark and by degrees it got lit up according to the dialogue which described various aspects of Ward's life. The finale came with a spotlight on the little dock and an actor (Gordon) assuming Ward's character as "King." Gordon, with crown on, sailed into the night as Terry read: "Like Ulysses he ever seeks new horizons, and when he sets sail his grateful people come down to the shore to salute him." The next morning after the party which lasted till the wee small hours, Ward went to sail his sunfish around the point to the beach. Phoebe Stanton who saw him set sail, alerted all the people on the waterfront to rush down to the shore and give "the King" a large ovation. About 30 people rushed down and saluted and clapped as he sailed by. He was very tickled.

Our Christmas parties were memorable, usually held at the Wilson's big house on the bluff above the beach. Everyone old and young came, and the littlest children looked adorable in their velvet dresses or black velvet suits. The singing of the carols was usually led by Roger Keefe who made up in spirit and volume what he lacked in tempo. Best of all was the competition for loudness between sections of "The Twelve Days of Christmas." I loved singing the German version of "Silent Night" which I knew, and of course the Schwarzenbachs sang it as it was written: "Stille Nacht, Heilige Nacht," and were gratified that I could join them. Bobby looked especially pleased.

Then on good snowy Christmas nights we would go out to the crossroad and build a bonfire and sing carols there. There's something marvelous about singing in the outdoors. Sometimes Roger would pile all the kids in the back of his open truck and they would go to peoples' houses and serenade them: "We are not daily beggars who beg from door to door, but we are neighbor's children whom you have seen before." Then back to the Keefes for hot cider and cookies and apples, and Roger would read "The Christmas Carol." Nice memories of nice people, and the girls remember those Chrismases fondly.

Molly O'Connor gave piano lessons at her house on the Point. She was a wonderful teacher and many of the kids came regularly to partake of her benign but professional instruction. I have always longed to play the piano, and although I can play a few pieces from sheet music, and several by ear, I am terrible. I decided to take lessons from Molly. When I went I waited on the bench in the hall for my turn and I would be sitting with little Tony or Robin or Sandra and others, none of them over 12 years old. I found it very hard, and I was nowhere near as good at learning how to read music as the youngsters. This was partly due to my playing by ear for so long. But finally I got the hang of some simple pieces, the best of which was "The Soldier's March" which Molly asked me to play in the up-coming recital. She had two pianos facing each other. I was to play the melody on one, and she, a very proficient pianist, would play the complicated accompaniment on the other. Well! Was I excited! It sounded wonderful to me, although Molly was doing all the hard part. I had the illusion I was playing the whole thing. But when the time came for the recital, Lyn and Margot discouraged me from performing, saying it was silly for me to do so amongst all those little children.

I have always loved theatre and am happy amongst theatrical people. Peter Bassone, who had been a student at my "Theatre Thing," came to see me about a year later. Peter had lied then about his age saying he was under twenty-one so he could join my acting school. He was dying to learn theatre with the wonderful cast of instructors I had assembled—Arvin Brown, Mildred Dunnack, Arthur Kennedy, etc. But now he contacted me to say that he and a couple of other young actors had bought a wonderful old building in Westport, Connecticut which had a theatre in the upper floor, a good stage, and kitchen facilities. He wanted to start a dinner theatre, and would I help. I was terribly excited and rushed headlong into the venture with my young colleagues. Ward generously found $3,000 for my participation, and "Upstage" was launched. Peter and Rick and I were partners. But as our theatre developed enormous complications set in. You couldn't think of two more difficult undertakings, a theatre or a restaurant, and here we were coping with both. I soon discovered mortgage irregularities, permits not valid, and the threat of being closed down as a result. I pleaded with the Westport officials, paid electric bills with my own money, and saved many bad situations in the nick of time. The Fire Department were going to forbid us to open one night when the restaurant was full, and the show about to go on.

But over and above these difficulties, a junta movement was formed which sabotaged my authority. Rick and Peter, sensitive homosexuals, would not bite the bullet when it was necessary, and felt my presence compromised their professional creativity. This was eminently unfair as it was I who had the capacity to produce backers, audiences, and outside talent. When push came to shove, Patsy England, whom I had brought into the project, never supported me, and Marcia Davis and Ottilie Kaufman, all of whom were recruited by me defected, and I was forced to quit. This was a power play. I didn't want power, but shared responsibility. The poison, however, had done its work.

The irony is that we did some marvelous shows. Peter and Rick and

Wendy and Alexandra were very talented performers. Our first production of "The Fantastics" was incredibly good. Rick, the male lead, had a marvelously exciting voice which was of Broadway calibre. But the highlight came for me when I got Geraldine Fitzgerald to try out her "Street Songs" at Upstage. It was a smashing success, and she later opened it at Reno Sweeney's in New York. To this day I can't go over the thruway bridge in Westport, from which you can just see the theatre, without getting a sinking feeling. Upstage folded completely a few months after I quit.

I first met Geraldine Fitzgerald when she came to Upstage and I picked her up at the Westport railroad station. I was excited to come face-to-face with this wonderful actress whose many films I had relished from "Wurthering Heights" on. I almost felt I knew her, but I wasn't prepared for the dazzling smile and the bright, laughing eyes looking steadily up at me. She said, "You look just like Virginia Woolf." She meant it kindly, although I thought Virginia Woolf too ascetic and serious in looks to be a desirable prototype.

Geraldine's show "Street Songs" was wonderful and I was very proud to have had a part in launching it. She is grateful to me for this and also because I introduced her to our own pianist at Upstage, Stanley Wietrzchowski, who later arranged her musical numbers, and whom she took with her to New York as her accompanist. Geraldine, and Stuart Shefftel, her husband, have become friends and we've been together several evenings for dinner when they've come to Washington.

It was Geraldine who arranged for my first visit to the White House for a congressional wives luncheon where she was performing which was to be televised. I won't forget that first visit. Not being a congressional wife, I couldn't attend the luncheon, but I could watch behind the television cameras with Richmond Crinkley, the producer. When I arrived at the appointed time at the White House, I was met by one of the uniformed pages, and ushered up to the Green Room where I was to wait until time to go into the East Room. The young page said to me, "Now just make yourself at home." This was not anything like my home. I gazed around the beautiful room and thought of John Kennedy. I looked out the window across the south lawn to the Washington Monument, and behind it in the far distance, the Jefferson Memorial. As I watched, an airplane took off from National Airport passing behind the Jefferson Memorial. As it followed the Potomac River, it gleamed in the sunlight.

IX

Washington, 1975–91

I was not at all thrilled when Ward told me he had been offered a job in Washington, D.C. running the Public Television Station WETA. Now that the girls were grown and pursuing lives of their own, I had more time to concentrate on my own life. I had had so many disappointments with my play, but I could now renew my energies and activities in that direction. How could I keep up with New York and all its theatre resources if I was based in Washington? And having devoted myself to painting in the agonizing delays between activities of my *Pilgrims*, I was getting somewhere in the art world. I knew I would never be a great painter, but I knew I was good, and the whole process was absorbing and fascinating. Washington was not known for its embracement of the arts, at least not in 1974. Although the Kennedy Center for the Performing Arts had just been built, it had not yet made its huge mark on the cultural climate of the Nation's Capitol.

But we packed up and moved. Our car was loaded to the gills as we lumbered out of Wilson Point. It was a bright sunny day, which helped. Inky stood up in the back practically the whole way down for nine hours. Just before Baltimore, going over that splendid river, the late afternoon sky was spectacular. It looked like a daytime aurora borealis, with shafts of red and orange piercing the clouds, a suitable backdrop for a Brahms Symphony. I couldn't help but feel that this fireworks display had been put on for my benefit as an omen of good things to come. And I was right. Although I had pawed the ground and snorted steam in anticipation of the move to Washington, it took me only 48 hours to realize that this was the most beautiful city, and that we would be very happy living here. And in the 16 years since then my enthusiasm has never waned.

I was afraid when we first moved here that I would not fit into this high-powered political city. Politics make me nervous. I don't feel at ease when talking to someone at a gathering, whose eyes are roaming around to see who else more important is in the room. I had not been brought up with current events as a high priority. I remember getting one of the lowest scores in Winsor in *Time Magazine*'s current events test. (Willy got the highest along with Miss Jencks the history teacher). Nor had I been accustomed to reading the Op Ed pages or James Reston. Ward is so well immersed in all this; he devours newspapers and is extremely well-informed. He has often said he would have loved to be a reporter, or also run a newspaper. He would have been wonderful. But I prefer what he does, which is to brilliantly run a public television station. This career of his has been marvelous for me as it cuts across all levels of society, hits high spots of art, music and culture, and is highly meaningful in the political arena. Washington is not exclusively a political town. And in the years we have been here we have seen its culture expand and grow. This has been largely due to the flowering of the Kennedy Center under Roger Stevens, the Washington Opera under Martin Feinstein, and to the huge impact of the magnificent National Gallery of Art led by its superb director J. Carter Brown. New York City, once the leader in all art and theatre, is strongly aware of the ascendancy of Washington. Many openings of plays and exhibits are now held here, when formerly Washington was deemed a cultural backwater. Good hotels and restaurants, once few and far between, are now many. But above all, Ward and I have made wonderful and abiding friendships with a broad spectrum of people, and these have been a great stimulus to our rich life here.

The first black tie dinner we attended was at the National Gallery, under the gorgeous domed rotunda. The tables were set around the central sculpture of Mercury, and with flowers massed in pots, and placed in gorgeous decorations on each candlelit table, with important gentlemen, and chic wives, the effect was dazzling. But also intimidating as I knew no one. I knew when we found Ward's place card at table numero uno and mine wasn't there that my table would be behind a marble column, somewhere near the service tables. I found my place, however, not too far away at table number two. But the only problem was that while other tables were filling up rapidly, no one appeared at mine for a long time. After I sat down, a man came to sit at my right, but he soon became engrossed with his other dinner partner, who was very glamorous. As our table got organized, no one came to the place on my left. I drank my water and fiddled with the bread, and made a design in the salt. I felt very uncomfortable. But just as soup was being served, in rushed Mayor Walter Washington, the black mayor of Washington, and took his place beside me. I was enchanted by his friendliness, and soon we were talking a mile a minute. He was telling me about how he idolized Lady Bird Johnson and how important Lyndon was to his life. Long after everyone else had finished their dinner and started to leave, Mayor Washington and I were still in deep conversation. I will never forget it, as I knew then that I could make it in Washington without any special eminence. One-on-one is the best ratio, and since then I have had many wonderful dinner partners, some of whom I will describe later.

Our living situation in Washington started out badly. Ward had once more "conned" a lady on Dent Place west of Wisconsin Avenue to rent us her house. She was impressed with his public television life, and offered her fancy digs to us at a reduced rate for a year. At the end of six months there I couldn't stand it one minute longer. She was unbalanced, and nearly crazy. She made life miserable for all her tenants, as I found out later, by popping in all the time, accusing us of stealing jewels which we had no idea of their whereabouts, and when we left, threatened to call the police if we didn't clean the house better. It was perfect, but she ran her finger over the top of the closet pole where the hangers hung and showed us the "grime." She took apart the interior of the stove with a screwdriver to show us years of collected soot. I had never been involved in being so unjustly accused—and by a mad woman—that it unsettled me.

I found a good house on P Street, with a superb location, a gorgeous patio and back yard in which I built the only vegetable garden in George-town. It was smashing with tomatoes, lettuce, peas, cucumbers, parsley and beans in an area about the size of one-fourth of a tennis court. There was a little fountain and pool in the patio. And I had a studio on the top floor. The day after we moved in, Ward came home and asked how I would like to have Jimmy Carter come to our house the next day, because Bill Moyers wanted to interview him on television as his presidential candidacy was in full swing. They wanted to be in a non-institutional locale in the privacy of a "charming" folksy home. Well! Things moved quickly. The secret service arrived and went through the house with a fine tooth comb, asking me what was where, and I told them I hadn't a clue as I had just moved in. Soon the television crew and equipment arrived, and set up shop right in front of the fireplace. There wasn't much room to spare. A huge black cable was brought in the front door about the size of a boa-constric-tor. The whole operation caused quite a stir, but it reached fever pitch when the secret service with walkie-talkies monitored the progress of Carter's limousine from the airport. "Now he's turning on M Street, coming up Wisconsin," etc. And pretty soon a huge blueberry blue limousine pulled up in front of our house preceded by black secret service vans. Out popped Jimmy, and shook Ward's hand. Then he opened the trunk in back himself to get his shaving equipment, much to the consternation of his guards for whom this manoeuver wasn't scheduled. A large crowd had gathered. He and Ward went up the stairs to the bathroom and Ward sat on the toilet seat while Jimmy shaved, chatting amiably.

The interview was fascinating and Jimmy later said it was very crucial to the success of his candidacy. Bill, a Methodist minister's son, and Jimmy ditto, talked one-on-one, no sham or frills, and they discussed topics never before broached in interviews. Our living room was so crowded that I had to watch from the doorway on my hands and knees looking past the legs of the secret service men. All the furniture had been moved into the garden. A police dog was sent into the garden to sniff for bombs, but he didn't pay any attention to a large bale of peat moss in which I could have easily concealed a lethal weapon. One of the secret service men stepped on one of Inky's messes, much to his revulsion. After the interview was over and Carter was preparing to leave, he took the trouble of looking all around the room crowded with technicians and equipment to find me, and when he did he waved over heads and said, "Thank you, ever so much for your trouble, Mrs. Chamberlin." I thought this gesture was very much in his favor. I voted for him, and he won.

We were in the P Street house about nine years. It suited us just fine. Black Inky our poodle died there, but we soon got Pushkin, a Schitzu-Maltese poodle, a gem of a little creature whom we got from Luvie Pearson. One day I walked him down to Neams Market, that ultra-grocer at the end of the street that I tried not to shop in too much as they were so expensive. I put him in the small shopping basket which he just fit into, when in walked Pearl Bailey. She was a frequent shopper at Neams, and all the clerks made much of her presence. She romanced them all, especially the butcher. She was herself marketing "Pearl's Fruit Cake," and deposited many little packets of it on the counter. She caught sight of my little puppy and remarked how darling he was.

Then she said, "Does he like fruitcake?" and promptly gave him a whole piece the size of a pack of cigarettes. He devoured it happily.

Then she said, "Does he like hot dogs?" and she promptly gave him a large uncooked hot dog. He devoured it happily. Pearl had about 10 pounds of broccoli in her cart, and 20 pounds of hot dogs.

I asked her why she had so much. She said she was going to Russia that night with her orchestra and they all loved Pearl's broccoli, which she would cook for them. As soon as Pushkin and I got out on the street, Pushkin was sick all the way home.

Ward liked Pushkin quite well, but was a bit puzzled by what he was. I said he was a Schitzu-Maltese Poodle, and not to pronounce it "Shit-zu," but "Sheet-zu" as it sounded nicer.

The first time Ward took him along for a walk down the front steps, as they got to the sidewalk, an old lady remarked, "What an adorable little dog. What kind is he?"

I heard Ward say, "He's a combination *shit-zu* and a Maltese Falcon."

I had also fallen madly in love with two huge brown standard poodles that lived down the street. I inquired if there were any more available like them, and sure enough there was a litter of nine of them on Capitol Hill. I went to see them, and there was nothing to do but I must have one. I was determined. Two dogs are better than one. I called Lyn and Margot and told them what I was going to do. That I would bring the dog home, and Dad was sure to fall in love with it. I wasn't going to tell him.

"You can't do that, Mom, it's not honest. You must tell him first."

The day I was going to get the dog, Ward was headed to New York and as the taxi arrived very early in the morning and Ward was getting in, I said in a loud voice, "By the way, I'm getting another dog."

"What!" he said. "You must be crazy." And off he sped to the airport, no time to remonstrate further.

I must say that Flora has been the apple of his eye, and their love affair started immediately. And Pushkin and Flora are the best of friends and the best companions imaginable.

We fixed up the basement of the P Street house so that we could rent it out. It wasn't deluxe, but the many young people who stayed there over the years seemed to like it, and it was never unoccupied. I loved the addition of an extra body to dog-sit and house-sit, and the association with the younger generation. We had Wick Sloane, Andrea Sehl, Bobbie Mussie, Ben Schneider, Walter Matthai, Julie somebody, Barbara Earle and I think Gordon Earle at various times. I remember once Ben Schneider, an intellectual and quiet, philosophical type, emerging from the basement to go to work, and as he retreated down the street to the bus I noticed a pair of my pink underpanties sticking to the back of his shirt with static cling. Many of these tenants were newly graduated from Williams College and seeking their fame and fortune in Washington.

Our visitors were many. One spring I volunteered to help house a group of Englishmen who were coming for the Bow-Rippon Society's annual meeting. These were conservative ministers of the House of Commons, and a Republican friend of mine was trying to find housing for them, in which I helped by finding several neighbors who would take one or two in for one or two nights. In gratitude I was given as my house guest the most distinguished of them all. Sir Peter Emory and Lady Elizabeth arrived, right off the Concorde. Naturally I had prepared cucumber sandwiches and tea and scones, which they politely made a stab at, having just probably had filet mignon and caviar.

Sir Peter brought me two bottles of scotch with the private House of Commons label. I clasped them to my bosom saying I would never let anyone have this scotch but me.

Peter said, "Nonsense, Lydia, drink it up and then fill them again with your own brand. No one will ever know the difference." Rather too quickly (Ward thought), we made friends. Sir Peter asked Elizabeth if he could recite the *London Times* poem.

She said, "Oh Peter, isn't it a bit too soon for that particular poem?"

"Nonsense," said he again. "I'm sure Lydia would enjoy it in the proper spirit." He said in explanation that a friend of his, Sir Geoffrey somebody, was an editor of the *London Sunday Times*, and during a summer lull he asked the readers to send in material on their definition of "Love." They got an astounding 49,000 responses, two of which they chose to print. One of these was this poem which he recited:

> "Flo, Flo, I love you so,
> Especially in your nightie.
> When the moon flits, across your tits,
> Jesus, God Almighty."

We have been to some memorable dinner parties in Washington. There are two, however, which stood out in my mind as the best. We were asked to the residence of the French Ambassador de Margerie to meet Yves Montaud, who was in this country promoting his two new films. The gorgeous residence, full of the best furnishings France has to offer—tapestries, marble floors, Louis the XVI everything, inlaid wood panels, paintings, French chateaux-like salons, huge urns of flowers, and very glamorous guests. After champagne we went into the lovely candlelit dining room and sat down. There were four round tables of about ten each. I found my place at Helene de Margerie's table and couldn't believe my position. I sat between Mistislav Rostropovitch and Jonas Salk, with Austin Kiplinger, Count Wilhelm Wachmeister and Mme de Margerie not far away. Salk is my idol. He told me he had a revolutionary experiment he was working on to combat AIDS, a different approach from everyone. I would bet my bottom dollar that he would succeed. Rostropovitch was very congenial, and we laughed together, but I don't remember what about. Ward, for once, didn't have such glamorous partners, though they were nice. I have never heard a more graceful and charming toast than the one the Ambassador gave for Yves Montand. It reflected his own superb grace, taste and charm, and he was so eloquent in his praise of this French actor. Montand stood up and in response said, "Vive la France, Vive l'Amerique" and sat down. Not good, what? Imagine! He should have done better than that. Sadly to say Bobbie de Margerie (most of his friends called him Bobbie, including his wife) died last week in early December. It is 1991. The world is diminished by the death of this marvelous, compassionate and lovely man. He had gone from Washington last year, back to Paris and the Art World, to Christie's International, I think.

We were invited more often to the British Embassy to parties given by Ambassador Antony Acland and his new wife Jenny. Just going up the circular staircase carpeted in deep red, with huge portraits of British monarchs staring down at you, was a treat. The one of Elizabeth II in ermine and crown was splendid. Antony and Jenny were very friendly to us, and particularly since Ward got Jenny's daughter Fiona a job in Public Radio at WETA. The long table in the dining room when set up for dinner was glorious to behold. Candleabras, flowers, four sets of glassware at each place, and starched napkins folded in flower petal shapes. At one of these parties I sat next to former Prime Minister James Callaghan, and Senator Alan Simpson, both lighthearted and easy dinner companions.

There was one party, however, given by WETA for the "McNeil-Lehrer Hour" where my party conversation was not at all up to snuff. I was totally at a loss sitting between Al Hunt of the *New York Times* and Senator Bob Dole, who had Helen Graham on his other side. Walter Cronkheit was on Hunt's other side, and you can imagine that none of the conversation was anything I was able to contribute to. But nobody seemed to notice but me.

Generally I really relish the dinner party format because your dinner companions cannot get up and move. They are trapped. And I am very good one-on-one on a personal level. Most men love personal questions and I am genuinely interested in their replies. I have made some lovely new men friends thusly. Ward seems to know that I am pushy when it comes to meeting actors and actresses. Once recently at a party at the British Embassy for Jeremy Brett (the wonderful Sherlock Holmes) Brett was holding court sitting in a chair surrounded by admirers. I picked my timing perfectly to go up to talk with him, and as I made my move, I heard Ward say to the lady he was talking with, "If you want to see a magnificent manoeuvre, just watch Lydia." I guess it was a compliment. Soon I had pulled up a chair next to Brett, and we fell into good conversation.

Ward's very close friends, John and Mary Douglas, gave a small dinner dance at their house in Bethesda one summer evening. John is a very fine lawyer and an old, old Princeton pal of Ward's. Mary was a trustee at Princeton the same time as Ward, and they are splendid people. As we came in the Douglas' front door we noticed the dining room was set up with three tables of eight, and we went through the living room out onto the terrace where everyone was assembled around the pool for cocktails. Much to our surprise the entire Kennedy clan was there, Ethel and Teddy and Pat Lawford, the Shrivers and Jean Kennedy Smith. Also present were the Robert McNamaras and a couple of more lesser lights like ourselves.

After an extended cocktail hour everyone was very spirited as we went into the small dining room. There was just room to squeeze into our places at the table. I sat next to Smith and Sargent Shriver. Ward sat next to Mary Douglas and Ethel Kennedy. Teddy was at that table, and soon the noise decibels were high with merriment. The Kennedys behaved as if they were kids at a summer camp. If someone got up to make a toast as Ward did, he was interrupted with wisecracks, almost derision, and couldn't finish his remarks for the Kennedy jokers. It was really quite astonishing to see the family in action, sufficient unto itself. After dinner the tables were cleared away and there was dancing. It was pretty free-form and spirited. I danced twice with Teddy and I must say he was a very good dancer. We danced to "Saturday Night Fever" with a certain amount of careless abandon.

One of the wonderful features of our life in Washington and a highlight of our stay here has been our association with the White House in connection with the TV series produced by WETA, "In Performance At the White House." As Ward was the chief we attended all of the performances, often sitting in the front row, or at least the second row near first, Jimmy and Roslyn Carter, then Ronald and Nancy Reagan, and finally with George and Barbara Bush. One can never be blazé about going to the White House, and even with the many times we went we were always excited. Even all the performers were agog, and because of all the hype connected with performing for the presidents, more often than not put on their best performances.

The East Room became a cabaret, and the best one you ever went to. There were only about 100 people at most sitting in rows on little gilded chairs, and there were always masses of flowers which showed to advantage on television, as did the gold and white ornate moldings of the walls, the huge mirrors and the three sparkling chandeliers. These as you might suspect, were removed when Mikhail Baryshnikov entered diagonally from the back corner and uncorked a dazzlingly high ballet leap. I got to know the camera crew who were veterans after so many White House performances. Little Glenda all in black working the big cameras, Julius the huge black engineer who, when things got quiet, focused on Ward and me, and there were Gary and Al, all wonderful technicians. After the show everyone went through a receiving line to meet the President and his wife, and there are many photographs of us doing so. Ward always looked spectacular, but I came across as a house-frau from the Crimea. Then we went into the gorgeous dining room for a reception. It was invariably lavish with a huge floral bouquet in the center of the long table which was laden with the best food you ever put in your mouth. Hot chafing dishes with broiled scallops, cheese puffs, fried oysters, and tiny barbecued skewers with chicken and filet mignon bites. Best of all were the huge glass bowls mounded with cold shrimp. The dessert table had every kind of cake, pastry and candies surrounding an enormous cornucopia of fruits. The bar table all along one side had everything you wanted. All served up by the "old family" black retainers who had been in service for many years. One of the senior butlers got to know me, and practically had my Dewar's Scotch with a splash of soda ready for me when I entered.

I loved talking with the entertainers, most of whom were there with their proud families. I've chatted with almost all of them over the years, Liza Minelli, Pearl Bailey, Mel Torme, Kathleen Battle, Kitty Carlisle, Robert Goulet, Mary Martin, Baryshnikov, Patti Austen, John Raitt, Bea Arthur,

Izaac Perlman. I've even held hands with Gene Kelley, who was friendly, out-going and positively edible. One summer "In Performance in the White House" was to be held on the south lawn, with a full orchestra, a chorus of little children and featuring Mary Martin and John Raitt. All of a sudden in the midst of a duet from "South Pacific" the heavens opened up into a downpour. We all ran for cover into the White House. The performance had to be resumed the next day. So back we came. I had struck up a friendship with Rosemary Raitt as we sat in the front row on folding chairs. She told me that she and John were heading up to Cape Cod in a few weeks as he was going to sing at the Cape Playhouse in Falmouth. I found myself suggesting they stop by on their way to our house in Westport Harbour.

One summer Sunday afternoon about a month later when I was up at our house, as Lyn and Mary and Margot were preparing to go back to Boston and Ward was away, the phone rang and this beautiful, deep voice said, "Hello, Lydia, this is John Raitt. We'll be there in an hour. Don't go to any trouble."

Whew! I dashed to the fish market, bought a huge piece of swordfish, put potatoes in the oven, got the grill set, made a salad, and soon they arrived. I was embarrassed that it was only me to entertain them as the girls had said a polite how-d'ya-do and left. But they were easy and John cooked the fish outdoors.

As we were eating I said, to make conversation, "John, how did you get into musical theatre?" Whereupon for one hour he gave me arias from "Oklahoma," "Fanny," "Carrousel" and "Man from La Mancha" and other musicals in which he had starred. There was just me, an audience of one, for this splendid voice. I wish I had had a tape recorder going.

When Jimmy Carter was President, he entertained Chinese Premier Deng Xiao Ping with dinner at the White House and a huge gala performance afterwards at the Kennedy Center. WETA was to televise the proceedings. I went the day before to watch them set up the Eisenhower Theatre for the event. There were cardboards on the seats to indicate the VIPs who would be sitting in them. Senators, congressmen, cabinet members, judges, etc. would attend. The night of the performance, Ward and I watched the entertainers warming up backstage in the Green Room. The Harlem Globe Trotters were horsing around tossing basketballs at each other sprawled on the sofas, a large chorus of Chinese children were getting their hairbows and neckties adjusted by fluttery ladies, Rudolph Serkin was pacing up and down, shaking his fingers to keep them from getting stiff, Leonard Bernstein was bouncing around kissing all the musicians, John Glenn looked very serious and when the presidential party finally arrived late, everyone backstage was in a state of nerves. Poor Dick Cavett who was emceeing on air had to ad lib for the half-hour delay. Ward, who went to the television booth to help him, told me to stay backstage, and not move till he came back. Well he didn't. But I didn't care. I watched all the proceedings from the wings. After the performance was over, the President and the Premier went up on stage to congratulate everybody. I was still standing obediently in the wings. The only other person around was a secret service man who eyed me kind of funny. Then the most extraordinary thing happened. The President left the stage with his party and headed out right toward me. The whole lot of them. Jimmy Carter spotted me and put his hand out to shake mine. So did Rosalyn. So did Amy. And good gracious, so did Premier Deng, thinking I must be important. Then little Mrs. Deng put both her hands in mine and with tears in her eyes, said, "Thank you velly much." And they passed on. I started to laugh. And was still doing so as Ward found me. "You won't believe what just happened," I said. I was right. He didn't!

Another occasion which I cherish was a state dinner for President Napolean Duarte from El Salvador. Although we had been many times to the White House, we had never been asked to a state dinner. It was splendid! Each guest was assigned a gorgeous, tall, white-uniformed and gold-braided gentleman of the staff to inform and help with protocol. "First you. . . . then you. . . . and after dinner you. . . . and after that you will. . . ." etc. It was nice, even though we got the picture anyway. The dinner itself was marvelous. I sat next to Loren Mazell, the symphony orchestra conductor, and there were other Salvadoreans and Cabinet officials at my table. On my other side a very elderly gentleman, whose name I never got, fell sound asleep right after the main course. I don't think it was my fault. President Reagan gave a very good toast to President Duarte, but in response Duarte stole the show with his heartfelt remarks. Beleaguered as his country was with violence and strife, and being agonized over the kidnapping of his daughter, he spoke with calm and conviction of his role to improve his country, his faith in justice, with the help of America. My heart went out to him. After dinner there was a little concert in the East Room, and after that everybody milled around. Ward and I headed toward the Green Room where the President and everyone else seemed to have congregated. We started moving around the fringe of the crowd, clockwise, and as we got in front of the fireplace, who should be coming toward us counter-clockwise alone, but President Duarte. I wanted to speak to him, as I had read he was a painter, and since I had had several paintings of mine shown in San Salvador representing the Estado-Unidos a few years before as part of a touring show. Ward looked a bit disapproving as I opened the conversation with Duarte. I told him the above items.

He said, "Are you a painter? How wonderful. Your paintings . . . I wish I'd seen in my country." And we got into more chatting. Ward looked more relaxed. Duarte said he painted late every night after his busy frantic days. It was the only thing that kept him sane. We talked about landscapes, which he loved.

Without thinking, I asked him if he ever painted on-the-spot in the countryside.

He threw back his head and laughed and said, "I wouldn't last one hour outdoors. I would be shot." We were still laughing when President Reagan came up to take him off to meet someone else. Poor man, he later died of cancer. When he was here in hospital, I wanted to send him a box of drawing equipment to while away the terrible hours. I wish I had.

One of the "In Performances at the White House" took place in California at the Reagan Ranch. It was a performance by Merle Haggard. It couldn't actually be held at the Reagans because their place was too small. So neighboring Jimmy Stewart's ranch was picked instead. This huge gorgeous property with rolling pastures, many horses grazing behind white paddock fences, and its large central barn was impressive. The audience sat on bales of hay. Ronnie and Nancy flew in by helicopter, and I watched the little aircraft land on the side of a hillside on a precise spot marked by a big white cross. The formal engraved invitation we received made us a little apprehensive because down at the bottom it said, "Attire, Western." There is a shop here in Washington which sells nothing but western garb, and I dashed up first to see what I could manage. I ended up looking a bit like Annie Oakley, with a white sombrero, a ruffled blue denim skirt, a vest, and white cowboy boots with purple fringes. Ward and Jerry Slater went up later to buy their outfits but didn't quite look convincing as Westerners, particularly as Jerry asked the salesman for "dungarees" which the young man had never heard of. They really looked like Eastern dudes, although Ward's faded blue shirt with snaps everywhere has become one of his favorites back home.

We stayed in a motel in the Valley below. All the secret service were staying there, and as we first looked out our window onto the pool area, the small pool was overflowing with the secret service men all drinking gin and tonics. We were boarded into buses from the high school nearby. The security checks were very careful. And on up the hilly terrain we went, across little rivers and onto the Refugio Ranch Road to our destination. After the Haggard concert, where Ronnie and Nancy were sitting on front row hay bales, we were served absolutely the best barbeque food I have ever eaten. Black huge tender steaks, ribs, chicken, salads, elaborate desserts and all the fixings. There were a lot of snazzy California types there in their "authentic" western attire. One pretty lady who stood next to me at the paddock fence as we watched the Reagan's helicopter arrive, was clad all over in molasses-colored suede (Italian-designer I'm sure) from her Spanish sombrero, to her fringed jacket, to her riding skirt, to her boots. She had also heavy gold necklaces and bracelets. As the Reagans walked down the path past us they waved to her. I have a picture of that, and it looks like they were waving at me. Beverly Sills and her husband sat at the Reagans' table, also another wonderful lady whose name was Mary something, who was a silent screen actress and had been riding horseback with Reagan the previous day. We got friendly with her, and Ward thought she was the cat's whiskers, which she was. She had on *the most* stunning silver and turquoise jewelry you ever saw. Of museum quality. Her appearance was totally authentic as if she belonged, which she did. On the other hand there was Jay Iselin, head of Channel Thirteen in New York, a friend of ours. We first spotted this huge round brimmed hat as big as a turkey platter walking towards us. Underneath it was Jay, smiling broadly, his small stature completely overpowered by his haberdashery. He had on a grey flannel jacket and blue jeans. I have a picture of him so outfitted. He was smashing.

This was a really fun event for Ward and me. I liked seeing the Reagans so much at home on their home turf. When we got to the airport afterwards to go home, I was waiting for Ward with our luggage while he checked in. A very familiar looking man walked by me, and seemed to recognize me, and after he had just passed by turned around to wave at me. It was Bob Hope. (His mistake.) Henry and Nancy Kissinger were on our plane, and while we were waiting to board I asked Nancy, whom I knew slightly, where they had been staying. She responded that they were at Walter Annenbergs. So much for our Western barbeque.

A very memorable evening occurred when George Bush was Vice-President. We got an invitation from the Bushes to a going-away party for our dear friends, Phillis and Bill Draper, who were moving to New York. It was to be held at the Alibi Club. I was very sad to lose Phyllis and Bill whom we are crazy about, and wrote a song for them, as I am wont to do at the drop of any festive occasion. I wrote this one to the tune of "Mem-

107

ories" from "Cats." It was a bit tricky, and I had figured I wouldn't do it unless just the right moment occurred, and only if it seemed appropriate. Unfortunately, Ward couldn't go to the dinner as he was in California. I hated to go alone, but did, and took a taxi to the Alibi Club. It was pouring rain. When we got to the entrance which is unmarked, exclusively, there were lots of secret service standing guard, getting drenched.

"You don't want to go in there, lady," said the driver.

"Oh yes, I must," I said and dashed in.

George Bush greeted me, calling me Lydge, which Barbara does ever since she was brought to our house by Flo Gibson to select paintings for the vice-president's house. Flo calls me Lydge. There was quite a collection of VIPs there, but at cocktails it was just like old home week. I was surprised when George started talking to me about the abortive and unsuccessful bomber raid on Libya, which had occurred a few hours before.

"You see, Lydge," he said, "our intelligence was no good. We didn't know our radar wouldn't work that close to the ground."

I nodded knowingly and said, "Oh dear, you didn't?" or some equally deft response.

When time came for dinner we went in and took our places at the large round table, and as at King Arthur's, no one was more noble than the next. Dinner was nicely homemade and normal, roast beef and carrots and beets, followed by salad, and ice cream with chocolate sauce. When it came time for the toasts, I began to get cold feet, however. The assemblage was a bit daunting even for me, although I love to perform. Phyllis was directly across from me sitting between George Bush and George Schultz. There were also James Buckley, Sandra Day O'Connor, Ambassador Wachmeister, and Cabinet members I can't remember. George Bush made the first toast, short and a bit perfunctory, not very spontaneous, though he meant well. Then another man got up and merely toasted "to Bill and Phyllis," and sat down. Wachmeister got up and in his rather formal Swedish way said something proper and short.

Then there was a long pause and in the silence you could hear spoons and coffee cups clinking. No one got up. Well, I had to. As I stood there clearing the lump in my throat, I was looking directly at the two Georges, but there was no retreating now. One of my lines was, "When you take on Muamar Quaddafi, when you shore up the third world, etc." (Bill was appointed to head up the United Nations Committee for Development of the Third World). I will hopefully find a copy of my song from my files, because it went over quite well. That is to say, I got through it. There was quite a lot of applause at the end, I think. I'm glad I did it, as it enlivened the party a bit for the sake of Bill and Phyllis.

We have met and gotten to know many of the very special cast of "Upstairs, Downstairs." Jean Marsh is now a good friend of ours, we have been with Alistair Cooke on several occasions, we entertained Gordon Jackson (Hudson) at dinner, Meg Wynn Owen (Hazel) has stayed with us when we were on P Street, Christopher Beenie (Edward the butler), I took on a sight-seeing trip of Washington, and Simon Williams (James Bellamy) and I had tea in Guildford when Margot and I were in England, Rachel Gurney (Lady Bellamy) attended a party we gave. I was in charge of a fundraiser for WETA, an elaborate dinner featuring many of the cast of "Upstairs, Down-stairs" and "The Adams Chronicle." The British Ambassador Ramsbotham came, and Hermione Gingold, Jean Marsh, and other notables, and it was a jolly affair. Those patrons who took a table were entitled to a celebrity at their table. We had thought that David Lancton (Lord Bellamy) was coming from England for the occasion, but he had to cancel. He was to have sat at Alice Acheson's table and she was thrilled at the prospect. I called him in England, in Chichester I think, and asked him if, for the fun of it, he would formally write his refusal to "Lady Acheson," signing it "Lord Bellamy." He did it perfectly, and with a great sense of enjoyment, particularly in that he well remembered Dean Acheson. Meg Wynn Owen was staying with me when I received Lancton's response, which was on the most beautiful paper. As I was taking Meg to the airport I had her deliver the note to Alice. Alice was enchanted to meet "Hazel" and they chatted inside for many minutes while I waited in the car, not wanting to spoil the illusion.

I took Jean Marsh to the "Treasure Houses of Great Britain" exhibit at the National Gallery. I loved watching her response to the "treasures," and we oohed and aahed at the richness of the objects and the glorious installation. We had fun gazing up at some of the huge portraits of Great Britons, and imagined what their personalities might be. She stood for some time in front of a huge portrait of a young Scottish noble in a green velvet jacket with one hand on his white satin hip in which he was holding velvet gloves. Jean struck the same pose, and asked me to notice his lips, which were full, and ripe and delicious. "All aristocrats seem to have full lips," she said. "Now notice how mine go straight across like a slit. For gener-ations we in the serving class have had to grin to bear it." And she pressed her lips tightly together thrusting her lower jaw out to prove her point. I loved it.

Jean had wonderful stories to tell about the televising of "Upstairs, Downstairs." She loved "Mrs. Bridges" (now dead) and also Gordon Jackson (also just died). Evidently Jean and Angela Baddely used to play tricks on ugly "Ruby" whom they were not fond of. When I took "Edward" on a Washington excursion and picked him up after he toured the White House, he remarked, "The White House is so small." He was comparing it to Buckingham Palace.

We also got to know several of the actors in "Brideshead Revisited," one of whom was Nickolas Grace who played the part of the flaming and delicious homosexual Anthony Blanch, one of "Sebastian's" and "Charles'" classmates at Oxford. At a party that was given for the show, Nickolas showed up in a shiny black suit, white socks and black shoes, no tie, and with him were two smashing females with orange and purple and green hair, skimpy dresses, and fishnet stockings.

Nickolas with his popping black eyes took a liking to me, as I did him. I told him that the British Ambassador was coming especially to see him. He became alarmed and when Ambassador Henderson and Mrs. H. showed up, Nickolas hid behind me.

"Go on Nickolas," I said, "you have to be polite. The Ambassador came especially to see you. You have to go speak to him," and I pushed him forward. Little Nickolas went up and stood before the big man.

He held out a limp hand, and assuming the part of his character "Anthony Blanch," who had a serious stammer said: "G-G-G-Good evening, M-M-M-Mister Ambb-bassadddor, you are a m-m-m-meaty boy!" There was a deafening silence. Then, he kissed Lady Henderson who blushed. The Ambassador threw his head back and roared with laughter, as Nickolas retreated backward bowing like a Chinese coolie. It was a superb performance. Nickolas and I have corresponded ever since at Christmas.

Of all the performers I know, I like best Geraldine James who played the part of Sarah in "Jewel and the Crown" and also opposite Peggy Ashcroft in "Passage to India." Geraldine was here doing a promotion and benefit for us at WETA, and I got to take her to museums when she wasn't otherwise occupied. She was pregnant with her first baby, and she looked wonderful and was game as a goat. People recognized her in the galleries, which pleased her a lot. We related to each other, and I so enjoyed her un-phoney attitude toward people, and her marvelous acting ability. We, too, have corresponded since then, and after Eleanor was born she came to New York to play Portia in the "Merchant of Venice" opposite Dustin Hoffman. Ward and I went to New York to see her in it, and went backstage after. She was wonderfully vibrant and strong in the part, yet soft where need be. As Sarah in the "Jewel" I find unforgettable the scene at the end, after all the mayhem and tragedy of the terrorists attacking the train, Sarah in her khaki uniform is going back home, saddened and disillusioned. Guy Perrin, the handsome officer is standing by as Sarah prepares to leave. They are deeply attracted to each other but events have been against them.

> Guy: "When shall I see you again?"
> Sarah: "What's there to see?"
> Guy: "A great deal."

It doesn't sound like much on the page, but it was dynamite emotionally, and I think a most exquisite moment of romance, more intense than a flaming sex scene.

There was a party at the Indian Embassy for the cast of "Jewel and the Crown" and "Sarah" was there and "Guy" (Charles Dance). I fell madly in love with Charles who is the most handsome man I've ever seen, and funny. We had our picture taken together hamming it up, which was a knockout, but sadly I spilled coffee all over it by mistake, and his glorious visage was ruined. Drat! When they were to leave Washington, Ward and Geraldine and Charles and I went to WETA together to watch the final episode of "Jewel." I sat next to Charles in the viewing room, on a small sofa, and he had his arm around me the whole time while we watched. He is something else! They were going to Philadelphia that same night, and Ward and I waved goodbye as the hired black limousine pulled away from the studios into the night.

I have had a pretty successful art career here in Washington. A great many people have bought my paintings and have them hanging in their houses. Early on I sold one to the Kennedy Center which has been made into a note card one can buy. Also Barbara Bush chose three of my paintings to hang in the Vice-President's house when they were there. One time I went there to a huge tea party for a national reading conference and learning symposium. Barbara stood on the staircase and addressed the group, and when she finished she said: "We have a very fine artist in our midst, Lydia Chamberlin, and I want you to all go into the entrance hall and see her three lovely works." It was so nice of her. I blushed becomingly.

I also have a painting in the National Museum of Women in the Arts. It is called "Prout's Neck" and there is a black and white reproduction of it in their catalogue on page 168. (In the index I am listed right below Mary Cassatt!) The painting at the present moment is in the American Embassy in Nepal on loan for the "Art in Embassy's" program.

A highlight of my "brilliant" career came when I was offered a show in London by a French lady, Suzel de la Maison Neuve, who owned a gallery on Eccleston Street near Victoria Station. I was never so excited and hardly needed an airplane to get over—I could have just flapped my wings. The gallery was charming and built in an old converted mill, with stone walls. The opening was exciting and long limousines pulled up to the front with Lord and Lady so and so, and lots of "honorables." I didn't sell much, but enough to make it worthwhile. One reviewer from the *Paris Herald Tribune*, in describing what was going on in London that week, first reviewed Andrew Wyeth who he found melancholy and dispirited. Then in a new paragraph he said:

"But Lydia Chamberlin, on the other hand. . . ." and gave me a glowing review. (I couldn't have written it better myself!)

After the opening, Ward took about ten of us to dinner in a tiny wonderful French restaurant, and after that Suzel treated us to Annabelle's, a disco where we danced till three in the morning. When I told our daughters about it later, they couldn't believe we had been to such a chic nightclub dancing till three in the morning.

I have described earlier how I was part of a traveling show to San Salvador. This came about through the "Washington World Gallery" where I had my first shows when I came to Washington. It was run by several Latin Americans. I have also had other shows. But the best shows I have had, I have produced myself. The problem with having a show with a gallery is that the gallery takes 50% off the top, I provide my mailing list and lure all my friends to the opening, I pay half the cost of the party, and often part of the invitation. If a painter is a stranger in a city and wants to get known, he has to be represented by a reputable gallery. But here in Washington I am somewhat well-known and I can dodge the system by selling out of my house and putting on my own shows periodically.

*Grandma Gifford
as a young bride.*

*Grandma Gifford
and my father*

My father

My mother at 17

*My father at the time
of his wedding, 1920*

My mother, 1920

Powder Point House, Duxbury, Massachusetts

Lydia's grandfather and grandmother Young in front of Powder Point House

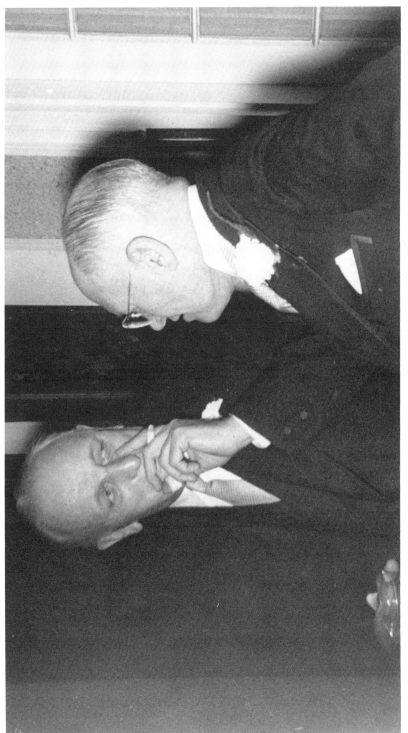

Stephen Gifford and Ward Chamberlin, Lydia and Ward's fathers

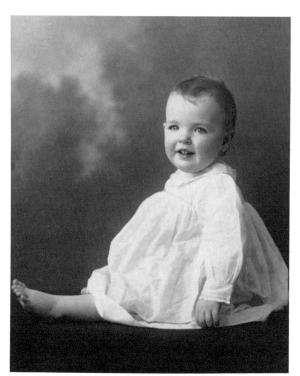

Lydia, 1924

Lydia and Steve,
1924

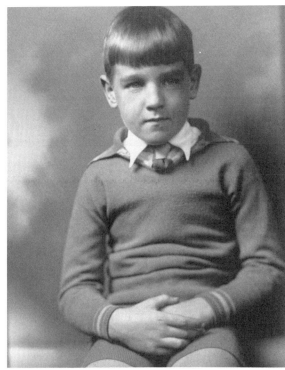

Steve at 5

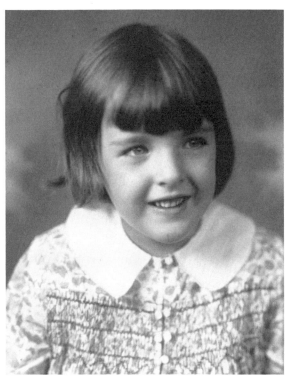

Lydia, 1928

Lydia, mother and Steve about to sail for Europe, 1930

Winsor School Baseball team, Lydia third from right in back with rumpled uniform

Bill Floyd, Lydia and Steve, Winter 1942

Mother's musical
H.M.S. Aft N' Fore,
Middle background:
Lydia, Bill Floyd
and Steve Gifford

Lydia and Steve in
Nice, France, 1930

Lydia and Steve

Summer 1941

Lydia, 1949

Our wedding.
Standing left to right:
Lydia's father, Lydia's
mother, Steve, Lydia,
Ward, Bill Sloane,
Ward's father,
Ward's mother,
Newt Schneck.
Sitting in front:
Bill Farrelly,
Sue Coleman,
Sam Bell,
Mary Ahern,
Alex Stumpf,
Ann Williams

*Ward and Lydia
at wedding with
Mrs. Gibson and
Allese*

*My father
at our wedding*

Lydia and Ward throwing bouquet from porch

Steve hugging Cousin Addy, with Johnny Johnson and Betty Johnson at right

*Lydia and Ward
seen in Lisbon
walking the boulevards
on October 12, 1951*

*Bobby Schwarzenbach, Lydia,
Bridget Schwarzenbach, and Ward
at costume party*

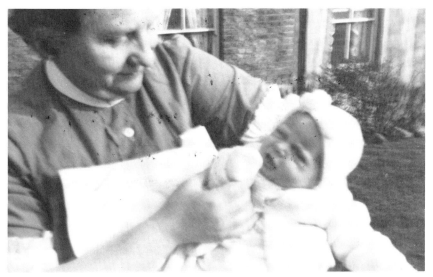

Nurse Holmwood and Lyn aged one month, The Boltons, London

*Lyn and
Margot on
the slopes,
Lech, Austria*

Lyn playing paddle tennis with Bobby Schwarzenbach

Lyn and Margot in their teens

Margot and Lyn, summer 1992

Margot and Alexandra aged 2

Henry Fonda and Lydia, New York 1968

Lydia and Ward with Jean Marsh

Ward and
Jean Marsh

Lydia and Diana MacLeish at the opening of Lydia's art exhibition in Washington Harbor, Washington, D.C.

Ward, Charles Dance and Geraldine James at cast party for Jewel and the Crown

Lydia and Geraldine James

Sharon Rockefeller, Marvin Hamlisch and Lydia

Lydia and Helen Hayes

Barbara Bush in front of Lydia's painting of Dumbarton Oaks

To the Chamberlains ~~from the~~ Bushes
With warm regards,
Gg Bush

*Winter
Solstice
Revels*

*"Four Kings from
Orient" at Winter
Solstice Party.
Bill Bruell, Tim
Hoopes, Hugh
Jacobson and
Steve Martindale*

*"Angel" chorus
on kitchen
roof at Winter
Solstice Revels*

*Lydia and
Colleen
Dewhurst,
Folger
Library*

Tea at Alice Acheson's. Alice Acheson (back to) in foreground with Lydia

Before a garden party at the British Embassy in Washington, D.C.
Left to right: Ward, Robin Jacobsen, Bucky Block, Lydia and Hugh Jacobsen

Our house in Westport Harbor, Massachusetts

Front porch with Patsy Ives and Lydia and Louis, Flora and Pushkin

Lydia and Ward, Western dudes

Ronald and Nancy Reagan arriving for television show

Lydia and Ward at Draper's costume party

Lydia and Ward during a lifeboat drill aboard the Royal Viking Sun off east coast of South America

One of these took place in Washington Harbor, a glittering, gaudy, new development in Georgetown right on the Potomac River. It looks more out of Tivoli Gardens than Colonial Georgetown, but with fountains and esplanades and decorative landscaping, and fancy expensive restaurants, it is an energetic and fun place to go. Often there are strolling minstrels, singers and street actors who appear there. I found an empty location that eventually was going to be an Italian restaurant, but as yet it was undecorated, with cement columns and rough floors on which technicians had painted directional arrows, with a lovely grass covered arcade looking right out onto the river. The management of the Harbor let me have it for a week, and we put on a smashing show, so original and right for my paintings. One of Ward's electrical geniuses came from WETA and lit the whole show with real class, with a spotlight for each of the 24 paintings. I almost cried when the lights were turned on for the first time. The paintings glowed as I have never seen in any gallery, where normally there is one spot for three paintings. We had musicians, and fabulous finger food, and it was a glamorous event. The place was crowded and the likes of Sandra Day O'Connor, Ambassador de Margerie, Paul Duke, Jim Lehrer. Evangeline Bruce came adding some class. I sold practically everything the first night.

A couple of years later, I did the same thing in an unoccupied house in Georgetown that a real estate agency was trying unsuccessfully to sell. They wanted people in, and I wanted their lovely blank walls. Also the quality of a private house enhanced the paintings so that people could see them in a living situation. I also practically sold out this show too.

I was given one commission which gave me great pleasure in receiving, but enormous difficulty in achieving. Bucky Block, a great friend of ours who heads a large insurance firm here, called me up late one beautiful afternoon saying that he had just flown in from New York and as the plane approached National Airport following its usual pattern along the Potomac, he saw a sight that dazzled him, a view looking down on the tops of all the famous buildings, along the Mall from the Lincoln Memorial to the Capitol. The afternoon sun touched the monuments with a gorgeous glow that he would never forget. Would I paint the scene, using my artistic discretion? Of course I would. And then I proceeded to go to the top of all the landmarks, and the highest buildings to get the necessary birds-eye view. The parapet roof of the Kennedy Center was the best, but it didn't get all the Mall. I went over to the USA Today building across the river in Rosslyn and inveigled my way up to the roof. The view was perfect, although I needed better telescopic equipment if I was to get the architectural detail required to capture all of the buildings involved. So I hired a friend who is a photographer to go and shoot it for me. I had told Bucky jokingly that in order to get this airplane view I would need to go up in a helicopter. He said, "Okay, go ahead!" But Ward said it wouldn't be allowed. I did a very good but difficult painting which took me weeks. It is now hanging in Bucky's office, and I am very proud.

My friend Phyllis Draper asked me to paint a painting of the view from Bill's office at the Import Export Bank that he headed at the time that overlooked Lafayette Square. I was to do the photographic research secretly while Bill was in South America as it was to be a surprise. His secretary greeted me, and I went to the windows to study the square, but found I couldn't photograph through the hermetically sealed double-glassed windows. There was a parapet up on the next floor, the 12th floor, which was open. The only access to it, however, was through another back office by going out a window. The man in that office looked a bit startled as I disappeared and like Quasimodo walked on the narrow ledge to the front of the building. Perfect . . . I could see everything, all the park and statues and the lovely Federal buildings on the far side. I could even look down on the White House and see all the defense installations on its roof. The street was far below. Wait a minute! Nobody knows I'm here. I could be a sniper! The White House security could easily pick me off with rifles. I beat as hasty a retreat as I could, envisioning the headlines in the evening paper. "Middle-aged Lady Sniper Shot by White House Security Guards."

Actually the photos I took were no good, and I had to go back another day. This time everyone was alerted. I had to get a pass, and a guard had to accompany me. As we crawled through that same window to go outside, this strapping big black guard looked a little pale. "Are you sure you want to do this, lady?" he said, and he only accompanied me halfway. But my mission was accomplished.

The various Balls that are given in Washington are very splendid and many. For the most part Ward and I can't afford to go to them as they can cost a bundle, like the Symphony Ball and the Cancer Ball. We have gone to the Corcoran Ball several times at great expense but did so because of its art orientation and because we liked the hostesses who asked us to sit at their tables. But in spite of two orchestras, lavish food and decorations, the ball was so crowded you could hardly dance, and you certainly couldn't hear the conversations you were trying to hold. We would say each year, not again. And we haven't for a couple of years now.

We are invited to many benefit dances, and WETA has itself held a couple of super ones. One that was held in the Pension Building was outstanding. Ward hosted a glittering group of celebrities including Mary Martin and Julia Child and Mayor Walter Washington. I got to pick who I wanted to sit next to, and it was Walter Washington. Gene Donati's orchestra was playing for the dancing, and Walter asked me if I liked to dance. I said I loved to. He then asked me if I liked to merengue. I said I loved to, not knowing quite what it was. When we got out on the dance floor, all the members of the orchestra plus Donati saluted the Mayor, and off we went. We were at first the only ones on the floor, and he guided me in this South American rhythm with mastery and grace. He was one of the best dancers I've ever danced with. I enjoyed it hugely.

We go about four times a year to the Waltz. That's its only name. It is a very exclusive group, and rather misnamed, because they only play a few token waltzes. There are dinner parties held beforehand, when it is not a dinner dance itself at the Sulgrave Club. I have not always enjoyed myself when the crowds around the bar are all hyper and chatting, and the men cluster together. Unless you are brave you stay on the outskirts, but then you may not get a dancing partner. I hate trying to be charming and endeavoring to market myself at this dance bazaar, particularly if some of my favorite men friends, the good dancers, have been there.

The best dancers in Washington have been for me: Walter Washington, Bob Barton, Elliott Richardson, Skip Nalen, Hank Strong, Bob Blake, Justice Lewis Powell, Justice Byron White, Bucky Block and Hugh Jacobsen. My evening has been made if I have had a dance with any one of the above. The trouble with most Washington men is they can't really dance and therefore they talk too much on the dance floor. You can't talk and dance. The resulting shuffle from side to side is hopeless. And when a waltz occurs most of the males would rather not. I love a partner who likes to swoop and improvise and is a little crazy, and gets a bit carried away. I'm a pretty good dancer and I love it even if I make a spectacle of myself from time to time.

In Washington where appearances count for a lot, I rate low on a scale of one to ten. In the first place, good clothes are created for the very thin, small and rich. Being large and poor, I have had a problem but I have solved it over the years. Quite satisfactorily. I never go out for lunch as that ruins my painting schedule, and would involve changing out of my slacks, sneakers and sweatshirt, which is my uniform. I often dress in the dark at 5:30 when I get up so that I won't wake Ward. This often produces some strange combinations. I have discovered that the Junior League Thrift Shop sold some very good stuff, and I bought a wonderful dressy, pleated, long silver skirt that I wore with different tops to many parties. Loehmann's is okay sometimes, but I can't stand the sales ladies with dandruff on their black dresses in the Back Room who are always talking to each other about illnesses and mean-spirited gossip. But my favorite of all stores is a Japanese store way up in Takoma Park that sells antique and second-hand Japanese kimonos. I must have at least 14 of them, varying from a tomato red with gold threads, and a white satin lining inside the droopy sleeves, to an ornate gold and silver chrysanthemum design with a pale turquoise silk lining, very dressy. With these I wear maybe a satin or nice silk blouse and black pants or skirt. I have had tons of compliments.

I have bought only two expensive dresses. One was for Margot's wedding, a lovely chiffon Hannah Mori, a delicate blue, gray and pink chrysanthemum design with a powder blue satin sash and covered buttons. I still love it! The second was a mistake. I thought I needed to buy an inaugural ball gown, for the Inaugural Ball. So I picked out a heavy white satin job. I went to tremendous trouble to get tickets for the ball, standing in a huge line downtown at the headquarters, thinking that this Bush bash would be memorable, and a not-to-be-missed opportunity. Ward (who didn't care about going at all) was a good sport and humored me. We decided to go by subway to the Pension Building which we were assigned to by ticket, as the parking for the millions of ball goers would be impossible. The ballroom was crowded and people walked up and down as best they could till the President and Mrs. Bush showed up. When they did arrive, they climbed onto a raised platform, said a few words and disappeared with their secret service through the throng. There were two orchestras at either end of the huge room, but the dancing was nearly impossible, and Ward and I soon left too. My friend Robin Jacobsen said, when I told her what a bust it all was, that I should have known better—nobody goes to the Inaugural Balls who has any class, or sense. She's an old timer here.

There was a quaint, second-hand shop on Wisconsin Avenue when we first lived here called Deja Vu. It had all the usual bits of clothing memorabilia, velvet hats with ostrich plumes, beaded handbags, yellowing ivory toilet sets with hairbrush bristles that were stained and brown, and racks and racks of dresses, coats and suits all jammed together. I went in one day with Inky, our ancient black poodle, to look around. Inky was intrigued by whomever it was in the "dressing room," which was nothing but an old curtain on a circular rod, like a shower curtain. The lady inside kept handing the items she was discarding to a very chic looking English lady in caramel-colored cashmere, who replaced them on the racks. Inky was now inside and this most elegant voice talked to him as one does to a friendly dog. Every now and then a long slim arm with gold bracelets would appear and the lady would say, "Not this one either, dahling, it just won't do." I had spotted a black velvet torreador's outfit with proper vest, pants and a balloon silk shirt with enormous silk sleeves. As I was holding it up in front of me and looking at myself in the long mirror, out came Inky and the lady. She was enveloped in an old-fashioned heavy ornate moire-black cloak which looked for all the world as if it had belonged to Queen Victoria. She was smashing in it. It was Irene Worth the actress, who was presently in a play at the Kennedy Center. She caught sight of me contemplating my bullfighter's rig and said, "Dahling, that is sensational, you must buy it." And I did. We both walked out with our Victorian and Spanish "treasures." I wore mine several times until the fragile silk blouse wore out and I got too fat for the pants. But I still wear the vest.

Although quite unconventional, nobody dresses like me. I go for clothing which is generally fun and spirited. Lili Pulitzer it is not. A fur coat I don't own, and during the day when I'm painting and walking the dogs, I look terrible. Also because I swim every morning my hair is a daily disaser, only to be remedied by Maria at the hair salon, within walking distance on 31st Street, when I have to go out in the evening.

One of the first dinner invitations we got in Washington was from the Belins who lived in "Ever May," that lovely Georgian estate on 28th Street. With its cobbled, circular drive and central marble fountain, its perfect architecture, its terraced lawns, its wisteria-festooned arbors, its many rose gardens, pergolas and a little summer house, it is the epitomy of southern aristocratic grandeur. I hadn't met Mary and Peter Belin yet, but Ward had now played tennis often with Mary on her marvelous tennis court situated below the house. After dinner at the long dining room table, we were getting along splendidly and I was making every effort to be charming and spirited. It had been a long cocktail hour, with wine at dinner and brandy afterwards in the garden room. Mary and I sat on a small sofa together having a demitasse; Ward and Peter sat opposite on a matching little sofa. Mary looked pleased, particularly because Peter seemed to be enjoying us along with his liquor.

Mary said to me in a confidential tone: "Lydia, I told Peter about you as we were getting dressed for dinner." I said, "Peter, you will like Lydia a lot. She's not much to look at, but she's a lot of fun!"

Dent Place, where we now live, is like an English mews street. Being a one-way street almost up to Montrose Park, it is quiet and very civilized, away from the Georgetown bustle. We know everyone on the street, and

I have made friends with our neighbors, perky Ruth next-door and white-haired Mrs. Shinkman next to her. Poppy across the street is the "Mayor" of Dent Place, and she organizes our yearly block party in May, and also the Crime Watch Program, which has been a model for other parts of Georgetown. The block party is a lively affair and everyone participates. The street is blocked off for the festivities and there is live music, and endless delicious homemade dishes contributed by all. Our little front garden blooms like mad with geraniums, impatiens, pansies, ageratum, azaleas, and flowering bulbs. I take pride in it, and many people stop and mention it as they walk by when I'm gardening. We have a beautiful holly tree that arches over the front steps.

One afternoon as I was out front cleaning our brick path and sidewalk I had made a cup of tea, and put it on my car roof to sip on as I swept. Pretty soon, Betty Shinkman appeared with a little plate of sandwiches. "You can't have a proper cup of tea without proper cucumber sandwiches," she said. She is British. Except for the terrible crime on the streets, Georgetown is a very civilized place to live in.

Georgetown is like a village and wonderful to walk in. I never get tired of gazing at the lovely houses, each one a variation on a Georgian theme. Each doorway is splendidly individual. The brass polished to a high gloss, and some are lit by flickering gas lamps. Almost every house has an enclosed backyard and garden, often with small swimming pools. We have a back garden which is raised up from the back alley and gets full advantage of sun, which most don't have. It has flower beds, and a circular raised brick planter in which we put geraniums and pansies and impatiens. It looks nice when seen from our little balcony above, that is, outside the French doors from our dining room. Ward, who is a sun worshipper, loves to sit on this little deck reading his newspapers or doing endless paper work on the weekends. We have four large white flower containers in which we planted rose bushes, which bloom profusely with huge Peace Roses, a white Queen Elizabeth, and a gorgeously fragrant orangy-pink Helen Traubel. Ward often picks a fat rosebud and takes it to his office, balancing it on his dashboard in a mayonnaise jar till he gets there. One should know when they buy a house here to always buy one on the south side of the street, because that exposure provides a south-facing garden. We sit in ours often on warm nights, and are able to barbecue all year long, except of course when it's snowy.

We are almost up to Dumbarton Oaks and its splendid gardens. I like to walk there especially in early spring when the fruit trees are in bloom, and the dogwoods light up the landscape with splashes of white and pink. Eyvie and Giles Constable paid me a huge compliment by commissioning me to paint whatever view I wanted for them as they departed Washington after Giles retired as head of Dumbarton. I relished walking all over the huge property with them as they pointed out their favorite scenes. A carpet of bluebells here, a silver trunk of a gorgeous maple, the Elipse Garden, the formal rose gardens, the Alleès, the beautiful carved benches, elaborate stone moldings and sculptured animals placed strategically along walks and patios. And the Orangerie, fragrant with gardenias and orange blossoms. I painted five views on one canvas because I couldn't decide which one aspect they loved the most. It was a bit peculiar, but I think overall it worked, and they seemed very pleased.

We are about three minutes away from the Safeway on Wisconsin Avenue. Most people don't like shopping, but I do, especially here. I dote on the vegetable and fruit departments with their fresh wonderful produce. I cannot walk by the artichokes, or the endives, or the asparagus, without buying. And I buy many more plants from the flower section than our tiny house can hold. Especially strong and lovely are the white cyclamen that look like nuns' hats and I have to put blinders on when I pass the gardenias. This is familiarly known as the "Social Safeway," and one can't go there without seeing friends or VIPs. Invariably I go right after swimming in the morning and hope I won't see anyone I know, but I always do. And as fate would have it, I have often bumped into beautiful Sigrid Spalding, she in her leopard coat with matching hat, perfectly coiffed, and with impeccable makeup. I met her thus one snowy day going into the Safeway. There were real snowflakes on her long black lashes. Oh dear, I had on my Georgetown University sweatsuit, and my once nice hair set had just flopped in the swimming pool.

One of the reasons this Safeway is so superior is that it is frequented by embassies, legations and diplomats from all over the world. Butlers and maids stand in the check-out lines with carts laden with exotic foods, expensive cuts of meat, and flowers for receptions. Also the various nationalities can find their native foods of China, Indonesia, Mexico, Thailand, Sweden, Vietnam, etc.

I count on my morning swim. I get up very early and do whatever house chores I have, walk and feed the dogs, and get to my pool before nine o'clock. I would like to make it by eight, but I don't. I swim anywhere from a quarter of a mile to a half mile. I love being in the water, and I do some of my best thinking and meditation while doing my laps. No matter how tired or how pressed I was before swimming, it has never failed that I felt buoyed and restored afterwards. After going there for several years now, I recognize faces of the many regulars, but I know only a couple by name. I swim in the smaller pool and often have it entirely to myself. I like swimming in the deeper water. The locker room and the shower room are very clean, and the pool beautifully maintained. The pool is at ground level, and a swimmer can see outdoors to the line of trees that surround the gym. The effect is lovely when there is snow on the branches, and you are warm in the water of the pool.

There are all shapes, ages and sizes of swimmers; some are handicapped. Young school children use the gym on a regular basis, although they don't often swim in the pool. I love the babble of the eleven-year-old girls from the convent nearby. They have blue plaid skirts and white blouses and dark blue knee socks, and they are chatting about hair, boys, emerging bosoms, being fat, etc. The little black girls are especially pretty and lively, although one of them is very fat.

One day I was showering after my swim in the open showers where modesty is only protected by white cloth shower curtains hanging loosely from rods. Nobody draws them much except the lady who had a recent mastectomy. Nearby was a young girl about 18 years old whom I had noticed before. She was Egyptian, I think, with a fantastically beautiful body, not curvy and sexy, but like Isis with a straight back and legs, and small bosoms. Her light olive skin was as smooth as alabaster. Her oval eyes looked out from beneath straight black eyebrows, inscrutable as a Sphinx. She was like a young goddess.

On an impulse to voice the positive things in life one feels, particularly if they are complimentary, I said, "You have a beauty that is worthy of the ancient Egyptian sculptors. You are like the young goddess Isis."

Whereupon the poor girl, startled as a deer, departed hastily into the locker room saying nothing. I haven't seen her since. Oh, dear! I had only meant to compliment her, not sexually harass her. As a painter I have painted many nudes in Life Class, analyzing them artistically, and dissecting them as cooly as a surgeon. People to whom I have told that story say I should have known better. Well, I didn't. But I was gratified by a conversation I had with Elvira at the pool only yesterday. Elvira is a Spanish lady, one of the regular swimmers, like me. She is quite elegant and aristocratic, and takes a great deal of time getting dressed and coiffed after each session.

I said to her, "Elvira, do you by any chance remember a beautiful young Egyptian girl that used to come here several years ago?"

"I certainly do," she said, "she was like a goddess. I have never seen anyone so unusually beautiful." And I told her of my encounter with her, which she understood and appreciated. I felt vindicated.

I must also mention the mockingbird that sits many mornings on a high perch on the corner of the roof of Yates Field House. He is the monarch of all he surveys, and if one could enter him in a song competition he would win hands down. He is the Pavarotti of mockingbirds, his repertoire is so extensive that I stand below amazed at his variety and voice control. I always know when spring comes, because there he will be, showing off. My heart leaps up when I behold him.

To round out my life in Washington, I play golf. Swimming is good for the upper body but in that I don't have a very strong kick, it doesn't strengthen my legs, the way walking does. Although I walk Flora and Pushkin twice, sometimes three times a day, they stop and go with so much sniffing and stalking of squirrels, that it isn't much exercise. So I often dash out to our Army-Navy Country Club and get in nine holes before dark. I mostly play alone, and therefore catch up to those playing ahead. I have met many splendid retired admirals and generals this way, some of whom ask me to join them. They usually play well, and are quite serious. They would never concede you a putt. One afternoon recently, I started off at the first hole, taking a golf cart, and when I got up to the second tee I had to pause for a foursome which didn't ask me to play through. As I sat patiently waiting, I noticed behind me another golf cart barreling along with the assistant pro in it.

He came right up to where I was and said, "Mrs. Chamberlin, do you by any chance own a blue Dodge Colt Vista?"

"Yes," I said.

"Well, it's backed into another car and you better come move it." We raced in tandem back to the parking lot and there were a cluster of men including Steve the Pro. I had forgotten to put my car in park. It was now resting against the rear of a brand new, black Rover jeep van. The owner, who looked like General Schwarzkoff, glowered at me. I had not hurt his car at all, but I had delayed his men's foursome by half an hour.

121

I said, "Sorry, just a stupid woman driver."

Steve said, "You said it, I didn't."

My medical and dental history doesn't warrant much discussion. Physically I am a combination of a hypochondriac and a Christian Scientist, and with the notion that an ache or pain will go away in time, I resist going to the doctor. When I do go, which is rarely, I go with the greatest apprehension, convinced that he will send me immediately to the hospital even though my complaint may be minor arthritis of the thumb. One time I went for a check-up. I submitted to all the tests that are normally given, feeling helpless in the face of all the impersonality. And those terrible "gowns" that you have to don! Why can't they come in pretty colors? Because I am so tall, they are much too short and further expose me to the elements. Well, I was in my gray gown, sitting on that cold stainless steel slab, with my legs hanging down waiting for the doctor to come in. He didn't come, and he didn't come. I passed the time reading all his framed certificates from medical school, analyzed those tin bottled remedies on the glass shelf like Alice, certain that one would be labeled "Drink Me." I would have done so if it would shrink me so I could escape through the keyhole. After a *very* long time in which I imagined my tests were being rushed to Johns Hopkins, I felt I must get a magazine from the waiting room. So in spite of my skimpy garb, I went to get one. As I passed through the doctor's small adjacent office, practically on my hands and knees, there sitting in the large wing chair was the doctor. He was sound asleep. He woke up with a start, and was so apologetic that I had to make *him* feel better for the rest of the appointment.

My dental history is a long one. I have terrible teeth inherited from my father. My brother Steve is like Mum with hardly a filling in his head. But I am a dental cripple and but for Dr. Baxter would be toothless. I cannot tell you how magnificent he is, and how I would fly to his dental chair even if I had to commute from Taiwan. He has been named the best dentist in Washington, and has a clientele you wouldn't believe, senators, ambassadors, Carter Brown, etc., and his devoted following of women is legion. You can't go to a gathering or party without a multiple of his patients being there. Baxter, therefore, doesn't go to social parties. And he is right not to do so. All the women are in love with him, including me. But I really believe that I have a special relationship with him. Not only has he bought two of my paintings which hang in his waiting room, but we talk as much as we possibly can during an appointment on every conceivable subject. He is very free with me, and interested in all aspects of living. I really dote on him, although that feeling has nothing to do with romance or sex. To have a warm relationship thus with a man is wonderful. It's a bit like when a woman is close to a homosexual. It is a relationship that is free and uninhibited by danger. Debbie, Dr. Baxter's receptionist, always adds 45 minutes to my appointment because of our inevitable chatter, and often is disapproving when the waiting room is piling up with waiting patients.

One day when I was sitting waiting in the dental chair reading "English Country Life," trying to choose which British freehold farm or house I would purchase out of the real estate section, in Sussex, or Cornwall, or on a loch in Inverness, somebody came in the door behind me, and a deep voice said, "I am your new dentist, and I am replacing Dr. Baxter for the morning." As he came around the chair, he gave me a big kiss. It was Senator Percy, tickled pink with his joke. He had just finished his session with Dr. Baxter.

I was walking the dogs along P Street one morning, when a lady in a car stopped in traffic, rolled down the window and proceeded to execute some sign language directed at me. It went like this. She made a large gesture with her hands to indicate a rectangle. Then she pointed towards her front teeth. Then she gave a thumbs up sign, after which she clapped her hands. What she was trying to communicate was that she had seen my paintings in Dr. Baxter's office and thought they were wonderful.

Halloween is big in Georgetown. Ghoulies and ghosties, wizards and witches, phantoms and Draculas swarm into town and congregate in alarming numbers along M Street and Wisconsin Avenue. The police have their hands full as things get rowdy. I myself am an old Scrooge. I put all the lights out and don't answer the doorbell. I do, however, give out apples to the little tricksters who arrive before dark.

Although I very seldom go for lunch with anyone because it breaks up the day, I have discovered tea-time as being a splendid time to see one's lady friends. Tea requires little preparation and fuss, and even if one makes homemade cookies and cinnamon toast, they aren't eaten by dieting females. One of my abiding joys is to have tea with Alice Acheson and Evangeline Bruce, either at their houses, or mine. This we do quite regularly and only today as I write, Evangeline called to ask me to come on Thursday, which sadly I cannot do. I love to go to her house which is my idea of perfection. It is the most gracious and civilized of any house in Georgetown, filled with luscious but liveable antiques, and oozing with charm and hospitality. All of it reflects the exquisite taste of those who have moved comfortably in elegant circles all over the world. Evangeline was the wife of Ambassador David Bruce who died several years ago. He had been the ambassador to France, and also Great Britain, I think. Vangie is divine looking, kind of Romney or Gainsborough-esque, cool as lavender, with a soft English voice, and a delicious laugh. We giggled uncontrollably the other day as we were going together to Alice Acheson's for tea, and we got confused in the elevator as to what floor Alice was on. We pushed all the stops, got out, reconnoitered and got back in again when we couldn't find the right apartment. We looked like a couple of undercover madams, and tied up the elevator for some time, laughing all the while. She is on everyone's most wanted list for parties, patronage and benefits, and graces all that she accepts. She is coming to my United States-New Zealand arts exhibition next Thursday for which I'm grateful. Stuart Alsop, after having been at tea one Sunday at Evangeline's started the rumor, "Evangeline Bruce irons her cucumber sandwiches."

Alice Acheson and I have been friends since we first moved here. As artists we relate to each other in a way some others can't. She is as special as anyone I have ever known. She is over 90 now and has been pursuing steadily her own interests since Dean Acheson died. She had devoted herself to his life of politics and statesmanship and all that entailed. But after he died she picked up her artistic interests, devoted herself to painting and being with creative people. She too is sought after by everyone, and cuts a charming and important figure in Washington. Although she doesn't drive anymore, I used to see her sketching and painting all over Georgetown, sitting in the front seat of her Rambler or perched on a bench in Dumbarton Oaks, or beneath the gorgeous flowering cherry on P and 31st Street.

I had an English painter friend who came to stay with us whose name was David Addey. Ward and I had bumped into him in France when we stayed in Honfleur and found him in a small gallery where he was exhibiting his work. Ward was rather astonished to hear me say to Addey, out of the blue and having only known him for ten minutes, "You must come and stay with us when you come to Washington." He was really very nice. We forgot about him until months later on a summer night when the telephone rang from England at three in the morning.

Ward answered it sleepily. (I was up in Westport Harbour.) "No, you must be mistaken, I don't know you . . . Who did you say you were. . . . Lydia asked you to visit? Oh good Lord yes. David Addey. And when are you coming? Next week!"

And so he came. The visit was a great success, as he was painting all around Washington for a show here later. He lived in our basement, and was really no trouble, although he stayed a month, rather than a week.

I introduced him to Alice Acheson and they became friends. They both loved to play "Scrabble." The last night he was here I cooked a delicious supper for him which we ate out in the garden, chatting about art and life. During dessert he kept looking at his watch, and the conversation seemed to thin out.

"David, have you got somewhere you have got to go?" I said.

He said, "Lydia, don't think I am rude to rush off, but I have a final game of Scrabble to play with Mrs. Acheson, and she is ahead." And off he went to Alice's.

Philip Bonsal lived down P Street from us, and when I first met him it was our dogs that provided the introduction. He had the prettiest white and tan cocker spaniel to whom our poodle Inky took a shine. Our first conversation was short. I said what a lovely dog you have, and indeed she was, having just been bathed and groomed at Chi-Chi's. I said she looked just like the cocker in *The Barrets of Wimpole Street*. What *was* that dog's name? Neither of us could remember. He walked on down the street in an opposite direction from me. By the time I had gotten almost to Neam's Market, I heard his loud voice shouting back at me, "Flush!"

Philip was wonderful looking, tall and straight, and although patrician had a spark and soft dynamic which was very attractive. One couldn't mistake him walking along Montrose Park as he did every afternoon wearing a grey felt hat and clad in a soft brown suede jacket, his long legs striding with measured confidence.

One morning I got up very early to walk to the corner to get the newspapers. Right in front of the Bonsal's house was a huge racoon dead in the street, all gory and mangled. Philip Bonsal came out his front door to pick up the newspaper on his stoop. He had on a silk foulard bathrobe, with neat pajamas and perfect leather slippers. How sartorially splendid to be so put-together on rising. He caught sight of the poor animal in the street, and did not see me. He walked down his steps, went to the racoon and picked it up lovingly cradling the bloody body in his arms. He carried it to a large ashcan and deposited it carefully inside. His bathrobe was stained, but this he ignored. I had witnessed a touching funeral. I have been devoted to Philip Bonsal ever since.

WINTER SOLSTICE PARTY

One of my favorite dates on the calendar, next to Valentine's Day, is the Winter Solstice. In the year-long journey of the sun it is the shortest day of the year. One rejoices that from then on the days will get longer by a minute each day. Ancient and pagan peoples have worshipped this moment since time immemorial, and it is not by accident that the birth of Christ was timed pretty close to the Solstice, give or take a few days. This might have been the fault of the screwed up calendar experts way back then, before astronomy or theology were too precise.

One of the best parties we ever gave was a Winter Solstice party on P Street a few years ago. It was smashing. We had an angel chorus, a troupe of young kids playing instruments, The Three Kings of the Orient in dazzling costumes, Joseph and Mary, and many townspeople in medieval costume. But best of all, Ken Fisher, an inspired extrovert, was Lord of the Revels, and the Lord of Misrule, a colorful Revel figure. I was the Lady of Misrule. He and I led the proceedings from the little balcony, outside the dining room, whilst all the guests stood in the garden below. I had rented a devil's costume for Ward, but he wouldn't wear the salient parts, and I found most of them behind the sofa where he had hidden them the next morning when I cleaned up.

It was a cold drizzly night as everyone filed in the house and out into the back garden. We had lit some fires which were cheery, but the hot punch that Ward had made from a World War I recipe of his Father's was more effective as a heating element. It was dynamite. After everyone had assembled, Ward carried out the enormous Mexican candelabra blazing with 21 candles and stuck it in the ground. It did look a little bit like a Klu Klux Klan meeting. Then came six angels swaddled in white over their long underwear with gold halos at rakish angles. They took their positions on the flat roof over the kitchen which they got to by climbing out the upstairs hall window. They were really game, particularly Phyllis Draper, who is afraid of heights. But they sang like angels, and looked like a Carravaggio painting silhouetted on high against the dark sky. The children violinists who I had found playing Christmas music in the Foundry were very professional and looked adorable in their Austrian hats and jackets, although I noticed one of the littlest boys wearing his gloves while trying to play his instrument. Anne-Marie was for all the world cherubic, fat like a baby robin, with her bright pink cheeks and she thrilled everyone with her rendition of Minuit-Chrêtien.

The three Kings from the Orient were splendid in lavish costumes. But as I had four wonderful male voices I invented a fourth King, and rc-wrotc the lyrics to include King Hamill (it rhymed nicely with camel). I gave this part to Tim Hoopcs, and drove up and left the lyrics at his house that morning. That afternoon through my mailbox were slipped his revisions of my lyrics. Of all the nerve! And they were nonsensical and unsingable. I revised his revisions as best I could, and resented having to take the time late that afternoon to slip them through his mailbox. When he arrived at the party I had no idea which lyrics he was going to use. But I almost forgave him as he wore a splendiferous costume, replete with flowing robes, crown and ermine fur. (Tim did sing his *own* version!) The other kings took their parts very seriously. Bill Buell had been practicing Caspar for weeks, but when it came time for his solo he blew it, forgetting his words. Later when I saw him at parties he would plead with me to cast him again next year. He vowed to do it right. Hugh Jacobsen was a robust Melchior, and sang with gusto. But the best was Steve Martindale as Balthazar with his gorgeous baritone ringing out clear into the night. Chris Herter was unrecognizable as Joseph when he walked in, and he relished his part, although he didn't have much of a role except to look adoringly at Mary (Alma Viator). We had constructed a little crèche over the little pool.

I had composed a welcoming song about the Solstice to the tune of "Ashgrove" which was effective. But Ken Fisher in his zany Revel outfit stole the show as the "Lord of Misrule." He also led the assembled multitudes in the complicated "12 Days of Christmas" and encouraged much competition for loudness amongst the 12 sections. Then it came to a climax with the refrain:

"Dance, dance, everybody dance, I am the Lord of the Dance, said he . . ."

Everybody was to join hands and form a snake line while singing like mad, they were supposed to go up into the house, through the living room and out onto P Street. It was time to go home, and it was an excellent way to get rid of everybody. So, led by Ken, they all filed through the house and out onto the street. The only problem was they all filed right back in again. The sleet had turned to ice, the steps were glazed and the sidewalks treacherous. The party went on for sometime. When it did stop, the going was impossible. I saw Ramsay Potts leading Caroline Simmons to her nearby house practically on their hands and knees. Ken Fisher could hardly get his car across Key Bridge as there were so many accidents. He helped untangle some fender benders still clad in his revel costume. Sue and Raz had to crawl up their steep driveway on their hands and knees almost not making it. I had many calls the next day telling me of other slippery adventures. It was a marvelous party!

X

Westport Harbour

Nothing has given more meaning and focus to our life than buying our house in Westport Harbour. Ward and I felt that we needed to coordinate with Lyn and Margot who were living in Boston, and this was hard to do being so far away in Washington. Although Mum was now in a nursing home, none of us wanted to live in the Duxbury house. Duxbury had changed a lot. It was growing by leaps and bounds as a suburb of Boston. There were now two post offices, numerous florists, fancy dress shops, etc. and although still picturesque was too cultivated for our tastes. Besides it was hard to get onto the beach, which was now so crowded that you were required stickers and permits, understandably. Furthermore the traffic on Route 3 from Boston was horrible on weekends, and too much to cope with.

Margot and I put our thinking caps on. We got out maps and made lists of each of our requirements for a place to rendezvous in the summer. Ward, we figured, needed two airports, a railroad station, a place to buy Barrons and the Wall St. Journal, and good tennis. I required a good swimming beach, golf, a garden and a safe place for dogs and grandchildren. Margot and Lyn would be happy if the place was not too far from Boston for a day round trip, also they too wanted a quiet beach, tennis, privacy and no hype. As we studied the map we realized that the Rhode Island and Massachusetts coasts were within the proper parameters. We did not, however, consider Cape Cod. Too crowded, too difficult, too tramped over for comfort, and impossible to get to with all the weekend traffic jams on Route 6 below the Canal.

So, one cold March weekend Margot and I explored, starting in Rhode Island. As we came north along the Rhode Island coastline we couldn't find anything. The exposures were wrong, and the communities along the beaches were tacky. Around Providence we went and headed to Little Compton, following the Narragansett Bay along the Sakonnet River. Little Compton was beautiful, and the town with its old historic houses was nice, but it didn't seem like "us." It was too perfect and manicured, and it was evident that there was much wealth there.

As we drove through Little Compton, heading East, we got lost in the fog. Not knowing quite where we were, we stumbled into Adamsville, Rhode Island and took a road along the Westport River. We both immediately felt that this countrified and unpretentious atmosphere was right. And as we explored further our suspicions were confirmed. And since then Westport Harbour has more than exceeded our great expectations.

We rented a house for two summers, then we bought a wonderful old 1790 colonial beauty, in 1981, I think, after Mum had died. We sold her house and with my share we were able to buy now in Westport Harbour. It was the best investment we ever made in our happiness. It was pure luck that I called the real estate agent when I did, as we were leaving our rented house. I must call Joan Dennis, I said, and even though she seldom had Westport properties, being entrenched in Little Compton, I thought I should phone her out of friendship.

She said, "Oh, Lydia, I'm glad you called. I know of a property in Westport Harbour that's just come up for sale. It is an old farm house that has recently had a bad fire, and the owner wants to sell."

We made an immediate excursion to see it. Margot and I wanted to check it out alone first, but Ward and Margot's then boyfriend Michael insisted on coming along. We turned from the River Road onto Cross Road which is the high road connecting the two roads that run south to the beach. It is the top of the four mile rectangle that encompasses most of Westport Harbour. There was only one other house on this road, and we turned down a long straight driveway lined with hydrangea trees, not bushes. You could just see a corner of the house way at the end. There were big fields on either side, in one of them were cows.

Ward reached over from the back seat and excitedly said, "Now don't appear to be too eager to the real estate agent," and it was he that was too eager. Margot and I laughed.

Our first view of the house stopped us in our tracks it was so wonderful. A big porch surrounded this lovely colonial. There was still honeysuckle climbing all over, a big central brick chimney, and a huge pine tree large enough for Rockefeller Center sheltering the porch from the East. The fire's devastation was very evident inside, but as yet the roof was still on. The ground floor had had water damage, and the second floor was pretty well gutted, but the whole structure was miraculously saved by the huge chimney which carried the worst of the heat up and out.

Well, we bought it on the spot. Borden Tripp the owner, now one of our closest friends with his English wife Maureen, were happy to sell it to us. And we were stunned to find we were owners of a big house with 6 acres of land, stone walls, peach trees, grape trees, cows in fields, raspberries, and blackberries. It is sunny and open, and you can't see another house. Margot remodeled the inside with wonderful expertise providing me with a studio and a gallery. Above the gallery is a little balcony, and a high ceiling with skylights. We later put in another bedroom. The effect was wonderful and the house seemed to smile from all the new daylight that came in, after all the little dark rooms it used to have. My studio is in the ell over the kitchen, and I too have a big skylight. The bedrooms were all re-floored and painted and the old beams preserved.

The only thing we had to do downstairs was paint and paper. My favorite room is the dining room with its beams and doors going out to a little grassy patio. I wasn't very experienced at picking out wallpapers because when I was married I was only interested in modern architecture and decoration. Margot picked out most of the wallpapers and with taste, but it was I that found the dining room paper. I knew I wanted a soft deep red, like in the Japanese prints, cozy and nice. I looked and looked and looked, to no avail. I was desperate as the man was coming soon to apply it. I was in Exeter with Ward, and while he was in a meeting, I went to a small paint store that had wallpapers. I lugged the huge display books to the table and thumbed through endless terrible designs of peacocks, windmills, and hunting scenes. Then all of a sudden I saw my red paper. Absolute perfection. I turned the page over to get its name and order number. It was called the "Lydia" pattern!

When we first discovered Westport Harbour, Mum was in the nursing home in Plymouth. I felt badly that we didn't want to live in Duxbury, and hoped she wouldn't be too disappointed. One day I tried to describe to her all the glories of the new place we had lost our hearts to. I went on at some length about how Pup would have loved the natural surroundings, how he would have doted on all the ducks and geese and boating and wild life and the abundant sea food. As I was enumerating these, Mother seemed dozing off a bit. She often went in and out of her concentration. Her eyes were closed, but I sensed she was listening. I went on about Ward loving the good tennis, and I the good golf at the smashing little Acoaxet Club. I said that although it was only a nine hole course it was very difficult.

Mum suddenly came to, and looked at me with her blue eyes smiling. "There are mushrooms on the third hole!" I cannot play that hole ever without thinking of her, and picking the mushrooms. She must have played the course fifty years before. It comforts me to think that she knows where we are now.

We were not looking for sociability or new friends when we moved there. All we required was a private focus for us and the girls in which we could be together in the summer and holidays. But we found a wealth of wonderful people and feel very much at home in this ideal community. There is no keeping up with the Joneses. Everyone is devoted to his own property and beautiful vista of which there are many. I have been commissioned to paint many "favorite" views of marshes, ocean, beach, riverscapes, and boatyards. I am hanging over many fireplaces, and if I had a show of all that I have done you would see a composite of all the splendid facets of Westport Harbour. One lady who has a river view I painted from her house takes the painting with her to Florida every year. Another lady regularly takes my painting of a field of Queen Anne's lace first to Michigan, and then to California. I am very proud of my work done in this wonderful locale.

People when they come to visit are so taken with this undiscovered part of the world that they immediately contact a real estate agent to buy property. This Nancy and Bob Page did, and others are still sniffing around. There is very little to buy, as most of the property is held and cherished by owners who have lived there for years. The summer rentals, when and if they occur, are snatched up immediately. Lyn has been lucky enough to find a super rental every year in August on Boat House Row, right near the Wharf, and so smashing for the children. It gives them independence from us, yet we are nearby with washers and dryers and Sunday dinners.

Once when a couple from Washington came to visit we swam, played golf and tennis and they were dazzled by the whole place. When she wrote an effusive thank-you note, he appended a P.S. This surprised me as he was not a man of many words. He said, "Westport Harbour is like 'Brigadoon' that in its magic will vanish and not come back for a hundred years."

Another man, who was a bit citified, relished the view of the cows and open fields from our porch. As we were having drinks and sitting in the large black rockers we could hear the sound of the waves coming into shore from the beach to our south. There had been a lovely storm that had just cleared.

He remarked: "I didn't realize you were so near the thruway. I can hear the roar of the traffic."

"You ninny, that isn't traffic, it's the ocean," I said.

None of the old-timers would think of putting their houses right on the water. In the old days all the farms were set back and their fields ran right down to the rivers and ocean. So, too, ours, and although through the years the trees, hedges and vines have grown up all around the margins of the properties blocking out the former expanse of ocean view, we can see out our second floor windows to Cutty Hunk and Martha's Vineyard. And the ocean is very much a part of our environment. Our wonderful beach at Elephant Rock is as superior as any I have seen for swimming. Its curve of about a mile and a half is all sand and the swimming is good even at low tide. It is one of the few south facing beaches and therefore not rocky, except for pebbles that come in after a big storm. But these soon disappear. We spend many happy hours on this beach, which is marvelous also for the children.

I won't describe all our friends, but we are lucky to have many. Aud Wicks warrants a mention, however. This wonderful, funny man, who has recently died, was a gifted artist. When we first moved to Westport, a friend said that I must meet Aud Wicks as he was an artist too. Oh Lord, I thought, we'll probably hate each other. But we arranged to meet. We liked each other immediately and shared photos of our work and views.

As I was leaving, Aud, who was very short, put his arm around my waist and said, "Lydia, I'm so glad you have moved here. We will now have an artist's colony of two!"

In the beginning, after we had moved into our house, and the renovations had been completed, we had a mini-open house for some of the local residents, particularly those who had known the house in the old days and had been to many parties there when the Tripps were in residence. Everyone was very curious about us, and whether we would fit in, and if we had violated the essential character of this historic manse. They all came and discreetly snooped and peeped into every corner, seemingly much pleased. One man noticed we kept our liquor in the same cabinet. One lady remarked our sets of Shakespeare and Thackery were on the same shelves. One splendid lady stood for a long time in my gallery upstairs gazing at the lovely skylights, the indirect lighting and the openness of the once rabbit-warren area.

Looking up at the little gallery balcony she said, "Now isn't that nice. We can have it for our musicians at our Christmas parties." I knew we had passed the tests.

Westport Harbour is undiscovered for many reasons. One is that there is no main highway running through it, and no public place to go to once you get there. There are no restaurants, or stores or hotels or gas stations, and the beach and golf club are private. There is one kooky old inn, the Harbour Inn, near to the beach, but it is run by a kooky lady who will not change its old-fashionedness for love nor money. It used to be an old post office, general store and gas station, and until recently the ancient gas tanks stood in their art-deco glory in the front yard. One of the suites still has the old post office boxes in it. The other rooms are named after dead presidents and generals and have the same by-gone aura. When Margot was married we rented the whole inn for the bridesmaids and ushers. They all had a ball!

Although Westport Harbour is rural and totally uncommercial everyone shops up in Central Village a few miles up the road. You turn left beyond the horse trough onto Main Road and there can find all the stores you need: the best supermarket, the best apothecary, liquor stores, two fish markets, a not so classy beauty salon (behind a garage and junk yard), a boarding house for dogs, and a marvelous Lebanese veterinarian. There are two huge nurseries for buying plants and flowers. At the beginning of the River Road at the crossroad is "Manchester's Restaurant," an old establishment with vintage charm, rustic wooden beams and fireplaces, very cheery to go to. Even though the food isn't gourmet, it's plain American steaks, chops and lobster. I like it better than my family does.

Just beyond is "Grace's General Store," where one buys one's newspaper and sundries. We still call it Grace's. She died recently at the age of 90 or so. She was someone to reckon with. She had her likes and dislikes, and it took several years before she acknowledged our presence. Everybody congregates there in the early morning for coffee and newspapers. She sold the best Vermont cheddar cheese you ever tasted, cutting off big crumbling chunks with a huge cleaver, which she rammed into the enormous wheel of orange cheese. She didn't like a lot of the summer folk. Maureen Tripp told me that when she married Borden, Grace never paid any attention to her even though Borden was one of the leading elder statesmen in town. Finally after several years they got an invitation to Grace's New Year's party, which she gave every year, and invitations were much sought after. Maureen was very pleased now to be included. She wondered what in the world to wear and decided to be non-fancy and non-conspicuous. When she got there the party was in high gear, everybody in their fanciest outfits, with the most elaborate foods and liquors. Grace met them at the door with champagne. She had on a jazzy sequined cocktail dress, much eye makeup and gold fingernail polish. Pretty good for 85 years old. Maureen felt like Mary Poppins. So much for a "rural" gathering.

We constantly count our blessings that we found Westport Harbour. It was Divine guidance, I am convinced, and it has brought us into focus so totally with our girls and ourselves, more than we could possibly have imagined. As I am writing now we have just heard that Margot and Eric have struck water. They are building a house on a piece of our property which gives us the greatest delight and satisfaction. Just because the parents love a place does not necessarily mean that the children will want to come there. Aren't we lucky!

XI

"Pilgrims"

I have been obsessed for years with the hope of producing a full-scale historical musical based on the Pilgrims. This crazy ambition has burned inside me for nearly thirty years, and during that time there hasn't been a day that I haven't thought about it. Every moment when I have vowed to give up altogether and banish the script to the top shelf of my closet, something positive would happen and there it would be yapping for attention. It will not go away.

"Pilgrims" is the story of the voyage of the Mayflower and the Pilgrim settlement in the New World. These full-blooded Elizabethans were our first Boat People. They had exiled themselves from the terrible tyranny of an English society which was in the dreadful grip of a corrupt king and a dogmatic church. The Pilgrims gave up everything to find an environment in which they could grow and prosper in freedom. They were not Puritanical fanatics.

The school pageants which get dusted off in time for Thanksgiving do not do justice to these energetic pioneers and the story of their exodus from England and subsequent confrontation with the "savage" New World is stirring and eminently worthy of a fine-spirited musical. The love triangle between John Alden, Priscilla Mullins and Myles Standish is the soul of musical theatre. Squanto, the "twice-kidnapped" Indian who had been captured and taken twice to England is a strong, made-for-Broadway role and the contrapuntal Saints and Strangers on the voyage make for vivid theatrical contrasts.

In the late forties when I was working in New York, Mother was writing a script for the annual Yacht Club Show based on the Pilgrims. It was a natural for this Duxbury audience as one could gaze across the Duxbury Bay to Clark's Island and Plymouth where the Pilgrims landed. Mum was a wonderful writer and had taken advanced degrees in playwriting at Radcliff after Bryn Mawr. She had studied under Professor George Baker at Harvard, an eminent dramatist and teacher. Here in Duxbury she collaborated with Foster Trainer who in his time at Harvard had composed music for several of the Hasty Pudding shows.

When the time came for the musical to be performed I came to Duxbury and was caught up in all the theatrical business and rehearsals. The title of the musical was "Pardon Us Plymouth," which Mum had named in honor of "PUP," which is what we called my Father. The night before the opening I rehearsed my brother Steve in the kitchen. He had the male lead John Alden, and I must say it was good casting. He had to leap over three barrels while singing "I'm a super-duper cooper, and a conscientious hooper . . ." We set up trash cans. It was quite tricky. In the love song "Speak For Yourself" Priscilla has a nifty rhyme: "You are outlandish, you, asking me for Myles Standish." This local musical was a smash hit, and even though provincial and amateurish, it had a wonderful ring to it. You could hear people saying as they filed out to the lawn and onto the piers, "Why, it's just as good as 'South Pacific.'"

I went back to New York with the feeling that here was a wonderful theme for a Broadway musical, if it was handled by professionals. After Ward and I were married, and the children were somewhat grown up, I set about trying to put a New York team together. That was almost thirty years ago, and I am still at it.

I began by establishing my own concept of the material and did a great deal of research. The more I knew about the period and the characters, the more enthusiastic I became. The dusty, boring facts on the Pilgrims that one gets in Longfellow and school books is enough to put anyone off. I was excited by the beautiful, simple English prose of "Bradford's Diary" which gives the only eyewitness account of this extraordinary odyssey. William Brewster, the Elder of the Pilgrims, had already exiled himself and a small band of Englishmen in Holland for seven years. And it was from Holland that plans were made to emigrate to America. Conditions in England were intolerable under James Ist, and with the tyranny of church as well as state, there was great discontent and outrage voiced underground in universities and dissident churches. There was no such thing as free press or free speech. Brewster started a secret printing press in Holland and gave implementation to the growing opposition. At the time that Brewster was to board the Mayflower there was a price on his head for treason and sedition, and he had to be smuggled on board the ship. And at that point my musical "Pilgrims" began.

My efforts to produce this play have been characterized by agony and ecstasy. The agonies have come from commissioning a series of writers to produce a book for me, none of whom were up to the task, and all of whom took endless months to produce the goods. Without exception I wanted to sink all the scripts to the bottom of the ocean. They strayed from my concept, the characters were hateful and ill-conceived, and none did justice to the full potential of the glorious subject. At the outset I was fortunate to find John Duffy a composer, and he brought Jan Hartman into the project. We then found a good lyricist Anne Croswell and things started out fine. But we needed money, and a decent outline of the libretto in order to raise the necessary funds. I am very good at raising money, and where my "Pilgrims" was concerned could talk my way into anyone's wallet. But it's one thing to talk about it. It's another thing to get the creative produce completed and read to sail. Also this team of mine had to be paid. There was nothing they did on speculation. And as we went along there was also Shelly Markham, the magnificent arranger of Duffy's music, and later still when we put a real audition together, there were the singers to pay. I raised all the upfront money to do this, and we had some very exciting auditions in New York and Connecticut.

One of my greatest encouragements came from a backers' audition we held in New Canaan, Connecticut. The performers were exciting and the music gorgeously presented. In forty-five minutes we had raised pledges of over $100,000. The audience of prospective backers raved about it and were eager to participate to the full. But these were pledges, and I wisely didn't convert them to cash until the script was completed and the musical score totally composed. Then my first agony occurred. Jan Hartman, the writer who was commissioned to write the full script, took almost two years to do so. When I finally got it the subject matter was unrecognizable and unacceptable. Furthermore, without telling me, he was working on another script of his own dealing with the Nuremberg Trials, a subject with which he was obsessed. He had no time to focus on "Pilgrims."

I presented several other backers' auditions which confirmed that if we could complete the work we would have good financial support. I found a co-producer in Joel Schenker, but he turned out to be a terrible disappointment. He wouldn't even share with me the cost of paying for the Security and Exchange documents that were required. Then in the next years I hired other writers. I gave Stephen Rosenfield three cracks at it and had to reject all three efforts. Then there was Gerson, Haney, Colby and Ashworth, all of whom tried and failed. It took the marrow out of my bones to inspire and motivate each one of these scriptwriters. I was able to ignite them but not insure a satisfactory end-product.

I did have an exciting flurry of success, however, when Hilary Elkins called me up from London saying that he had heard about my musical and wanted to be a part of it. He is a New York producer and is married to Claire Bloom. He said he was returning shortly to New York and didn't want me to sign with anybody else before he got home. He said we could make another "Fiddler on the Roof," or a "1776" and all we had to do was put a creative team together. Well! This was a switch—to be courted! When he got back we started collaborating in earnest and put an excellent team together. The first time we all assembled in Hilly's office there were my composer John Duffy, our lyricist Anne Croswell, Ed Sherrin, a director married to Jane Alexander, and Sherman Yellen, a writer, and Elkins. While we were sitting there a call came in for Hilly which he took. It was David Merrick on the line. Hilly said he was sorry he couldn't talk now, he was with Lydia Chamberlin. Merrick blasted from the other end, "Who the hell is Lydia Chamberlin?"

The team was ready to move forward. And about a week later I drove into New York from Wilson Point to finalize our agreements. As I was going over the Triborough Bridge, I couldn't believe this turn of events. It was Big Time stuff, and I had been the catalyst of it all. My play was finally going to be produced, and by pros. Two days later, before all the legal papers had been drawn up, I was crestfallen to read in the theatre section of the *New York Times* that a new play "Rex" was just being mounted with William Adler money, produced by Hillary Elkins, directed by Ed Sherrin, and written by Sherman Yellin!

That's show-biz for you! I took all my marbles and went home. "Rex" opened in Washington about a year later, just after Ward and I had moved here. We went to the opening at the Kennedy Center, and I took great comfort in the fact that it was an unadulterated bomb. I bumped into Ed Sherrin between the acts as he was mingling with the crowd to determine audience reaction. He looked shaken. I said, "Wonderful show, Ed. Too bad you didn't do 'Pilgrims' instead."

After all the cajoling, hand-holding, re-writing I had done over the years, I realized when I came to Washington that there was only one person in this world who could write the script and that was me. For better or worse that is what I have done. I think the script is good enough to stand on its own if it could be shaped and tailored and crafted for the stage. I have had to leave Duffy and Croswell, and go back to square one with the music. I have completed enough of the lyrics for a composer to work around. And this very day I am expecting in overnight mail a completed score by Stanley Wietrzchowski who has been working on it for over a year. He was my composer, pianist and arranger way back at Upstage. He has taken on the assignment with the greatest enthusiasm although I'm afraid, from the little I've seen of his efforts, that he is not creatively up to the richness of the task. It's one thing to play Gershwin like a musical genius. It's another thing to be Gershwin.

Maybe it's just as well I have never been able to put this musical on. It would have changed my life totally, and I am not thick-skinned enough to weather all the double-crossing, the vagaries, the disappointments, the agonies of producing a Broadway musical. I have noticed how original concepts, good as they may be, get screwed when the going gets rough. The powers that be sit in a hotel room in Chicago and try to "fix" what's wrong. One will say the left arm has to come off. Another the right leg; a third says, "no . . . off with it's head." You cannot be creative by committee! I couldn't stand it! I've talked many people into believing this musical could be done. I agonize over the realization finally that it possibly cannot, at least not by me.

I have now received the musical score from Stanley. It is much better than I thought. It is wonderful to hear one's lyrics encapsulated in music. We may have a chance, but there is still much to be done.

XII

The Shakespeare
Authorship Question

A belief which I hold very strongly is that William Shakespeare from Stratford-Upon-Avon could not have, under any circumstances, written the dramatic body of works ascribed to him. I am a strong advocate of Edward de Vere, the 17th Earl of Oxford as being the true author of the plays. The concealment of Oxford's authorship is one of the great unsolved mysteries in the history of literature. Many people have doubted the Stratford man's claim, including Bismark, Thoreau, Benjamin Franklin, John Galsworthy among others, and the band has been growing steadily over the years.

The case against William Shakespeare from Stratford-Upon-Avon is based on the great gulf between the man's life and the works themselves. When you consider that the works of Shakespeare are the greatest treasures of literature in the English language and you try to "marry" these with what is known about the author to whom they are attributed, you are overwhelmed by incredulity. I was! Many times when I have brought up this question of authorship with people as yet un-grabbed by the stunning possibility of an author other than the conventional Stratford man, I have winced when they say, "Who cares who wrote them; we have the plays, and that is what matters." It isn't the only thing that matters, and I care very much.

There is no way that an artist can write from anything other than his own experience. Great ideas do not just spring out of one's forehead as if touched by God, or by being immaculately conceived. True creativity emerges from the marrow of one's life, strengthened by education, nourished by association with other great minds, and tempered by the creative and scientific environment in which it is born. I will not believe that these masterpieces of literature could have been produced by an uneducated man whose four different known signatures on separate documents are scrawls, no better than illiterate marks, who in his will could only leave to his wife his pigs and his second-best bed. No books, no manuscripts, nothing to indicate the accoutrements of a pre-eminent literary genius. When "Shakespeare" died there was no fanfare, nothing to mark the passing of a great man. And Elizabethans loved and honored their poets and dramatists above all people.

Some say, "You don't have to be highly educated to write great poetry." No, but if you look at Chaucer, or Robert Burns, or Robert Frost consider their subject matter—they are writing from their experience and their own rural environment. "A Miller's Tale," a "Cotters Saturday Night," "The Hired Hand," "Stopping by the Woods on a Snowy Evening," "Birches." These are all gorgeous works, but they are not "Hamlet, the King of Denmark," "Richard the Third," or "Henry V." To talk about a mouse as a "wee timorous cowerin' beastie" is one thing. Talking about kings and royal relationships, law and falconry, chivalry and court manners, Ovid and Plautus, is another. He added over 2,000 new words to the English language, an accomplishment not in the capability of an ordinary mortal. Milton only added a couple of hundred.

The plays reveal an intimate knowledge of court life at the highest levels, and indeed suggest noble privacy to Queen Elizabeth that could not have been enjoyed by anyone less than an Earl or a Duke. "Hamlet" is thought to be autobiographical, with Polonius modelled after William Cecil Lord Burghley who was Queen Elizabeth's principal minister. Ophelia and Laertes are most surely Robert Cecil, Burghley's son, and Ann Cecil, Burghley's daughter who married the Earl of Oxford, our candidate for authorship. Oxford's life closely parallels Hamlet's. And you can't just dream up the soliloquy in Henry the Fifth the night before the battle of Agincourt "Upon the King."

I first became aware of this authorship question through Mum who was a staunch Oxfordian. I read the material she had and wasn't particularly galvanized until I discovered "Shakespeare Identified" by Thomas Looney, written in 1924, which could well be the greatest bit of historical research by a non-academic professional ever accomplished. Looney (pronounced Low-ney, but unfortunately no one does) systematically went through

144

all the plays and sonnets recording what kind of knowledge and experience would a dramatist have to have in order to write such subject matter. What did the plays reveal about the author, whoever he might be, and what contemporary author in England could match those requirements. It is impossible to conceive the gentleman to be dull Bacon, or unsubstantial Marlowe, and anyway if they had been the author, we would have known it. But the man who fit the profile to a tee was Edward de Vere the 17th Earl of Oxford, a Renaissance man, a recognized poet, the highest Earl in the land, a patron of several acting companies which played often at Court, a scholar, a soldier, and a swashbuckler.

As it was dangerous, ungentlemanly, and un-politic for a nobleman to sign his plays, most of the plays are unsigned, and only at a later date did someone affix the name Shakespeare to them. It is thought to have been a pseudonym, assumed to decoy identity from the real author.

No manuscript has ever been found to prove or disprove whether "Shakespeare" or Oxford wrote the plays. Only Folios, or printings remain. It is thought that the originals were systematically destroyed by Lord Burghley to wipe out all traces of Oxford's identity. He was "in disgrace with fortune and men's eyes," an outcast. Not only had Oxford divorced Burghley's daughter, but also some say that after a flaming affair with Elizabeth, the Queen gave birth to a baby boy. This does not fit the hype Burghley created as a public relations master stroke, the image of Elizabeth as the "Virgin Queen." Elizabeth's pregnancy could have been concealed by going on a "Progress" which she did frequently to manor houses all over England when it suited her, sometimes for months at a time. Also the costumes she wore could conceal a baby elephant. It is further suggested that the child born thus to such eminent parents was the Earl of Southampton, to whom the glorious sonnets are dedicated. These sonnets, if read with this possibility in mind, take on new meaning and lustre.

The two most ardent supporters of the Oxford claim in Washington have been David Lloyd-Kreeger and myself. Although David died last year in 1990, he and I have talked many times at parties together about our shared conviction. He put in a great deal of time and effort into organizing "The Great Debate" at the American University, a debate between a Stratford advocate and an Oxford advocate, the outcome to be judged by three justices of the Supreme Court, William Brennan, Henry Blackman and John Paul Stephens. The format was an original one and the event which took place in the huge church near the University was remarkable for the huge crowds that showed up. The nave was jammed and there were people standing in the aisles. There were a thousand people inside and a hundred or so standing outside. The judges looked very impressive in their black robes.

But the problem with the whole thing was the choice Lloyd-Kreeger made in the two advocates who were poorly prepared and uncommitted to their subject. They couldn't have cared less and were only mouthing arguments that they had so recently been presented with. Ward had interviewed them sometime earlier and he was startled to find how little they knew and how totally unconcerned they were about the outcome. Oh, for a bit of conviction. And many convincing arguments were ignored. The judges quite rightly handed down the opinion that the burden of proof could not be established for the case of Oxford, and so had to maintain the Stratford status quo. There was a dinner afterwards at President Berenson's house for all the judges and other participants. Charlton Ogburn who wrote the huge impressive volume *This Star of England* in which a strong scholarly case is made for Oxford was there, but I must say our camp was terribly depressed and seemingly discredited. Lloyd-Kreeger was master of ceremonies, but he was paying attention to protocol and the judges, and never once made an acknowledgment of Ogburn's lovely presence. I was waiting for him to do so as I had a good poem made for our team and would have followed the lead. But for one of the only times in my life I was tongue-tied, and went home with my poem un-sung. I have regretted it, for I very much wanted to honor Ogburn, as well as Oxford.

Passions are aroused over this authorship question. Ironically, I have come to realize that the academics are the most entrenched and close-minded of all. They would have to fear for their academic lives if it were proved that someone other than the Stratford man authored the plays. Take for instance Professor A.L. Rowse, an eccentric old lady of a Shakespearean scholar who will not even discuss the matter and dismisses the subject as crack-pot. Ward and I went to a small dinner party at which Rowse was guest of honor. There were two tables of six. Ward was relieved to see that I was not seated at the Rowse table. He had instructed me to keep my mouth shut and not get involved as it would spoil the evening. I was dutifully silent until I heard Rowse holding forth about the great Victorian poets of England, and stating that background and education were paramount to the development of the greatest poets. I turned my chair around and when I began saying, "If you hold that opinion, Mr. Rowse, how do you account for. . . . ," when Ward leaped up and interrupted by asking me if I would like another cup of coffee.

At another small dinner party in Connecticut I was seated next to Louis Auchincloss, the novelist and writer who has written on Shakespeare. It was a disastrous placement. Apart from being dour and dyspeptic and uncharming as a dinner partner, it didn't help that he took an instant aversion to me. I couldn't resist asking him what he thought of the possibility that someone other than Shakespeare of Stratford could have written the plays. I said nothing more incendiary than that. He turned absolutely purple, said something scathing to me, threw his napkin on the table and left the party altogether. Ward said I must have said something impossibly rude to him. I did not.

Somewhere somehow an original manuscript will be found in one of those stately libraries in the stately homes of England tucked unseen for years in a copy of Ovid, or Plautus, or Holinshed's chronicles. All traces of the manuscripts of the greatest plays ever to be written in any language could not have been erased altogether. Perhaps there are hidden papers in the funeral monument urn at Stratford-Upon-Avon where the "bard" is buried. But no one will ever know what's in it until one storms the citadel, for it is forbidden to open it. I would love to be a part of a night raid on this bastion. Poor old Stratford would sink into the Avon like Atlantis, never to be seen again if its native son were discredited.

XIII

Philosophy and Religion

I am a Unitarian at heart. I do not subscribe to the dogma of religion, and find when I go to even an Episcopalian service I cannot bring myself to say the words, "I believe in the Father and the Son and the Holy Ghost." I don't. (I used to tell the girls, when we went to a wedding or some service that celebrated the Trinity, not to say these "I believes.") The fundamental belief of a Unitarian is just that, the unity of God and Man, and that Christ was no more "divine" than man himself. Only he was better at it. No man is more chosen than another by God. That eliminates Popes and Cardinals and the concept of Special Eminence. I don't believe in original sin, and am horrified with the Bible when Satan is mentioned, or the story of the expulsion from the Garden of Eden, or when in the Baptism ceremony a tiny child must be expurgated of the original sin bequeathed to him from the time of Adam and Eve. I must add the definition of a Unitarian that makes me smile. "A Unitarian believes in the Unity of God, the Divinity of Man, in the Vicinity of Boston."

I am not a voracious reader, but there are a few books that I have metabolized well, and which have developed strong concepts in me. One of these is *The African Genesis* by Robert Ardrey. In it Ardrey examines his own and other genesises and comes up with a philosophy that was a breath of fresh air to me. Like Darwin he believes that living organisms developed by evolution, and like Leakey he sees man's origins as evolving from animal primates. At the end of this book he says that he is much encouraged to find that he "descends from risen ape rather than fallen man." Isn't that nifty!

A second book of Ardrey's which I found illuminating was *The Territorial Imperative*. In this he expounds the theory that man is impelled in life by three imperatives—Territory, his Status, and Sex—in that order. An animal or a bird will defend his territory more vigorously than he would defend his position. He would defend his position in the pecking order before he would defend his mate. And his sexual imperatives were defended last. Isn't that splendid, too! I always thought that sex as such was greatly overestimated as a priority. Although I do believe Love is at the top of all human needs. The ability to love generally separates humans from animals.

There is, however, much in the Bible that has animated my life. Some of the old prophets in the Old Testament I can relate to better than in the New Testament. I can't stand preachy St. Paul, and I'm not too crazy about the holier-than-thou Apostles. I will have to look up in the Bible, however, where the phrase "the peace of God which passeth all understanding" comes from. This remarkable condition implies the existence of order and demands true non-intellectual belief in the existence of God. When the going gets tough, and life seems all out of kilter, and forces are descending over which one has no control, then I pull out this phrase and feel more able to cope. It works like magic.

Martin Luther King in one of his sermons in Alabama, a Christmas sermon, I think, struck such an affirmative note when he called on his congregation to lift up their souls, in spite of earthly misery and violence, to the heavens where they could plug in to a "cosmic companionship." That knocked my socks off. Isn't it a superb phrase! And the use of the word "companionship" is dazzling. The millions of stars all move in the heavens without colliding with each other, that order had its genesis somewhere, call it what you will. It's a pity that on our own crowded orb we are bumping into each other constantly.

In life one can't fathom the why of magic, but one can instantly recognize when magic occurs. I have written earlier my indebtedness to Shakespeare. I particularly value Henry V which I practically know by heart. It was all due to the Laurence Olivier movie version of this great drama which I probably have seen fifteen times, and have been in love with Olivier all my life. At the drop of a hat I can recite the great soliloquy *Upon the King* spoken the night before the terrible Battle of Agincourt, also the moving speech that fires up the troops: *Crispin Crispian*, and the gorgeous "Once More Unto The Breach, dear friends," calling for new vigor during the battle. When Ward and I traveled with Margot and Eric to France a few years ago I experienced two bits of cosmic companionship not unlike magic.

We were in two cars as we left Paris. Our first stop was Honfleur, and then to Bayeux on our way to the Loire. I was totally unprepared for the unbelievably splendid Bayeux Tapestry. In all my "proper" education no one had done justice to this wonderous woven object. The beautiful installation enhanced the excitement, as one followed the story of the Norman Invasion of England by William the Conqueror. I for the first time totally emphasized with the Norman's claim to the throne and scorned miserable Harold. After all Edward the Confessor on his deathbed told Harold his unfavorite nephew, to go to France to get William to sign the succession papers (thereby bypassing Harold for the succession). Everything was in order until on his return home the Saxons convinced Harold that he should double-cross the King's wishes. Forget William, be King yourself, they said, and the Norman Invasion of England began. I now had a new hero in William, and I was crazy about Mathilda his wife, who with her ladies wove the marvelous tapestry, the true eyewitness story. When it came time to leave Bayeux I hated to go. Ward and I got into our little white rental car, with Margot and Eric in theirs, early one sunny morning. As Ward got in the driver's seat he asked me to look at the map, and also check our mileage. I looked at the mileage on the dashboard. It registered *1066*.

When we got to the Chateau district of the Loire we stayed in an old remodeled convent, on the banks of the Loire. This inn was very beautifully situated, as it was high up and had a gorgeous view down to the river and across to a little town set on the water's edge of a huge flat cultivated plain, dotted as far as the eye could see with tiny farm houses. These lodgings were very atmospheric, and very expensive. After a delicious dinner we went to bed. I woke up during the night to find a full moon shining directly on our bed. I got up and threw open the casement windows whose mullions formed a diamond pattern in the moonlight on the floor. I leaned out on my elbows and gazed like Rapunzel at the incredibly beautiful view below. The air was very still, it had a champagne feeling and the moon was so bright that you could see the little town, the church steeple, the quiet Loire, and the fields beyond. I was entranced. Then it happened. A rooster crowed three times. The bell in the church tower struck three times. As when on the night before the Battle of Agincourt:

Henry says:

> The cock doth crow, the clock doth toll
> The third hour of drowsy morn.

As we explored this lovely part of the Loire I was constantly on the lookout for Eleanor of Aquitaine whose vast realms in Aquitaine and Anjou and Poitou in the 12th century made her one of the richest and most influential women of France. I had read Amy Kelly's biography, *Eleanor of Aquitaine* and was fascinated by this beautiful, fiery, energetic woman. She went on crusades with such a lavish retinue of people and equipment that even Cleopatra would have been stunned. Eleanor wheeled and dealed with the highest rank of nobles and prelates of the Church, always manipulating events in her own favor. Before she was ever Queen of France or of England she held in her own right a province beyond the Loire as sovereign as any king's. Eleanor divorced King Louis of France to marry Henry of Anjou who later became Henry II of England. Henry was the first of the English Plantagenets.

I found out where the word "Plantagenet" came from. I discovered that Henry, Duke of Normandy's mother, Mathilde, had married a rich duke of Anjou, Guy de Fouques. Mathilde was the granddaughter of William the Conquerer, from whence came Henry's claim to the English throne. Guy de Fouques was something of a dandy and when he dressed for occasions he always stuck a jaunty sprig of broom in his cap. Broom in French is "genet," hence "plant-a-genet." Henry, when he came courting Eleanor in Anjou, carried on the family "dress code:"

> "When Henry came riding his stallion over the bridge
> of Moutierneuf he carried a falcon on his wrist and
> a sprig of genet in his bonnet."

I've digressed a bit but I've sensed a bit of magic companionship in these stories.

I don't want to seem unconcerned about formal religions, but I think that Catholicism, Judaism, Protestantism, Zen Buddism, and all the isms make schisms which separate people from each other. God couldn't have fashioned all those different rituals, rites and regulations for *His* contemplation. When one goes down any Main Street, USA, one sees the various churches valiantly trying to keep their identity and their congregations together. The Baptist, Congregational, Episcopal, Catholic, Christian Science, Methodist, Latter-Day-Saints, Mormon, Greek Orthodox Churches are all preaching their separatist doctrines. It seems to me that as in *Onward Christian Soldiers* "all one body, we," though not necessarily Christian.

It would be callous and obdurate of me, however, not to acknowledge the immeasurable debt of gratitude one owes to the great religions of the world for their majestic contribution to Art, Architecture and Music. Strong faith has produced transcendent art, and in a sense this is magic.

A man who had just completed a phenomenal feat of sailing solo around the world (I think), was interviewed on television and was asked all the normal questions as to how he could possibly have managed all the lonely hours, the danger, the violent storms, etc. When responding to the question, what was the worst moment of all, he said it was not the storms that bothered him the most but the endless days when he was becalmed. The frightening nothingness in a vast sea, hour after hour.

He did describe one terrible storm when his mast broke, his rudder came loose, and he had no power to keep the boat into the wind and was helplessly tossed around like a cork in the raging seas. He thought to himself that he was not even half-way on his journey, and he was very far from land. He began to lose his confidence and the conviction that he could survive. He began to estimate how much longer he could stay alive. As he looked to the future he determined a month more would be unthinkable, a week more would kill him. He would go out of his mind in even two more days. But, he reckoned: "I know I can make it for the next two hours." And he put a succession of these two hours together, and survived.

This is a philosophy worth remembering when the going is tough, and you do not know how you can cope. When the long pull seems bleak, and you are in danger of falling apart, you find that you do have the strength to cope with the next two hours.

*   *   *

There are paintings that I would make pilgrimages to see. The portrait of *Genevra Benci* by Leonardo da Vinci, right here in Washington is probably my most favorite portrait in the world. This young contemplative girl has eyes and eye-lids of sheerest exquisiteness, and a mouth whose lips defy verbal analysis. The smooth hair, and the glow of her skin are so beautiful, as is also the Tuscan hill town of Urbino in the distance behind her. To my way of thinking she is far superior to the Mona Lisa, and nicer.

Worth a special trip to Cortona, Italy is to see the *Annuciation* of Fra Angelico in a tiny museum near the central medieval town square. All *Annunciations* are not created equally, for even the greatest masters sometimes miss, as Leonardo did with one of his *Annunciations* in the Uffizi in Florence. The problem is to make the two figures an artistic whole, and this can be done only by a third mystical element which is the Spirit. Mary and the Angel are only linear without the third dimension, an equilateral triangle is what is needed. This is superbly accomplished in Fra Angelico's wonderful masterpiece. This Renaissance treasure is beautifully mounted on its "altar" in the Diocesan Church in Cortona whose marble and gold installation heightens the spiritual and dramatic effect.

Piera Della Francesca is high on my list of favorite painters. His greatest paintings are collected in his Tuscan hometown of Sansepulcro where in the *Museo Civico* are two of his greatest master works. The fresco of *The Resurrection of Christ* is heart-stopping, but my favorite is the many pan-elled *Madonna della Misericordia*. Not far from Sansepulcro is Monterchi where in a cemetery chapel all by itself in a field is Piero's *Madonna del Parto*, the only pregnant Madonna in any Italian painting. It is a fresco not to be missed. I have always loved the profile portraits in the Uffizi in Florence of the *Duke of Urbino* and his *Wife Battista*. All five paintings by Della Francesca warrant a whole trip to Italy.

When Ward and I were in France in October, we chanced upon a splendid museum in Rennes on our way from Paris to Brittany. There we found the surprisingly good *Musèe des Beaux-Arts* which has one of the best collections of paintings outside Paris including a Sisley, a Van Gogh, a Caillebotte, a Seurat, etc. But it was Georges de la Tour's *"La Nouveau-Ne"* which totally knocked our socks off. This gorgeous painting of the Madonna in a red dress, with a baby wrapped in white, and the profiled attendant holding the concealed candle is now my favorite painting of all time. I had never seen it even reproduced before, and I have been on the lookout for Georges de la Tours for a long time. I must send to the Musee for more reproductions of it, for I cherish the only one I have.

I must include Goya's paintings on my most favored list, although no one emerges as a top runner. The unforgettable *"Dos de Mayos,"* the huge painting of the massacre of the peasants who led an uprising against the King is unforgettable, and I admire the Goya engravings *"Los Capprichos,"* and also the lovely Spanish señoritas sitting on their balconies, who are not really hiding behind their fans, is splendid.

I have mentioned how I love the Japanese woodcut prints that I was introduced to in Paris at the Carlhians. The beautiful Utamaro's of the lady courtesans are top favorites still. But also memorable are the Japanese painters Hiroshige and Sharaku, and I would be thrilled to be in their presence at any time.

The wonderful Museum of Fine Arts in Boston has a John Singer Sargent portrait of the *Boit Sisters*. These lovely children in their pinafores and "proper" little girl dresses capture a just-gone-by era of manners, nannies, nurseries and privilege, but they will never be dated. Their moment in time is perfection. This huge canvas is to-die-over.

I have always loved the American luminists, Fitzhugh Lane, Martin Heade, Sanford Gifford, and Thomas Eakins. What a wonderful exhibition of Luminists was here in Washington. Although no one stands far above the rest, I favor Fitzhugh Lane's various paintings of boats at anchor in Boston harbour. I love the parchment colored sails against the grey misty skies. Whites and blacks are the most traditionally difficult colors to employ in painting. But I think that grays are. And how seldom they are used effectively.

My wild, uncontrollable erotic nature is dazzled by Gustav Klimpt, that erotic Austrian painter, whose erotic, wild, decorative canvasses exude beauty and sensuality. Fortunately his genius as a painter transcends his subject matter. His color orchestrations are electrifying.

There are two small Vermeer portraits in the National Gallery of Art which I would gladly sell my soul for. These two girls are so individual and unmistakably Dutch that you would recognize them immediately if you ran into them walking along a dike in Amsterdam.

There is a radio show that we carry on WETA-FM called "Desert Island Discs." It is a copy of a BBC show that has been running in England for many years. In it a "cast-away" is chosen to imagine he has been marooned on a desert island. There is food, and miraculously a stereo record player available, and a complete set of Shakespeare and the Bible. Beyond that the cast-away is asked to pick the eight records of pieces of music he would choose to be with him on his remote desert island. I have selected my records already in case they should ask me to be on the show:

1) Piano Concerto #2, by Sergei Rachmaninoff
2) The Brahms Requiem
3) From Bach's Anna Magdalena Notebook: Du Bist Bei Mir
4) Romeo and Juliet Fantasy Overture, Tchaikovsky
5) La Boheme, Puccini
6) Strauss Waltz: Either Blue Danube or Tales From the Vienna Woods
7) Dein Ist Mein Ganze Hertz
8) Begin the Beguine or All The Things You Are or In the Still of the Night

After that you are allowed one luxury item. In that food is already provided I assume I don't have to bring Belgian Endive, fresh asparagus, artichokes and Hollandaise sauce, or Zablione.

But as a special luxury I would bring the Olivier recordings of Henry V, Hamlet, Macbeth, and hopefully memorize all the parts I don't know. (I would also need a year's supply of Dewar's Scotch, if that wasn't too much to ask) (and a case of Lark 100's).

XIV

Who Is Who?

There may be some additions to make to the narrative part of my life, and I will insert stories as they occur to me. But I must move on to describing those people nearest and dearest to me. I am finding it hard to synthesize thoughts on my Mother and Father. They were two such different people, but each were integral in my life in their special ways.

MY FATHER

Mum and Pa (or Pup), as we called him, met in a mixed-foursome club golf tournament in Duxbury. Mum acknowledge later that although Stephen Gifford was the handsomest man she ever saw, she was a bit put off at first by his loud argyle knee socks and his plaid knickers. Furthermore he was chewing gum. They were runners-up in the two-day tournament, and after that he courted Mum every day for the rest of the summer. Mum's family summered on Powder Point in a glorious new house which was featured in articles in the architectural magazines. It had two wings that sloped gently away from the central body like a well-built airplane. It embraced a lovely garden with a tiny round pool and grape arbor in back. It was here that Ward and I were married. My father's family owned an old mellow Cape Cod cottage on Cedar Street off the main street into town. We have lived in and loved both of these houses, although during the Depression we had to rent out the Powder Point house to make ends meet.

I remember the upheaval caused in my family when it was learned that

the Catholic Church was going to build a large new church right opposite
our Cedar Street driveway in a field that always had Mr. Mosher's cows.
My father was apoplectic to think that there was any need for a church
other than Unitarian in this tiny New England town. My brother and I revelled
in the new construction of the church and would climb all over the rafters
and beams like monkeys. One day when we came to climb, our pet chicken
Maizie followed us over to the church. She pecked around below as we
scooted far up into the scaffolding. Some Portuguese family came in to
view the construction and soon Steve and I heard some piercing squawks
and saw a young boy chasing Maizie. We climbed down as fast as we
could, only to see the car they were in disappear with Maizie peering out
the back window.

After the church was built and the Sunday services began, Pa would
have early breakfast every Sunday and commence his vigil and patrol along
the sidewalk in front of our house to see that no Catholics parked there.
I think he rather enjoyed getting all steamed up once a week.

My father was tall, dark and handsome, a cross between John Barry-
more and Lord Mountbatten. His good looks had come down to him from
the Gifford side of his family, strongly New England, but as beautifully
symmetrical as a Greek statue. My grandfather had posed for one of the
Minutemen in the famous statue in Concord. Pa's brothers were both wonderful
looking, Robert with his dark mustache was like a matinee idol, and Chandler though more homespun was stunning. Florence, his sister, must have
been lovely when she was young. Pa was a great favorite with the ladies,
and loved to flirt, and although Mother kept an eye on him at parties, she
didn't have anything to worry about, I'm sure. In the days when they were
first married, and later too, there were many parties and dances and mas-
querades, and treasure hunts and bridge games. Entertainment was then
created at home, this being a time before the onslaught of television. For
any birthday or anniversary there were poems and songs contributed by
each member of the family for the honored one. Mother was marvelous at
this, and composed fun and original material, especially for Pa's birthday.
She spent long hours writing her poems and they tickled my father to death.
He got the greatest kick out of her efforts. I, too, was writing doggerel at
an early age.

We used to take family picnics in the car. Mother prepared a large
hamper of food, and she and Pa and Grandma Gifford and Steve and I
would pile into the old chewing-gum colored Franklin and head for the
Cape or to one of the gorgeous freshwater ponds in Plymouth. Pa thought

the Franklin a high tech state-of-the-art car in that it had an air-cooled engine like an airplane. The back seat was much higher than the front seat, like a chariot. When we went to Long Pond, or Boot Pond in Plymouth, we parked under the pine trees right by the edge of the water. I adored the swimming and jumping into the water from the pine-needle beach. It all smelled wonderfully piney, and the water was sparklingly clear. On the way home we invariably stopped and got ice cream cones at our favorite Dutchland Farms. My father's favorite was ginger. I loved the frozen pudding. The Cape Cod canal was completed in the thirties, and I can remember when the Bourne Bridge was opened over it, and there we were crossing it in our tan Franklin.

I sometimes wonder how Pa's life would have been different if the Depression hadn't taken place, and the economy been strong. The first years of my parents' marriage (in 1920) were so promising. My father was in the wool business as a wool broker and he bought and sold wool "tops," as the unprocessed wool was called, from South America mostly, and Australia. He was a good businessman and had the charm to sell anyone anything. He also had the bearing of a diplomat, beautifully but understatedly dressed in his imported English suits. He looked like the Ambassador to the Court of St. James. When he got dressed in the morning the final touch was to sprinkle 4711 cologne on his handkerchief and tuck it just so in his breast pocket.

Pa never had a college education, and this he regretted, I know. He was determined that his children would. This also caused him to have a bit of an inferiority complex where intellect was concerned. I can remember him saying when asked a question he didn't know the answer to, "Oh go ask your Mother, she is the brains of the family." And I dare say that was true, but it didn't keep Pa from having an intuitive judgment and a natural intellect which guided him through life. It did, however, make for a bit of lopsidedness in my Mother and Father's relationship. There was so much that they couldn't share together. She was an avid reader, loved theatre, and had many literary and theatrical friends. He almost never read a book, and never went to the theatre or the movies that I can remember. He was a marvelous card player. When he and Mum played bridge she could bid like a whiz, but he was the one who could play the cards like a pro. He went in and out of Boston every day on the train. There was a club car on the train where all the men played hearts or bridge in the morning, and again at night. All of his cronies lay in wait for him hoping to beat him, but they seldom did. They called him "old goof," and he would always "shoot the moon" or make a game doubled and redoubled before they got to Kingston where he got off. A wild bid, double or nothing type was called a "Monponset bid" which was the station stop just before Kingston. Pa had many friends, young and old, and he gave his friendship unquestioningly and affectionately to those people he loved. This included Mother and Steve and me. He was very proud of his family and doted on us, but no one so much as Mum. Although they bickered and quarreled, especially when Pa's business was going down the drain, I never once thought that they were not happy together in marriage.

My father loved good food, and in that Mother became a very good cook who catered to his every whim, he always sat down to delicious meals. He craved seasonal specialties and would go to a great deal of effort to get the best and freshest peas, for instance, from whichever local stand had the best and freshest. These he would relish every day for weeks, until the crop went by. The same was true of corn, peaches and strawberries. When the scallops were running in the bay, we had scallops in every conceivable way for days. Pa especially loved seafood. I can remember when we lived in the house on the Point, he getting out of his pajamas in the morning, putting on his oldest swimming trunks and, gathering a bucket and clam rake, went across the street to the little beach and dug some clams for his breakfast. These he fried in a cornmeal batter and had with his orange juice and coffee. The aroma wafting up from the kitchen was delicious.

Often he would bring home with him on the train a large sack of lobster knuckles which he bought at the Boston Fish Pier. These knuckles he could get for about thirty-five cents a pound and they had a lot of lobster meat in them if one had the patience to extract it from the shell. He did. I can see him now spending a couple of hours at the kitchen table working away, and collecting a sizeable mound of the delicious pink meat which he later made into a wonderful lobster stew.

His specialty as a fish cook, however, was his Oyster Stew. He was very proud that he had been elected a member of the exclusive Union Club in Boston. Every year they held an Oyster-Stew-by-Gifford luncheon, and my Father would go into the kitchens at the Club, put on a large chef's hat and white apron, and concoct a culinary masterpiece. He put on quite a show, and all the old club members made much of him, relishing every mouthful.

Towards the end of his life he couldn't get around too spryly, and Mother and he would go out for long outings in the car. Sometimes they had a mission, as for instance to go pick Mayflowers in the woods back of the cemetery. Pa could find these elusive beauties as unerringly as a pig searching for truffles. They grew under oak trees, covered by the fallen leaves, and appeared at the end of April. They are the loveliest, most fragrant of flowers, and when in a room, pervade the air with a heavenly scent. One time he and Mother went to pick beachplums on the main road to Kingston where the bushes were especially laden with fruit. Mother parked the car off on the siding and while Pa sat in the car watching, she proceeded to pick the beachplums a little way off. She got absorbed in what she was doing, and was startled by a screech of brakes, as one of their friends stopped and came running up to her. "Is Steve alright?" the man said. There was my Father who had gotten out of the car and was lying on his back under a large bush where he had spotted masses of beachplums. Mother later said that she feared the man had thought her nonchalant to keep on picking while Pa was dead by the side of the road.

When I was little, about ten or eleven, I used to love to go to the Yacht Club to watch the grown-up dances. We were allowed to peer down from the little balcony above the dance floor. Mum and Pup were wonderful dancers, nothing fancy, but smooth as cream, gliding and turning with grace and confidence. Their fox trot was effortless, but it was the waltz that I especially loved. They covered a lot of territory as if on ice skates. But the only problem was that Mum had her eyes shut as Pa guided her through the steps. This embarrassed me. One's parents can be embarrassing sometimes.

A couple of years later, even though I went to Miss Jones' dance class, I wanted to learn more than that prissy lady could teach. And the little boys in the class looked so uncomfortable while dancing, nothing like my father. I asked him if he would teach me. He was pleased to do so. We fox-trotted and waltzed around the living room at a great rate. I remember him giving me some good advice. "Lydia," he said, "you are a very tall girl, and if you want to have lots of dance partners you must learn how to be as light as a feather. Don't press heavily with your left hand on my shoulder, nor with your right hand in mine. Hardly touch. Just sense the motion." He got me off to a good start, and I have followed his advice ever since.

When I went to dances and debutanté parties in Boston, one of my favorite dance partners was Mac somebody, whose name I forget now. He was much shorter than I, but we didn't care at all because we could synchronize so perfectly on the dance floor. One time he told me the secret of our success was that I could "block" for him against the taller couples. Another partner I danced with frequently was Dick Dole from the Hawaiian

Doles. We neither of us liked each other, but we were a good dance pair, and especially did well with "Begin the Beguine." But God forbid if we got stuck with each other in an intermission.

A lovely dance story I must tell. My parents were friends with the Rossells from Boston, Henry Rossell was a massively huge man, and Agnes very small and thin, and very plain-looking, although she dressed beautifully. I got talking to Mrs Rossell one evening at our apartment on Chestnut Street in Boston, when I was on my way to a dance and waiting to be picked up. I was surprised when she said that in her youth she too had adored dancing and that she and her beau and another young couple spent every moment they could dancing. The other girl, she said, was very blond and very beautiful. And while Agnes herself was no beauty, they were equally avid dancers. They didn't have much money, but one summer they saved enough to go to New York to the Astor Hotel to see Vernon and Irene Castle dance. Agnes' mother had made her dress, the other girl however had a white bunny fur cape, which was eye-catching. They ate sandwiches they had brought on the train, and changed into their party clothes in the ladies room of Grand Central. When they got to the Astor Hotel, they had a ringside table in the ballroom, which thrilled them. Agnes was no match in looks for Miss Bunny Fur, who caught many eyes as they sat down. Then with much fanfare out came the Castles who dazzled everyone with their dancing. The little foursome absorbed it all with great concentration, and were the first on the dance floor as the general dancing resumed. When they sat down there was a drum roll from the orchestra and out came Vernon Castle. A spotlight on him, he said loudly: "There are some guests here tonight who have been copying our steps and dances." He looked cross. Then he walked across the dance floor right up to where our young friends were sitting, and passing by Miss Bunny Fur, looked down at Agnes. "You are one of the most graceful dancers I have seen. I wonder if you would favor me with a dance?" And the ugly duckling turned into a princess dancing in the spotlight alone with Vernon Castle.

I rewarded my Father for all his affection toward me by producing his granddaughter, Lyn, on his birthday. Although Pa wasn't the kind of person you took your troubles to, he was always there to applaud your triumphs, whether he understood them or not. I can see him cocking his head to one side, after I related a story that pleased him and saying: "That was really slick." He was a very sentimental man. Every year on Valentine's day when I was at college, a large box would arrive, kind of soggy. In it wrapped in now semi-damp newspaper was a bunch of violets, which he had carefully wrapped himself. When Lyn was born on February 6 in London, several days later that familiar package arrived from overseas. The violets were a bit dried out, but it made no difference. When I think of my Father, that wonderful poem of Leigh Hunt comes to mind:

> Jenny kissed me when we met
> Jumped up from the chair she sat in
> Time you thief who like to put
> Sweets into your list, put that in.
> Say I'm weary, say I'm cold
> Say that health and wealth have missed me.
> Say I'm growing old, but add
> Jenny kissed me.

MOTHER

Mother adapted to the changing times with fortitude. Having been born with a silver spoon in her mouth, she made the best out of the reversal of fortune that occurred as Pa's business declined. Mother's own inheritance from the Youngs was scandalously frittered away by her older brothers who invested unwisely and greedily into nefarious schemes. What money she had she managed carefully, but she was always giving a financial injection to my Father, or to her brother Harold, or to a nephew Frank. When the going got really tough she did tutoring. I can remember all my boy friends' bicycles parked on our front lawn as they came for their tutoring lessons in French or Math or English, endeavoring to get admitted to the next grade, or Harvard. I would sneak by the living room and make faces at these poor struggling swains who hated to give up their precious summer hours that could have been better spent at the Yacht Club or the beach.

Mother was a natural born public speaker. She designed her own lecture series reviewing books and plays. These were very good, and locally well-attended. She was also asked to speak at colleges and universities. She told me once she never felt so fulfilled as when she was speaking in front of an audience. Her intelligence and humor were manifest, and she could improvise her material according to the moment. Her finest speech of all, she said, was at her Bryn Mawr's 50th reunion, where she was keynote speaker. She had the audience eating out of her hand, alternately laughing and crying.

One time when I was at Winsor in one of the lower classes, I had to give a treasurer's report before the whole school. I was petrified. Although it only was a listing of an athletic department inventory and costs, I knew it was a perilous undertaking. I asked Mother's advice.

She said: "Lydia, think of it as a marvelous moment of strength where if the audience is 25 people you multiply yourself by 25. If the audience is 200 people you multiply yourself by 200."

This was not helpful, I was thinking of subtraction of self, rather than multiplication. When it came time for my "performance" I tried to deliver my itemized list in one breath. Unfortunately my one breath lasted only halfway down the page. I could not inhale, and therefore the final items were inaudible.

When Mum was confident and on top of things she was a whiz, the life of a party, the focus of any gathering. She was so generous giving presents to her friends, most of which she had made herself, and which were a labor of love. Months before Christmas her "Santa's" workshop got going and one could hear the endless whir of her sewing machine. She made silk ties for all her boyfriends. Pup and Hector and Phil received bow ties at which she was as proficient as Brooks Bros. My brother Steve and Ward always got pajamas made of wonderful cotton with piping in the expected places. At one time Ward had in his closet twelve pajama bottoms and fourteen pajama tops that he had collected over the years. They were practically new as he wears pajamas only occasionally. I rather sadly threw out the last remaining green and white checkered top just a month ago, after 40 years of collecting.

She had learned how to sew beautifully and I remember all the smocked Liberty lawn dresses she made for me. Lyn and Margot were also beneficiaries of these. Mum made many of her own clothes, even suits and hats. This pretty good for a lady who had once bought her dresses at Worths in Paris, or Mainboucher. But she had learned how to economize. It used to sadden me, however, when I would buy her a nice blouse or scarf or nightie and she would leave them in her bureau saying they were too nice to wear.

There was a different side to Mum which I found hard to bear. She was often "laid low" with some malady or other, often imagined. This unfortunate characteristic she inherited from the Youngs, and especially her Mother. It was a form of depression which expressed itself in hypochondria. It was never severe, but it was omnipresent, especially in her later years. Her "heart trouble" emerged at various times, and she would take to her bed, feeling, I think, that any action or activity drained the body of strength that could only be renewed by bed rest. She often became sick when she visited us.

After Margot was born, Mother came to New York to help me out with Lyn and Margot. Poor Mum. It was too much for her, and after 24 hours she had to go home. I felt concerned about this hypochondria or whatever it was, and it made me very upset. But there was nothing one could do. I visited her often and waited on her hand and foot, and jollied her up as best I could.

I dreaded it one time when as soon as I arrived she announced she had to get two wisdom teeth pulled out the next day. I was sure this would kill both of us. She was now about 83 years old. But this was not imaginary and she marched bravely into the dentist's office cracking jokes and joshing with the nurses. She, I realized, was better coping with reality than with her imagined ailments.

One summer she had a disintegrating disc in her back which was real and really painful. It became so bad that we had to call the ambulance to take her to the Plymouth hospital. She was moaning in pain at every motion of the stretcher as the attendants took her down the stairs and placed her in the ambulance. I was to follow her in my car. It was a terribly hot August day, and when the driver started up the motor, clouds of smoke gushed out of the engine. We formed a bucket brigade from the kitchen with water. There was old Mrs. McWade, Mother's babysitter, and me and the men passing the water from hand to hand. Mother was still inside the vehicle getting hotter and hotter. But finally the engine cooled down enough to start, and off we went at a high rate of speed, through the back roads of Duxbury to the Route 14 highway. I had a hard time keeping up. About two miles away from the hospital, with the sirens going full tilt, to my horror I saw flames coming out of the back of the ambulance. I honked like mad but couldn't make myself heard. The only thing to do was pray that we could make it to the hospital before the whole thing blew up, with my poor Mother immolated like on a funeral pyre inside. We screeched into the hospital emergency entrance, and Mother was as calm as a cucumber as they took her inside. I was the wreck! As I left the hospital grounds later and was driving down the narrow road that leads to the main thoroughfare, there by the side of the road was the ambulance all blackened and still smoking. It looked like it had been hit by a bomb. It had indeed blown up a half hour before.

One time when I was visiting Mother, I drove her into Boston to do a bit of shopping. After going to Shreve Crump and Low, where I bravely parked right in front, and ditto with Walpoles where she was going to buy some sheets, we were headed to meet my brother Steve for lunch at Eddie's

Pier Restaurant down by the waterfront. As we passed by the South Station and got to the little bridge that went over the railroad tracks we saw big DETOUR signs saying we couldn't go ahead where we intended onto Summer Street and right by my Father's old office building. I felt I knew how to get around this road block, and wasn't much worried. But it was the noon rush hour and there was a lot of traffic. I went down back streets following the signs and my nose, but every time I thought I was getting somewhere near our destination, I arrived right back at the Detour sign where I had started. After twice trying I was getting desperate. Mother looked very small and pale sitting next to me. I spotted a large policeman on a huge motorcycle just beyond the barricade, chatting with a lady policeman. I called to him out the window, and he walked over to my car.

"What's the trouble, lady?" he asked. I told him I had been round and round and couldn't get to Eddie's Pier Restaurant. He said, "I'll personally escort you there." He winked at Mum. "Do you want the full treatment, or only half?"

"Full," I said, not knowing what that entailed. Whereupon he put his helmet back on.

"Follow me closely," he said. And after he took the barricade away we were off. He put his sirens on full blast and we careened down the narrow streets, one of which was one way the wrong way; people rushed to the side of the road as our little convoy hurtled along. Well! Mother and I were laughing so uncontrollably that I thought we would both have heart attacks right then and there. I could hardly see the road for tears. Mother blurted out, "I only hope that Steve sees our arrival." When we got to the restaurant all eyes were on us as the policeman pulled right up under the canopy and motioned for us to also do so. We were still laughing so hard as the policeman kissed both of us, and a valet parker disappeared with our car. We could hardly do justice to the story when we told Steve who arrived late; too late to witness our escapade.

There was a whimsical side to Mum which emerged on April Fool's Day. She used to dream up all manner of practical jokes to play on Pup. This was aided by the fact that Pup never recognized April 1 when it came around each year. There were two tricks I remembered. One was when she put a small spool of thread in his breast pocket with just an inch or so of thread emerging from the rim. He being very sensitive to lint or dog hairs or spots on his clothes would immediately on noticing the thread try to brush it off. Then he would pull it and discover it was endless. Another time Mother got a copy of the Boston Herald and removed all the inside pages keeping the front page intact. She would then stuff month-old pages inside. Poor unsuspecting Pa would read the front page, then go to the other pages reading normally until he got to the Sports page. When an article of some Boston Red Sox game played weeks ago was featured, he would have a fit. Mum would be sitting on the sofa knitting, watching him and waiting for the light to dawn.

Every year when all the "summer folk" returned to Duxbury from their winters in Milton, Brookline, Cambridge or Chestnut Hill, the post office and Sweetser's General Store had a population explosion. It always irritated Mother to bump into so many casual acquaintances whose conversational abilities were limited to: "Oh, Marjorie, when did you get down?" Then when Labor Day came it was: "Oh, Marjorie, when are you going back?" She was highly critical of these bland individuals. And if they ever asked her how she was, she responded archly, "Little improvement."

After my Father died we were concerned as to what Mother would do. Her main wish was to live at her house with a companion. We had asked her to live with us, and so did Steve. But she would not do that saying she didn't want to become a burden. Over the ensuing years, however, it was terribly hard to keep a companion partly because Mum was very fussy about who she could live with, and partly because she felt it not necessary to pay much in salary. Mother was of the opinion that anyone who came to live would be lucky to live in such a nice house for free, and would hardly have any work to speak of, although she insisted upon having her breakfast in bed, and her meals on time. She also assumed that the companion would cook and help keep the house in order when Margaret who only came every other week, was not there to clean.

We had a whole bevy of dames try out this "privilege" of living with Mum. There were a couple who stayed one week. There was Mrs. Evers who died on a trip to Scotland. There was Jane, a young girl who loved Mum. There was Mrs. McWade who lied about her age saying she was 70 when she really was 80. And there was Julia.

As far as I was concerned anyone who would stay with Mum for a reasonable amount of time was a blessing. I could take care of her for short periods, but I couldn't stand it over a long pull being away from my life in Connecticut with Ward and our girls. It was always such a relief to get on the highway again headed south after hiring "companions" for Mother, and praying that they would stay.

Young Jane was the least likely candidate for the job, being about 18 years old, but she wanted it very much and she and Mother got along like a house afire. She had the good instincts of a nurse, and was very solicitous. The reason she stayed for almost a year was she didn't want to live with her family in Duxbury. But she later moved to Washington for a real job. I've lost track of her, but am eternally grateful to her.

Mrs. McWade answered an ad we put in the paper. She showed up just in the nick of time when it looked like nobody was available, and I couldn't stay in Duxbury any longer to help out. Mrs. McWade was somewhat elderly, but she looked cute as a button as she came into the house for an interview. She had on a jaunty straw hat like caramel popcorn, and a green and white checkered dress. She talked to Mum for a long time, not the greatest conversationalist and probably not up to Scrabble, but she didn't balk when the subject of salary came up, and when asked when she could start, she said she could come that night. I nearly fainted. I walked her out to the car which was a bright red Volkswagon, and told her how pleased I was she would come.

She said, "I lied to your Mother about my age. I'm really 80 years old, not 70. I was afraid she wouldn't take me."

I said, "Your secret is good with me." She was the perkiest individual, and she stayed a couple of years, serving with distinction even though the only thing she could cook was "Potato Buds."

Julia was something else! She charged into Mother's life with vigor and good spirit. She looked like a "Madame," or like the goodhearted saloon-keeper in a Western movie. She had come from a "good" Hingham family, but had free-wheeled around, and was anxious to settle in with Mum as she was ditching a pesky husband. There was no gloom and doom with Julia around. She loved Mum and cheered her up in every possible way. She changed every evening into one of her many brightly colored caftans, which suited her full figure, and she was really companionable with Mum laughing and talking a mile a minute. She was a wonderful cook, and around the kitchen there were all kinds of signs of life: a huge sign on the fridge said "Smile," avocado pits on toothpicks were sprouting like mad in jars on the kitchen window, other plants she had salvaged from somewhere were blossoming alongside. She played card games well, and was a favorite with Mum's friends. She adored Steve, and doted on him when he came to visit.

Julia's kids, however, were a problem to her. She had two sons and a daughter. They were a bad lot, and I was worried about them for drugs.

They came sometimes to see Julia, but Mum didn't seem to notice anything extraordinary. After Mum died at the nursing home in Plymouth and Julia had left and I came up to settle the house, I am sure that the son had been living in the house, and had just evacuated out the back door as I came in the front. Also the beautiful peacock iridescent blue Tiffany bowl that Mum had given to me had disappeared. It was very valuable. One time when Mother's house was burglarized of silver and the old banjo clock, and some jewelry, I suspect it was Julia's hippy son, and an accomplice, but we never could prove it.

But that was at the end of Mum's life. And it is well not to remember the declines after so much achievement. I like to think of her in her prime, giving and coping and making a happy environment for Pup and for Steve and me.

I do think, however, that Mother's happiest and most fulfilled times seemingly occurred in her four years at Bryn Mawr. She often reminisced about her college days, and spoke of her activities and friends there glowingly. Although she never complained about being a wife and mother, she did not ever reach the full professional potential that was exhibited in her writing and lecturing and with her strong organizational abilities. But that was a different age, and women did not emerge from their households into careers. Besides, there was enough challenge to cope with on a day-to-day basis. I think she did well under the circumstances, and she created for Steve and me an atmosphere in which we could grow. She was very proud of us, and was a pillar of loving support.

At Bryn Mawr she had entered into all activities with enthusiasm. She loved the annual Gilbert and Sullivan operettas, and sang the leads often. She was Yum-Yum in the Mikado. In her senior May Day pageant of Robin Hood she was Robin Adair. She was good at athletics. Once in a track meet she had to substitute in the shot-put for a girl who was sick. She didn't know much about that sport, and was mad at Miss Appleby, the famous athletic coach, for forcing her to participate. She was irritated enough to "put-the-shot" wonderfully far. In doing so she broke a world's record! We had the silver mug for a long time on the mantlepiece, until the burglars stole it.

Mum just loved Lyn and Margot. When she was with them they laughed and giggled, and made merry with her wonderful sense of humor. We gave a New Year's Party one year and I had written a play in which everyone could choose their parts. These roles were listed on a cardboard, and when you came in you signed up for a part. These were variously "Frère Jacque," "Little Miss Muffet," "An Angel," a "Doubting Thomas," "Charles Lindberg," a "Reluctant Camel," etc. Mother chose the "Reluctant Camel" and she and Margot disappeared into the guest room, where they created a camel costume. They stuffed pillows for humps. They filled a nylon stocking with tissue for the neck, and although it drooped more like an elephant's trunk, the effect was sidesplitting, and Mum carried off her part with panache. She was uproariously funny.

I have remembered a story about Mother I forgot to tell. When I was just starting at Bryn Mawr, Mother and I decided to go on a toot together for a few days to see Williamsburg. Mother drove our car to New York where I joined her and we plowed on south in our rather ancient black Desoto that looked a bit like a hearse. We had a super time en route as she was such good company. I remember sitting in a beautiful garden back of the small inn we were staying at in Williamsburg and we ordered a champagne cocktail and toasted each other. The southern atmosphere beguiled us cold northerners and the charm of the southern people warmed our souls.

I had two boyfriends at the University of Virginia in Charlottesville, one whose name I now forget. I saw him briefly then, but only for lunch. But my other friend was Gabriel Ferdinando Salazar. The entire clan of Salazars and their cousins the Saenzs had come to Duxbury one previous summer, and had rented a huge house on the water on the way to South Duxbury. They were from Bogota, Columbia, and both families were wealthy, influential and charming. When Gabriel found I was coming south to Virginia he asked me to go out on a date. I said I would love to but I had my Mother with me. "Don't worry," he said, "I will get her a date." Good Lord, a date with my Mother? Gabriel arranged to pick us up at our motel on the edge of town.

Mother was unusually jovial as she got dressed for the evening. I never knew her to take a shower, but there she was with the steam pouring out, like Blanche in "A Street Car Named Desire" and singing sections from Iolanthe. As she was putting on the final touches and a discreet dab of L'Heure Bleu behind her ear, we chanced to look out the tiny transom of the bathroom window. There coming down the driveway in a large open touring car with its top furled on the back seat were Gabriel and Jim. They looked just like Sebastian and Charles in "Brideshead Revisited." Jim looked very dashing and eminently presentable. Mother and I started to laugh and only just got control in time to go out and meet our dates.

Mother climbed in the back with Jim, and had a hard time keeping her hat on as we dashed along the road to a roadhouse frequented by Virginia students. Gabriel had brought a bottle of whisky in a paper bag. Set-ups were provided. By the time we sat down at a crowded little corner of the bar, Mother and Jim were chatting like mad, obviously enjoying each other's company. I found myself tongue-tied and could hardly say anything fascinating to Gabriel. When I came back from a trip to the ladies room there was Mother reading Jim's palm, inventing all kinds of delicious nonsense. A small group of students gathered around to listen, and soon Mother had four more candidates to have their palms read.

There was a Fair on the other side of town that we went to. I could not believe my eyes when I saw Mother and Jim lining up to get on the Ferris Wheel. Mother can't stand heights. But sure enough, on they got. Gabriel and I wandered around listlessly, we went to a shooting gallery, tried to pitch balls at a doll, but our hearts were not in it, besides we couldn't find Mother and Jim. Finally we caught sight of them staggering along a path between the booths, laughing their heads off. Mother said, "Imagine coming all this way and losing my hat on a damnable Ferris Wheel." That night as we went to bed in our motel, I heard Mother giggling as she pulled the covers up over her. She and Jim corresponded for years, and he came to see her twice on Chestnut Street in Boston.

Mother enjoyed telling a story about a time when she was visiting us at Wilson Point. One snowy cold morning we were all outside playing paddle tennis. Little Victoria Keefe, aged five, got too cold playing in the snow, and I told her to run over to our house to get warm, and that my Mother was there. Tory arrived and Mum made her some hot chocolate, and afterwards sat her in her lap to tell her a story. As Tory was listening she looked up at Mum's neck, and started fingering the loose folds of skin. then she said thoughtfully: "No bone."

I have deliberately written these Memoires without referring to notes or research material. I wanted to search my being for what has stuck, without props. This is what is meant by "Memoires." But in doing so I am aware that many relevant facts have not been metabolized that would be meaningful. This superficial account of Mum is a case in point. Someday I will write a more in-depth profile of her, utilizing her journals, her lectures, her poetry and her letters as references. For the time being, however, I hope she knows how very grateful I am for her being all things to me.

WARD

Ward and I have just this past October celebrated our 40th wedding anniversary (1992). I cannot do justice writing about this marvelous human being who has been such a steady and loving companion for all these years. My new New Zealand friend, Witi Ihimaera, asked me one time what was the secret of our long marriage. I had never been asked that question before and didn't know how to answer it. But I said that I thought it was because both of us wanted to help each other make our lives work. It also has something to do with making the other person look good, and feel good. This I think we both have done.

Ward's professional life has been outstanding, and he has run station WETA Public Television here in Washington with the greatest distinction. There are few people who could have come into this maverick industry as well-equipped to handle the myriad problems of fundraising, producing quality programming in the fishbowl of the Nation's Capital, and coordinating highly motivated creative egos and personalities. He has a rare quality of being able to step back from a situation and giving it his best judgment without the complication of ego or personal self-involvement. Rare this is in an age where everyone is thinking of how events effect them, and the "me-ism" in art and literature. As he has just retired as C.E.O. he is receiving all kinds of congratulatory testimonials, all of which he so richly deserves.

Before these last kudos, however, he has gotten two outstanding awards, one from his school Phillip Exeter Academy, and one from professionals in the television industry. They warrant quoting. And from my point of view they are absolutely right on.

The John Phillips Award is the highest award the school can give, and it is not given every year. It states its purpose:

> To honor from time to time an Exeter alumnus whose life and contributions to the welfare of his community, his country and mankind exemplify. . . the nobility of character the Academy sought to promote.

The Ralph Lowell Award is public television's highest recognition of merit.

Ward Chamberlin has been a key force in public television. His wisdom and deep-seated beliefs in the values of public televi-

172

sion have been the major impetus behind many of the most notable accomplishments as an industry.

At every point in public television's history Ward Chamberlin has been there showing us a way—a better way—of fulfilling the dream of public television.

BUT! HE'S JUST MY WARD!

(To the tune of "*All the Things You Are*")

This guy abhors the thought of routine
He hates to go down any route twice
He won't consult his handy road map
Getting there for certain would be *so* nice!

    Won't wear galoshes when the snowstorm pelts
    Won't even wear a hat as ozone melts
    Someday he'll find his twenty raincoats
    And someday he'll know that moment profound
    When all those things he's lost are found.

His brain is much above the average
His brawn is like a boy in his youth
His sense of right and wrong is model
And his love of others, also his love of truth.

    BUT!
    Why must he don each day his old school tie
    The one with bearnaise sauce from meals gone by
    Some day he'll buy a whole new wardrobe
    And someday he'll know that joy in life
    When he's not badgered by his wife.

This man would make the greatest President
He'd run the country just like a whiz
He'd win the blacks and the Latinos
And women just by telling it like it is.

    BUT!
    He never signals when he's in his car
    And as for matching socks, they never are

Someday he'll notice gas is empty
And someday he'll know that moment divine
When all those parking fines are mine.

Our life together has been smashing
I'm charmed by all the things that we share
But if he ever had a mistress
She never would put up with his mess that's there.

He sops the bathroom floor, leaves hairbrush wet
Which straightens every strand of my new set
Some men are simply too too perfect
And I'm glad that at this moment in time
That all the things Ward's not are mine.

BETTY

Betty was a much prettier baby than the rest of the two year-olds espaliered in various attitudes on their mother's laps for the photograph that I remember so well in the album. Ten little cherubs, immaculately conceived for the picture, astride ten mothers, crisp in their summer Liberty Lawn dresses. They smiled for the man, or most of them did. My brother appeared to be more interested in getting a firm hold on Winsor's sailor collar. Stevie looked as if he were about to cry, and Johnny was. But Betty, wreathed in golden curls and smiles, was the star of the show. My mother didn't look too fat, but she must have been, as she was to produce me in a couple of months. Betty was the only girl in the group. This proportion later made Duxbury a very swell place to grow up in, for there were lots of boys, with the ratio at four to one. The females in our small crowd indeed had a monopoly, which we jealously guarded. I'll never forget the summer that two Richmond, Virginia girls moved into our territory with their family. They were renters. They were southern. They were fascinating, and we hated them. The boys made perfect asses of themselves over these stupid, fluffy, drawling beauties, who didn't even wear blue jeans, and did not know how to play touch football. Betty had a solution. We girls would make ourselves scarce. We would not only play hard-to-get, we would play impossible-to-get. Under no circumstances would we go to the Yacht Club dance on Saturday night. We would not go to the big beach picnic, no matter how big the bonfire, or how great the singing. We would take monastic vows, whatever that meant, we would swear celibacy, whatever that was, and we would head for Clark's Island in our boats, and camp out for the rest of the rental season. We never got very far, for the southern girls threw a big dinner dance, which we could not resist.

Betty lived right across the street from me. Her house was on the bay. Although she was my older brother's age, we were fast friends. My earliest memories were of sitting at the ocean's edge with her, playing in the sand. She had endless talent for making sand structures, and I marvelled adoringly. When I was about six I asked my mother why I was bigger than Betty when she was older. My mother answered that Betty would grow no bigger than she was right now. Betty was a dwarf. And as I subsequently turned out to be something of a giant, we made quite a pair.

My first overnight away from home was glamorous. Betty's grandmother, wanting to do something especially nice for Betty's birthday, lavishly took the two of us to Newport for a weekend. Betty was twelve. We drove down in a huge, black, chauffeured limousine to the spiffiest hotel in town. The bathroom in our suite was dazzling. The marble walls, the faucets of gold, the thick blanket-sized towels, the Roger-Gallet soap, all contributed to our frenzy of delight. But it was the bathtub that transcended all. It was enormous, and could have held two adults comfortably. It was like a duck-pond for us kids. We filled it to the brim and got in together. Betty had to get the bathroom vanity stool and lower herself down. It was so deep she nearly drowned, but we squealed with delight when we found that I could float without touching, and she could almost swim, being so small.

We would have stayed in all evening, but her grandmother fished us out, and spirited us away to the dining room, our fingertips looking like peachstones. All eyes stared at us as we walked to our table under escort from an intimidating headwaiter, who was dressed up as my father did only when he was going to a ball. It was the first and last time I felt uncomfortable in Betty's presence. Everyone watched as Betty climbed up onto the gilt chair that was being held out for her, but she handled the protocol like a princess.

She soon became completely hidden behind the huge menu that was presented to her. I was awestruck by the atmosphere, the silence except for clicking forks and the tinkle of glasses, and the waiter, who was waiting. I looked across the table for help from my friend, who just at that moment peered around her menu at me. Such an expression of devilment and glee on her face, her eyes dancing. She started to giggle. I did the same. And soon we were out of control. Our laughter could not be suppressed as much as we, or her embarrassed grandmother, tried. We must have succeeded, however, for we did get our dinner. We walked out of the dining room afterwards to a much different march than before. I remember people smiling and nodding pleasantly as we passed their tables. Betty's head was carried as high as she could carry it, and she beamed at all her subjects. This was a characteristic mesmerism that she had all her life. When she walked into any room all hearts stopped a little bit, so did conversations . . . then gradually people left whomever they were talking to, and gravitated to Betty. Although in Newport at age ten I had no idea what sex appeal was, she had it. The attention she got had nothing to do with people being sorry or patronizing her for shape and size. She just plain connected with everyone. She exuded warmth and concern, and one felt better in her presence than before. She had two beautiful tall blond sisters, but it was Betty who was radiant.

There was very little that Betty could not do. She had a pony named "Maybe," who was halfway between pony and horse in size. She could saddle him without help (from a ladder) and she rode him all over the back roads of Powder Point, her little legs sticking out from the saddle like sugar tongs. Often we would ride double on Maybe, me behind, holding onto Betty's non-existent waist, and I can remember the thrill of cantering on the beach in the early morning at the edge of low tide on the hard sand.

We had sailboats, too, little gaff-rigged beetle cats, which we sailed on Duxbury Bay. We raced regularly in all kinds of weather. Betty's main problem was getting out to her boat in the little rowboat with shortened oars. Her father, who was a doctor, was an avid racer in his Duxbury Duck, for which he always won prizes at the end of the season. When the wind was very heavy he took on extra crew, often Betty and me when his regular crew was not available, or the hour too early for the race—race times were dictated by the tide, which went completely out leaving behind nothing but bare flats. If one was not doing well in a race, and if then the wind dropped completely, this could be a problem, for one might have to wait several hours aground on a mudflat waiting for the tide to come in. One time I remember shouting to my mother far away on shore to call up my date Bill and say that I would be late for the dance. But when the doctor took us on as crew for a race, we almost always came in first. Betty was very agile in her position right over the centerboard, and because of her size could maneuver well under the boom when we tacked. I can see her now lying on the deck on her tummy as we run before the wind. I held one sheet of the spinnaker, she the other. We were miles ahead of the rest of the fleet and the waves broke over the bow regularly inundating Betty who looked like a little triumphant carved figurehead.

Betty's tennis was not great, but she was much sought after as a partner in the scrambles, which were always hilarious. She had the greatest net shot. When the opponents would least expect it she would reach up with her sawed off racquet and intercept a driving forehand, and pop it off into the alley for a winner. Everyone would crack up with laughter, especially Betty, who prided herself on this specialty she had developed. But she was an accomplished pianist. All her family was musical and she would provide any accompaniment that was needed for singing or playing of other instruments. She did not use the piano stool, because then she could not reach the pedals. She stood in front of the keyboard which she could just reach, her arms in line with her ears. She had incredible dexterity, and her hands looked like little fat spiders darting up and down. She could even manage octaves by rolling the notes at high speed so you didn't notice. Music was to become a major resource of her life. She had a very true singing voice, and when she sang she looked very much like a fat baby robin.

We sang a lot in Duxbury—on the beach, in cars, around the piano—not the greatest concert quality, but we all loved to harmonize and our crowd had some good voices. In the summer of 193 my mother wrote her first yacht club show, adapting Gilbert and Sullivan with local color and references to Duxbury. We were all in it. It was the happiest time of our lives. In the "Pinafore" section, we couldn't amass all twenty of the "Twenty love-sick maidens," but there were six of us including Betty, and we were all dressed like The Graces in sheets, with flowers and ivy entwined in our hair. We knew we were enchanting.

The highlight of the evening, the show stopper, came when Brad who sang wonderfully well, and who was devastatingly handsome, sang a love duet with Betty. She stood beside him as he sat on the edge of the stage with his legs hanging down into the non-existent orchestra, only a piano accompaniment nearby. None of us will ever forget "Bury, bury, let the graves close o'er . . . the days that were that never will be more," ringing out into the back of the hall. There was not a sound from the audience as Brad and Betty in perfect harmony hit the highest notes with grace and ease. It was an evening engraved on our memories, particularly because in a few months the war was to break out, and indeed these were "days that were that never will be more." Soon all of the boys were signed up for the R.O.T.C. at Harvard or elsewhere in preparation for active duty.

Our world changed unalterably, but for no one more than Betty. Our sheltered, idyllic, private, unconcerned, uncommitted, unthinking, pleasure-seeking romp was over. The outside world would be frightening to all of us. For Betty it would be even more of a challenge. Could this butterfly survive outside the sheltering cocoon of family and friends? She had a master plan. And by stages, like a deep sea diver, she prepared for the pressures to come. She had a car adapted to her short legs with lengthened pedals, and a knob contraption on the steering wheel, and she drove with skill. She enrolled at a junior college in Massachusetts. The first day at college her roommate was aghast at being allotted such a "freak" to live with and promptly went to the Dean to ask to be reassigned. The Dean said that there was no room at the moment to change and that she would have to stick it out for the first term. The girl returned before the term was up announcing that under no circumstances was she going to move, for it was the greatest privilege of her life to know Betty.

After college Betty moved into the next phase of emergence. She was accepted at The New England Conservatory of Music. She drove to and from Boston in all the rush hour traffic, sometimes even coping with the subway in bad weather. This period in Betty's life was, I suspect, the most satisfying and rewarding for her. She did wonderfully well and made friends from all walks of life. On weekends in Duxbury students and professors from the Conservatory would flock to her house. This collection of gifted, devoted people all singing and playing violins, pianos, guitars was a mini-Tanglewood on Betty's back lawn.

Betty and I had a passion for a culinary marvel which we had invented. We had to concoct it when my mother was not around, as it smoked up the kitchen and ruined several toasters. We would butter bread lavishly and put it in the toaster. We would then spread strawberry jam and peanut butter on the hot toast and reinsert it into the toaster for just an instant. The trick was to take it out in time, before it became unremovable. Sometimes we missed. I can see her now coming down the driveway to my house for breakfast, often carrying the bread, for her mother had outlawed this activity altogether. While munching on this "delicacy" we would usually talk about important things on our minds. There was something about the atmosphere that made us philosophical. Usually the subject was about boys. This particular morning in August I sensed that there was going to be a good bull-session. She arrived with a pile of fat letters which she deposited on the kitchen table as we prepared our mess. At this point in our lives there was not an able-bodied male left in Duxbury. They were all overseas. She was a more faithful letter writer than I, and therefore received many more letters. We reaped mail from France, Italy, Austria, the Solomon Islands, the South Pacific, and many camps throughout the United States and

Great Britain, etc., and were very proud of our vast range. But this morning, as Betty wiped her sticky little fingers on the already sticky paper napkin, took a large slug of milk, she said simply, "I'm in love."

This statement in itself was nothing new, as we were always in love with somebody or something. But the tone of her voice made me look up from the peanut butter jar and stop chewing, like a cow lifting her head from the grass at the approach of danger. She went on. "His name is Johnny. My mother and his mother were at school together, and his mother wanted me to write to him in New Guinea because he was so lonely and hated the war more than most. He is very artistic." She proceeded to dump out onto the table some wonderful crayon and watercolor drawings that Johnny had done in the jungle. "I am truly in love. We have been able to say things in letters that we have never said or felt before. And Johnny is coming home on leave in four days. I am going to meet him. You will have to help me decide what to wear. I want to dash home now and get going at the sewing machine to make something very nice and sexy."

My jaw was in an unshuttable position. My mind was racing. Fortunately I could not speak, for I had one big question to ask, which never got asked.

The morning arrived when she was to drive up to Cambridge in her car alone to meet him. She felt it would be easier to rendezvous outside the subway at Harvard Square than to cope with the South Station traffic. She looked aglow. We had chosen the color blue, and her hat had small bright flowers on it. Her freshly curled hair shone like gold. I helped her to wash her car, and it too was shining in the hot summer sun. She had a red carnation wrapped in wet paper on the seat beside her. I asked what that was for. She replied, "So that Johnny will recognize me." And off she went. I could do nothing for the rest of the day. I went to the beach alone and walked way, way down, past High Pines. The evening passed slowly. The night was even slower, as I did not hear from her by the time I went to bed. The next morning I woke early and on my way to the refrigerator for orange juice, I glanced out the window to see a small figure running down the driveway, turn the corner by the bridal wreath bush, and come dashing into our kitchen. Breathlessly she threw her arms around my waist and announced that she and Johnny were going to be married in December.

There is nothing more to add other than that they lived happily for years, more radiant in each other's company than any couple I have ever seen, and complete unto themselves.

XV

People Worth Mentioning

FAMOUS PEOPLE I HAVE MET

W. H. Auden
Bea Arthur
Ambassador Acland
Dean Acheson
Alice Acheson
Licia Albinese
Michael Baryshnikov
Richard Bissel
Yul Brynner
Lauren Bacall
Sen. Dale Bumpers
Ken Burns
Leonard Bernstein
George Bush
Barbara Bush
Justice Wm. Brennan
Pearl Bailey
Jeremy Brett
Evangeline Bruce
Christopher Beeney
Jimmy Carter
Roslyn Carter
Prime Min. James Callaghan

San Salvador Pres. Napoleon Duarte
Mildred Dunnock
Colleen Dewhurst
Charles Dance
Sen. Robert Dole
Queen Elizabeth
Jimmy Ernst
Amb. Rawdon Dalrymple (Australia)
Chinese Premier Deng Tiaow Ping
Jose Ferrer
Pres. Gerald Ford
Geraldine Fitzgerald
Henry Fonda
Amb. Tim Francis (New Zealand)
Fred Gwynne
Alec Guiness
John Gardner
Rex Harrison
Hurd Hatfield
Sir Edmond Hilary
Averill Harriman
Pamela Harriman
Susan Hampshire

Claudette Colbert
Kitty Carlisle
Jacques Cousteau
Joan Crawford
Alistair Cooke
Julia Child
The King Singers
Nancy Kissinger
Edward Kennedy
Robert Kennedy
Ethel Kennedy
Andre Kostelanitz
Clare Booth Luce
Charles Lindbergh
Jim Lehrer
Loren Mazell
Yves Montand
Prime Minister Brian Mulrooney
Mary Martin
Liza Minelli
Robin MacNeil
Jean Marsh
Amb. E. deMargerie
George McGovern
Giovanni Martinelli
Robert Motherwell
Amb. Denis McClean
(Lawrence Olivier)
Just. Sandra Day O'Connor
Lily Pons
Sen. Charles Percy
Vincent Price
Itzak Perlman
Just. Lewis Powell
Anthony Quinn
Pres. Ronald Reagan
Nancy Reagan

Lillian Hellman
Julie Harris
Marvin Hamlisch
Geraldine James
Derek Jacoby
Gordon Jackson
Chief Justice Renquist
Sen. & Mrs. Jay Rockefeller
Diana Rigg
Billy Rose
Mistislav Rostropovitch
Isaac Stern
Beverly Sills
Jonas Salk
George Schultz
Alexis Smith
Jimmy Stewart
Sen. Alan Simpson
Max Shulman
William Schumann
Helen Steber
Elizabeth Taylor
Margaret Tysack
Mel Torme
Just. Byron White
Eli Wallach & Anne Jackson
Simon Williams
Meg Wynn-Owen
Irene Worth
Sen. Lowell Weicker
Sen. Tim Worth
Mayor Walter Washington
Theresa Wright
Treat Williams
Count Wilhelm Wachmeister
Ardeshir Zahedi

My "love" list would be much longer than my "hate" list but there are a few outstanding individuals that I must mention for their special achievements. Song: (from *The Sound of Music*)

THESE ARE A FEW OF THE PEOPLE I HATE

Nixon and Begin and Muamar Quaddafi
J. Edgar Hoover and Joseph McCarthy
Blue-stocking rich folk who think they're so great
These are a few of the people I hate.

Most of the Popes, and especially the Piuses
Bigoted people with mean racial biases
Douglas MacArthur who faded too late
These are a few of the people I hate.

   When my heart sings, and the sun shines
   And life all seems swell
   I simply remember these pains in the neck
   And then I don't feel so well.

Saddam Hussein and Iran's Ayatolla
Drat Hostess Twinkies, Wonder Bread and Lite Cola
Think of the homeless with lifestyles so bad
These are the things that are driving me mad.

Northwestern Airlines that first banned the smokers
Patrick Buchanan and like-minded jokers
Elected officials just not up to snuff
Please stop the world I have had quite enough.

   When the day dawns and the buds bud
   And there's sign of spring
   I simply remember the things that I hate
   And then I forget to sing.

THESE ARE A FEW OF MY FAVORITE WASHINGTON MEN

Amb. Antony Acland
Edwin Adams
Ken Burns
Phillip Bonsal
Bucky Block
Father William Byron
Bob Blake
Judge William Brennan
Ed Campbell
Hugh Jacobsen
Skip Nalen
David McCullough
Paul Duke
Ed Eckenhoff
Amb. Bobby de Margerie
Amb. Tim Francis
Witi Ihimaera
Ramsay Potts

MY FAVORITE ONE-OF-A-KIND LADIES

Alice Acheson
Evangeline Bruce
Mac Herter
Betsy Lefferts
Luvie Pearson
Dotty Kidder
Sister Spaulding

THESE ARE TEN OF THE MOVIES I LOVE

Brief Encounter
Casablanca
Henry V
Waterloo Bridge
It Happened One Night
Any Fred Astaire
Any Shirley Temple

Wuthering Heights
African Queen
Rebecca
Philadelphia Story
The Sound of Music
Any Laurel and Hardy

Lydia Chamberlin

THESE ARE A FEW OF MY FAVORITE THINGS

Lamb chops and freesia and soap made by Yardley
Cherry trees in April whose buds are out hardly
Snow covered chalets and Paris in Spring
These are a few of my favorite things.

Hollandaise and endives and artichokes al dente
Haagen-Daas with chocolate sauce, and please put on plenty
Beaches all sandy with surf full of foam
These are the things for which I would leave home.

    When the tooth hurts and the gas quits
    And my child has mumps
    I simply remember my favorite things
    And then I'm not in the dumps.

Tiri Tekanawa and L. Pavarotti
Summer frocks of linen, or silk polka-dotty
A calf running free or a swan on the wing
These are the things that will make my heart sing.

Gondolas in Venice, Big Ben when it chimes
Playing golf in Scotland, and Vodka with limes
Sitting on our front porch—Lyn, Margot and Ward,
Without these to live with, I could not afford.

    When the rain falls and it is Easter
    And I've spoiled my gown
    I simply remember my favorite things
    And then I don't feel so down.

Learning to tango, perfecting my waltz
Expressing my real thoughts without any schmaltz
Remembering my Mother, and my dear old Pa
There's nothing nicer than what these things are

Making a slam that was bid and then doubled
Sleeping at night with my spirits untroubled
Finding the policeman was not chasing me
These are the things that now fill me with glee.

    When my face tans, and my hair's curled
    And I've lost some weight
    I then count my blessings
    And thank the dear Lord
    That my life has been so great.

XVI

*Would You Believe
That I . . . ?*

Would you believe that I have:

> acted on the same stage with Julie Harris
> conducted Leonard Bernstein
> directed Henry Fonda
> sung for George Bush
> had Jimmy Stewart as a dinner companion.

When I was living in New York before I was married I joined the Amateur Comedy Club. The first production I was in was "The Devil's Disciple," directed by Jose Quintero and starring Julie Harris in one of her first-ever roles. This was a splendid play and all the cast was exciting to be with. Although I was only in the mob scene, I gave it my all. On opening night at Hunter College, when it came time in the last act for Dick Deadeye to be hung on the gallows the mob rushed in registering despair and fury. I summoned up these emotions with all the conviction I could muster. In the process I lost my shoe, a large black Capezio, right under the gallows where it rested gleaming in the spotlight for Julie Harris's next big scene.

Many years later after Ward and I had moved to Washington the same Jose Quintero, now a famous director, gave a surprise birthday party for one of his dearest friends, Mary Ahern. Jose lived in one of those superb Beaux Arts apartments on the West Side, and it was a marvelous place for a party. All kinds of theatre people were asked including Leonard Bernstein who arrived late, almost bumping into Mary in the elevator. We all scurried to the balcony overlooking the huge living room, and hid, peering through the banisters as Mary arrived unsuspecting below. Like a bunch of kids we barrelled down the stairs shouting, "Surprise! Surprise!" And while Mary sat down dumbfounded, we presented her with songs and skits. One song was a group song which I had composed and led, and among the singers was Bernstein who obediently followed my beat.

I must add another story about Bernstein and Mary. Mary had worked with him on the great "Omnibus" shows, and she got to know him very well. They often worked late into the night on scripts and scores and she was a major force behind his wonderful lectures at Harvard called the "Norton Lectures." One late night in New York he asked her to come back to his apartment for a nightcap. They were both exhausted. When they got into the apartment he pointed proudly to a new abstract painting that he had recently bought which was hanging over the fireplace. He asked her what she thought of it.

Mary, zonked with fatigue, looked at it through tired eyes and said, "Lenny, it looks to me like it had been painted by a chimpanzee."

Lenny said, "Goddamit, Mary, you are the first person to recognize the painter, everybody else has told me what a masterpiece I have." It *was* painted by a chimpanzee, and Lenny's quite naughty trap for his friends.

At Wolf Trap, that wonderfully successful theatre outside Washington, started by intrepid Kay Shousse, a huge gala benefit was held to celebrate Leonard Bernstein's 60th birthday. It was quite an affair with a glittering bunch of people from the theatre and music world on hand to honor this genius. Isaac Stern, Yehudi Menuhin, Lauren Bacall, Lillian Hellman, Betty Courden and Adolph Green, and many other dignitaries I can't remember. There was a lavish party afterwards at Kay Shousses' to which all the performers came. Everybody crowded around Bernstein and he held court regally. I stood for a long time in line before I got to speak to him. When I did I wanted to keep it short and I said,

"Lenny, you won't remember me, but I am a close friend of Mary Ahern's. . ."

Whereupon he dropped to his knees and put his hands together as if in supplication and said: "Mary Ahern is a saint!"

When we lived in Connecticut I was a member of the Board of Trustees at the Long Wharf Theatre in New Haven, Connecticut. I loved this regional professional theatre and spent many happy hours on the board and attending their fine plays. I organized a Bryn Mawr benefit (why, I don't know) at Long Wharf and we put on a very successful evening with good actors and actresses participating. I almost got Henry Fonda to come but he had a conflict, and instead I was asked to go to Fonda's apartment in New York where he would give a taped interview and pose for pictures. His agent John Springer said Fonda was crazy about Long Wharf. So I and a photographer and technician went to his gorgeous apartment on East 75th Street, and there was Fonda looking absolutely splendid, tanned and bright eyed. We had a photograph taken of the two of us on the terrace after the interview. I bent my knees the teeniest bit, as he was about an inch shorter than me. We had written a bit of dialogue for him to say.

Among them the lines from "Mr. Roberts:" "Now hear this, now hear this," etc. His first go through was rather perfunctory.

So I said: "Mr. Fonda, nobody on shipboard could hear that even with a megaphone. Give it a bit more oomph." Which he did, and blasted it out with vigor the next time.

I have described earlier the going-away party the Bushes gave for Phyllis and Bill Draper where I sang a song I had written for the occasion. I have never sung for a president, but I have sung for a vice-president.

I have written up in a separate section about my glorious dinner companion, Jimmy Stewart, at the Hafts. I couldn't believe it when I saw my place card at Jimmy's right. Mary Haft was on his left, but since she has the quietest, softest voice and he can't hear out of his left ear, he conversed with me the whole time. It was like being on a date with him. When it came time to go, he gave me a big kiss, followed by a big hug, and said, "I really meant that!"

XVII

Up-To-Date

Another bonanza trip for us. We are in Boca Grande with Newt and Anne Schenck for the second year in a row having come last February to stay in Ruth Lord's house which she has so generously donated to us. She is devoted to Newt with whom she has been associated at Long Wharf, she as its benefactor and President, he as Chairman of the Board, recently resigned. Ruth has two houses. The bigger one we stayed in last year, which was splendid, and so unusually constructed. It had a labyrinth of corridors and small rooms having been added on to every which way, charming and illogical. This house which is just next door is smaller, logical and perfection. The patio is nicer in a sense of being more private and sunnier, and the house just right for us. The Schencks in one suite, and we in a corresponding one on opposite sides of the house. The kitchen has everything, and a good pine table to eat at which is so convenient and right. In the patio are many pots filled with geraniums, impatiens, gorgeous parsley and lettuces. There is the smoothest straightest trunk of a palm tree on one corner that reaches way up to the sky. A lovely butter yellow hibiscus climbs up and around the white-washed walls.

I was thinking this morning that I have been writing these memoirs, my *Tres Riches Heures* a little more than a year and I am almost finished. I'm over three hundred pages. I had started it on our cruise on the Royal Viking Sun up the east coast of South America, the biggest bonanza trip of all time. I then realized how many places we have been since then. Ward and I have had many rich hours, almost without expense thanks to Frequent

Flyer bonuses, Frequent Friends' hospitality, and several business confer-
ences. We have been to Buenos Aires, Rio de Janeiro (Ward twice), Bermuda,
Montego Bay, Jamaica, Orlando, San Destin, Boca Grande (twice), Tempe,
Arizona, Nantucket, Paris, Brittany, Burgundy, Oslo (Ward). All of these
places have been delicious to visit, and our minds are full of nourishing
sights and sounds. But when I finish my writings I can't wait to paint again
after a long period of not doing so. The place I shall head for first at my
easel is France. The trip that Ward and I took there in October went deep
into our sensibilities and we renewed our love affair with that beautiful
country. It was like seeing an old friend again. When I am in Italy I think
there is no place I would rather be. But when I am in France I know that
it is my favorite country of all. The French people have changed. They are
a lot nicer, and they even try to be helpful to strangers. Paris was sparkling
as they have cleaned many of the public buildings, especially the Louvre
as it surrounds I. M. Pei's dazzling pyramid. I have three paintings in mind.
One of a busy town market around a small cathedral in Saulieu on a rainy
Saturday morning. The second a sunny afternoon in the Luxemburg Gardens with the old men playing boules, carrousels, children rolling hoops,
French ladies in black sitting on benches, and the chiaroscuro of dappled
light shining through the canopy of green foliage. The third is a scene of
village through which runs our newly discovered favorite river the tiny
Ouche in Burgandy, a little bridge and cows grazing on the river banks. I
hope I can do justice to the visions that are in my head.

I don't know what to entitle this next chapter, but it warrants a section
all its own. It could be called perhaps the *MacLeish Connection*. It has a
quality of good fortune mixed with an eerie magical inevitability that makes
it such a memorable story to me.

The genesis of this is Aunt Rosamond, my Mother's younger sister.
Aunt Rosamond was a dynamo, and to be around her was stimulating and
sometimes maddening. As an opera singer she achieved no great international stature, but her trained voice was very effective. She attracted a lot
of professional attention and operatic disciples in New York. When she left
New York she bought an old inn in the Berkshires in New Boston, and ran
it for several years. She was a marvelous cook, but she overdid her generosity, and did not know how to economize to make ends meet. In the
inn's best days it attracted a lot of celebrities and also a whole bunch of
her New York musical friends who often came and free-loaded on her. It
was near "Jacob's Pillow," and there was a wonderful interaction between
the dancers and the opera singers. On a Saturday night it was a lively place
to be. The rafters were ringing with impromptu arias around the bar. I heard

Rosamond sing sections from Wagner's "Rheingold." She was a perfect Brunhilda and I was very moved. One time Mother and I went up to visit at the New Boston Inn. We had a marvelous time. The place was full, and Mum made an instant friend with young Steve DeBaun. I was astounded to hear the two of them singing the love duets from "Sampson and Delilah." They were very good, and hammed it up skillfully.

Rosamond and my Father had a love-hate relationship. When she was coming to visit he often announced that he was going to leave the premises, as her opinions were quite outrageous, and she often elaborated on them to get a rise out of my Father. He stalwartly defended his New England status quo, and during cocktails the conversation was heated. But when the smoke died down they were still friends, relishing the debates, and underneath it all fond of each other. Mother always got agitated when the two of them got going.

I had a friend when I lived in New York in the '40s, Rod MacLeish, who worked at ABC also. We did many things together, and he was always a willing and eager escort to functions. Although we were good pals he was not a "boyfriend" as such, but very good company. I said to him one weekend that we should go to visit my Aunt Rosamond at her inn in Massachusetts. It was a good idea and off we went. Rosamond's daughter Diana was there when we arrived and before I knew it Rod had fallen instantly in love with her. They were married in the summer at the inn with bagpipes playing their gorgeous tatoos, and I was a delighted bridesmaid for my cousin. They subsequently moved to London, he working for Westinghouse Broadcasting.

Time passes. Ward and I took our girls skiing in Austria with a stopover in London. Lyn and Margot were about eleven and nine years old. We paid a quick visit to Diana (Rod was away on assignment) and met their two young children Sumner and Eric. We then lost track of the MacLeishes for years. Rod and Diana were divorced and Rod had a few more unsuccessful marriages, although he and Diana remained close friends.

Time passes. Aunt Rosamond *finally* dies after a prolonged old age in a nursing home. A funeral was held for her in Boston, and I planned to go. I was surprised when Lyn said she would also go with me to the funeral. Margot didn't want to go but Ward decided he would come too. My cousins Diana and Bunny organized the service well, and were very gracious. I had seen little of them in the intervening years and found them nice and great fun to be with.

As we were graveside and Aunt Rosamond was being lowered into her grave, during the prayer Lyn poked me and whispered, "Who is that attractive guy opposite us?" "I don't know," I said. "It must be a MacLeish relative." Lyn said, "Wouldn't he be good as a beau for Margot." "Oh, Lyn," I said scornfully. "Don't match-make, it won't work." The attractive guy turned out to be Eric MacLeish, Diana's son, and he was very lively and fun to talk to afterwards at the reception. Lyn didn't lose any time. She organized a dinner party for that very week to which she asked Eric. He promptly accepted and she sat him right next to Margot at the table. It didn't take much time. Eric fell instantly in love. His courtship was very compelling. When Margot asked him for Christmas we knew things were serious. Eric took Ward aside as we were preparing to open our presents under the tree and asked him to save his two gifts for Margot until last. When that time came there were two little packages. In the first one two round-trip tickets to Alta, Utah to ski, folded inside a ski hat; in the other one two round-trip tickets to Tortolla pinned to a bikini bathing suit. This was a very persuasive tactic, and Margot was bouleversíed. They went skiing first, and before they had been in Utah long they called home to say they were engaged to be married.

Margot has had an unusual facility for orchestrating her boyfriends. The guys who were devoted to her before her marriage are still devoted to her now. Michael and David and B.G. and Richard have all been a part of our household at one time or another, and with the exception of Michael whom we don't see much, are still on the scene. When B.G. finally decided to marry Beth, Margot threw the bridal dinner at her house. When B.G. got up to make his toast he said, "Beth and I decided not to have any wedding attendants, but if I were to have a best man, it would have been Margot."

I can't think of any life that I would have rather lived. Although I'm not crazy about growing old, I shall not carry any great unfulfilled longings to my grave. "Je ne regrette rien," as the Edith Piaf song says. There isn't the greatest chance in the world that my musical *Pilgrims* will ever get produced, but I shall keep at it, and who knows what might occur. I have given it all I have got, and that is the best anyone can do. I have put too much of my limited resources into it already, to throw much more in. But if I had just $10,000 I could mount a pre-production group where it could be seen in all its glory, and perhaps then get propelled towards a full-scale production.

My painting career is satisfying and rewarding. Although I am not a great painter, I am very good. I have largely taught myself my technique and while I have had instruction from individuals from time to time, I have avoided formal art schooling which I find stultifying, often giving one "vocational" training rather than creative impetus. An environment in which to express what is distinctly and uniquely one's own vision is the sine qua non of creativity. No two painters can ever be alike, and as snowflakes differ, it is the mandate of the teacher to encourage this unique diversity.

I believe that every human being has the potential to be creative. God does not point his long finger at mortals saying, "Now you shall be an artist, and let's see, you over there, and you in the back of the hall shall be a genius." Leonardo, like Christ, just did it better than anyone else, and also Shakespeare. But each of these geniuses was pulling from within himself for self-expression, working within mortal parameters. And each worked like crazy day in and day out, with volumes of words, and gallons of paint. Even though the greatness of their works will never be equalled, there are stations along the scale of excellence that any human can aspire to. Every time one opens one's eyes in the morning one exercises balance, detects colors, evaluates relativity of objects, and is as sensitive as a heliotrope to light and dark, sun and moon. Most people's lives are involved in other pursuits than art. Only a minimal number make a career of art. And the very few people who do allot some of their life to creating art don't spend much time at it. I know that some people are born color blind, or tone deaf, but that is not important. Anybody, if they are willing to give up their time, can be creative. I think one of the greatest tragedies in education is when a school budget gets in jeopardy and when cuts have to be made that the Arts are the first to go. The Arts should be the last to go--let's throw out home economics, motor mechanics, sociology, physics and chemistry first. Perhaps the people of the world who are privileged enough to get an education would be better human beings and more compassionate if they could study Philosophy, Religion, Literature, and the Arts rather than Economics.

A painter once described what an artist did. "He creates something that could not otherwise be seen." The operative word is "otherwise." Other than he looked, chose, abstracted and cycled a vision through his own being it would not otherwise exist. All painting is abstraction. Look at any "realistic" painting or the most objective art. You will see how much the painter has eliminated in order to focus his vision. The finest example of this would be any Vermeer. Or any de la Tour. Essences have been preserved, not photographic reproduction.

I have just read in the *New York Times* an article entitled "Pondering the Riddle of Creativity." Although I believe that like the Sphinx the riddle will never be divulged, nor when the Earth began, nor the mystery of life's beginning, but there is much in the article that I find meaningful. The article says that when one is involved in "creation" there is a state of super alert, where time dissolves and a day passes like an hour. Psychologists call this the "flow state," an altered awareness found when one is performing at one's peak. The most successful creative people are those who savor the joy of painting itself, valuing the process more than the product. Painters must want to paint more than anything else, and when they experience the "flow" they are driven to push beyond their limits. It is when one's skills are in perfect balance with the challenge.

I have said that I believe everyone has the capacity to create, but unfortunately most people because of the pressures of just making a living do not tap their creative resources. There is an attitude also that there is a mystique to art, the secret of which is given only to "artistic" people. I have so often heard the lamentation, "Oh, I never could paint, I cannot draw a straight line." Well really, who can! I can't, and that's what a ruler is for. I would love to give a painting class for men only. Men have been so totally immersed in their work ethic that they are tyrannized by schedules, meetings, bottom lines and the dynamics of business. I know many men sensitive to beauty and nature who would readily respond to recreating it. Isn't the word recreation a good one. It has a meaning much deeper than vacation and fun and games.

Ward and I drove to Annapolis recently and I remembered that two of my paintings were hanging there. I had painted a long horizontal rendition of a Bermuda scape that I had cut in two and framed doubly. They were bought by two friends who lived side by side. They had fun by rushing their guests at cocktails from one house to the other to get the full effect.

There is a magic, mystical "happening" in painting that occurs very seldom. It happens only in the best of paintings, and I have experienced this phenomena in perhaps only one out of ten of my works. It is when the whole is greater than the sum of the parts. When in the process of assembling the parts on the canvas, some magic force takes over to which you submit. This force guides one's hand, one has no control over its inevitability. Each stroke of the brush, each color mix is integrally connected to the previous ones and no other options are sanctioned. When a painter feels this magic "take-over" it is akin to a state of grace.

One has to like the process of doing whatever it is one chooses to do.

The end result is the least important part of creativity. When I have finished a painting I like it alright but it is no longer a part of me. Someone said to me once, how can you bear to part with your paintings. I said that it was like a litter of puppies, you can't keep them all. But I could not justify the many hours I spend on each painting if I was not totally immersed in the fascination of the process. I can't even make the process cost-effective. A paralegal secretary makes more per hour than I do. And if I were not totally subsidized by Ward for rent, food and clothing, I could not be free to paint as I do. And although I have made some money in recent years, I can only augment our income, not be self-supportive.

I have not marketed myself as professionally as I might have. I have not entered into competitions, nor put myself in the forefront of the art market. But I do sell well, and have been proud of the number of patrons that I have. People are not art-hungry. Most individuals treat a painting like a piece of furniture. They don't buy because they already have a painting over the fireplace, and it's been there for years, probably inherited, and probably a hunting scene. It is also a great pity that people don't have more portraits painted. Think of all the gorgeous portraits by Gainsborough, Romney, Copley, Stuart, Sargent, Hals, Leonardo, Holbein, Velasquez, and all the others who graced the homes of their patrons. Alas, you can count on one hand the good portraitists of today.

I feel that art transcends nature, and is more essential than the object or scene painted. Even if you were to be in Arles when Van Gogh painted you wouldn't have seen the same landscape. If you were to go today to Provence you would not encounter the Cezanne countryside. But having seen the paintings of these masters is having an indelible print in one's mind of the beauty of nature which is more real than the raw materials themselves.

I have become a painter because I have seen many beautiful things in my life. I have wanted to put some of this beauty back that I have taken out. I feel beauty can make life palatable. I'm not good at effecting social change. I am not good at expressing anger. But I think it terribly important to recycle beauty.

XVIII

In Praise of Romance

I have been a romantic all my life. I would have been right at home in France with the Troubadours and Trouvères (whoever they were). The thought of young knights serenading with lutes under their damsels' windows putting their longings into poetry and song is splendid. In *Cyrano de Bergerac*, Roxanne is mesmerized by the exquisiteness of Cyrano's words and indeed falls in love with her stupid suitor thinking that he is the author of such gorgeous verbalizing. Whatever happened to Romance? Movies and television don't know the language of love. They only know the language of sex. True courtship is out of fashion, and way beyond the sensibilities of most men. And today a man can't even compliment a woman, or say anything remotely personal for fear of sexual harassment. What a pity!

I love old-fashioned historical movies where during a ball the courtly dances are performed. A minuet or gavotte gives a woman an opportunity to flirt like mad, and be very provocative within the parameters of the formal dance pattern. There is that wonderfully romantic sequence in *The Sound of Music* where Maria is outside on the terrace while a ball is going on inside, and she is overseen by Baron von Trapp teaching the children the steps of a beautiful Austrian folk dance. When the Baron interrupts and dances with Maria the resulting emotion is lovely to witness.

I am not crazy about explicit sex, in movies or television. It makes me uncomfortable to see people thrashing around in bed. Sex has gotten to be so cliché as to lose all the dramatic power of the real thing.

I'm afraid Ward thinks I'm prudish. I'm not at all. I think the true expression of love is cheapened by the commercial exploitation of sex. There is a marvelous scene in *Brideshead Revisited* where Charles first makes love to Julia on board ship when they are returning to England. All the passengers, it seems, but they are seasick in a violent Atlantic storm. They consummate their strong attraction to each other in Julia's cabin while the storm buffets the ship. Waugh writes the scene with great understatement, yet never sacrificing the marvelous dramatic impact of their intercourse. In an otherwise perfect screen adaptation, however, what does the director do? He has them thrashing around, puffing and gasping, revealing bare shoulders and bosoms. It was not nearly as effective as the written episode which I went back and re-read to see if I still believed it to be superior. It was.

The contemporary proliferation of ghastly sexual extravagances is horrifying. Little wonder that children can't see straight with warped vision of what is acceptable behavior in society. Look at Mike Tyson. Some role model! Look at Mayor Barry! Look at the revolting sex lives of many of our public elected officials. And what about Magic Johnson! Great though he is, and sad though his case of AIDs, his sex life was not exemplary.

But you cannot legislate morals. It is worse to suppress the distasteful, the immoral, the ugly, the lowest common denominators in society. Then you get the Mappelthorpe affair, the demise of the National Endowment for the Arts, the witch-hunting, the righteous ascendancy of Middle America with their holier-than-thou moral rectitudes. It's not a good situation. But the best alternative to ugliness is beauty. The best alternative to evil is good, and to violence, compassion. These can only prevail by example. I believe strongly in the trickle-up theory. Nothing is more contagious than love. Nothing defeats bigotry more than enlightenment. Any human being who displays these qualities can make a difference. But where are the leaders in our vast upset country who embody fine human instincts who can make such a difference, who stand for the best in human behavior and can give alternatives to the political crap that is presently mouthed?

There is a fine example of words that can make a difference in one's life. This is probably not the right location for this anecdote in my memoirs, but so what. I have relished all of the *Masterpiece Theatre* presentations on television from the BBC, almost without exception—*Upstairs, Downstairs, Anna Karenina, The Pallisers, War and Peace, To Serve Them All My Days, Brideshead Revisited, The Jewel and the Crown, Passage to India*. One is eternally grateful to these rich, intelligent, beautiful representations of the human condition. One of the first of these dramatic BBC shows was *The Forsyte Saga*. It set a perfectly splendid beginning for the marvelous hours we were to later devote to our TV sets on Sunday evenings. It was outstandingly fine, and being that it was an innovation at that time to do literary drama on TV, a reporter asked the head of BBC, Huew Weldon, what made them do it. Weldon responded that a young man had camped out on his office doorstep for months, and the secretary kept refusing his request to see Weldon about a show. But the young man was persistent. Finally, mostly to get rid of him, Weldon agreed to see him. The man outlined his idea to do a television series on *The Forsyte Saga*. And thus the great show was born. Weldon said at the end of the interview with the reporter:

"The trick in life is not to avoid error at all costs, but to give triumph a chance."

I have said that I thought the ability to love separated humans from animals, and that the ability to express love is one of the highest forms of communications. Words have the power to alter the chemistry of the body. When one hears an inspiring person speak, or reads a beautiful poem, or responds to words of love, one's blood has changed. Love is as psycho-somatic a condition as blushing is when someone walks in the room to whom one is attached, or afraid as when one sweats with fear. There have been so many instances in history and literature of "fatal attractions," and it seems that the most exciting love affairs always end badly. But there is nothing that Antony and Cleopatra, or Elizabeth Taylor and Burton, or Anna Karenina and Vronsky, or Ingrid Bergman and Rosselini could do about it. They are caught in a chemical, unalterable alteration of selves from which the only escape is ultimate burn-out. But I think it is magnif-icent to witness such flaming passions, which are not within the grasp of most of us ordinary humans. Poor Jean Harris had no alternative than to kill the faithless Doctor Tannower. Her being and her reason had been altered by the chemistry of jealousy and jilting. All of us have like Jimmy Carter lusted in our hearts. But as far as I'm concerned I couldn't manage a flaming love-affair, and I'm glad that some of my lustful fantasies have never materialized. I find my love life is fine the way it is.

I have been very happy writing my memoires. Sometimes I have been surprised by what has surfaced, and confess even enjoy re-reading what I have written. I shall miss myself when I am finished. I believe it is impor-tant to "make a joyful noise," and although I have chosen not to recall the dark side of life which is omnipresent, I am aware of the downs. I was walking down Lexington Avenue one day with Ed Sherrin and I was being very sympathetic as he was describing a miserable divorce he was going through.

I said, "Oh Ed, how do you survive such a rotten situation?"

He said, "Lydia, it is important to cope with the downs so you will be *ready for the ups* when they come."

We all know individuals who infect all around them with their doom and gloom. I think good spirits are equally contagious. One of my friends who was very ill said to me, "You always make me feel good when I am with you." I took this as a great compliment.

I anticipate with great excitement the movie that is about to appear based on the novel *Howard's End* by E.M. Forster. This has been one of my favorite books for many years. The two words in the dedication have been with me as talismans: "Only Connect." More important than anything is to stay connected with people. It is all too easy to walk away from something you disagree with, tossing your curls and harumphing, saying, "Who needs that person, or idea,or situation." Such alienation is so sad to see especially in families where a child does not live up to expectation, or does something "unforgivable" and the parent may say "never darken my door again." Disconnection is the worst. All over the world people are disconnecting, Arabs and Jews, Irish Catholics and Protestants, blacks and whites. And I believe that religions have a great deal to answer for separating humans from each other.

This has been brought home to us just recently by a terrible situation involving Lyn. Lyn has been in charge of the television operations at the Christian Science Monitor in Boston. In a violent Junta movement the orthodox members of the Mother Church have forced the resignation of the prime movers behind the huge television system recently initiated at the Monitor. Lyn is not a Christian Scientist, but she has been integral at the highest level in managing this important television endeavor. As a lay person she has brought to bear her many organizational talents, her marvelous executive ability and her beautiful personality. But when the opposition was mounted by the Church members to the growing financial burden of this most expensive of all media, television, she was a prime target. Not only were underhanded methods used to discredit the television venture, a huge attack was launched in the press. As a result of these attacks and because of her prominent position on the Monitor Channel, Lyn received threatening letters, her car tires were slashed and one of her female bosses received a death threat. What a way for church members to behave! I shall never respect the so-called Mother Church again. And I strongly object to them calling themselves "Mother."

I have not written as much about Lyn as I would like. She, like Ward, warrants more space than I have allotted. She has "star-quality," as our friend William Schuman once said. It has not been easy for her these past few years. Her marriage to John Earle collapsed when he left. This past week has been memorable, in fact incredible. It was Monday, Black Monday, when the Monitor Channel debacle occurred. The next day, Tuesday, Lyn went to court to receive her final divorce decree. Some forty-eight hours for her! But she has been unbelievably resolute, strong and philosophical, and it does her great credit. She has two wonderful children—Joby and Derry—smart and attractive and with great potential as human beings. She devotes herself to them and is a wonderful mother. I only hope that the road ahead is smoother and easier for her. She certainly deserves it.

Lyn has great intelligence as well as beauty. Her skills are awesome and varied. She could run the Pentagon, command a clippership and direct anything she put her mind to. And do it all with sensitivity and compassion. Under full sail she is something to behold. Some day, soon I hope, she will find a man who appreciates those qualities and can keep up.

I have been lucky to be married to Ward, who knows who he is and is unthreatened by women. In fact, he applauds them. There are others, however, whose macho image is blurred in the presence of an achieved female. These men are not only resentful, but stymied from using all their cylinders, thus inhibiting parallel growth. I believe strongly in the balance inherent in the principle "I'm okay, You're okay." When a woman grows at a faster rate, that is trouble. Over-devotion to work, money and fawning parents and associates often make a man distance himself from his marriage. What a bloody shame to take the line of least resistance! My husband, on the other hand, is confident in himself and his surroundings. He is like the Energizer Rabbit, banging his drum as he leaves everyone else standing still. What is more, he relishes every moment of his life, and mine.

As I come to the end of my memoirs, I realize that I have forgotten to mention the inspiration for my title: Jean duc de Berry's "Très Riches Heures." This dazzling medieval treasure written in the fifteenth century is a collection of gorgeous, illuminated manuscripts commissioned by Jean depicting the life and times of this rich prince of France. Many of these colorful masterworks are of his estates and castles painted in various seasons with fields and fountains, rivers and forests. Laborers are harvesting, reaping, swimming, fishing or shearing. Nobles and their ladies in gay attire feast and frolic, parade or celebrate a saint's day. Jean duc de Berry loved his life and this is a rich testament to it.

XIX

"Me, Too"

All during this process of writing I have held to the belief that an ordinary person like me can write about an ordinary life and make it worth the telling. Mostly famous people write their autobiographies. Olivier's *Confessions of An Actor*, Augustine's *Confessions of a Saint*, Katharine Hepburn's *Me*. But it's easy for those celebrities to write, for they already have a pre-fabricated audience for their well-known careers. But I have a scoop on them, for it seems to me that "normal" people can relate to my life and empathize with, hopefully, some of its situations.

I might have entitled my work "Me, Too." Maybe if I continue another tome I will call it that. But I have come to this stopping point which is the present, Spring, 1992. Whatever happens in the future which I think worthy to write about will take some distance. You can only create as Wordsworth said by "recollecting in tranquility." Only after a passage of time can you see what has metabolized within you, letting extraneouses fall, and savoring the nourishment of existence. One cannot clearly interpret the moment until it passes, for there is too much barrage in a current event to fully understand its long-time impact. All one can do is live each day as fully as possible, savoring the moments, keeping one's fortitude intact when the going gets tough, and trying to make a joyful noise. I have just noticed a little bit of advice printed in my calendar for March, 1992. "The best way to pay for a lovely moment is to enjoy it." I hope that there are some moments in my *Très Riches Heures* which are enjoyable.